UNDER **PENALTY** OF **DEATH**

RED ⚡ LIGHTNING BOOKS

UNDER PENALTY OF DEATH

The Untold Story of
Machine Gun Kelly's First Kidnapping

—◆◆—

KEVIN E. MEREDITH

with David W. Hendry, Jr.

This book is a publication of

Red Lightning Books
1320 East 10th Street
Bloomington, Indiana 47405 USA

redlightningbooks.com

Manufactured in the United States of America

First printing 2023

Library of Congress Cataloging-in-Publication Data

Names: Meredith, Kevin E., author. | Hendry, David W., Jr., author.
Title: Under penalty of death : the untold story of Machine Gun Kelly's first kidnapping / Kevin E. Meredith with David W. Hendry, Jr.
Description: Bloomington, Indiana : Red Lightning Books, [2023] | Includes bibliographical references and index.
Identifiers: LCCN 2022047977 (print) | LCCN 2022047978 (ebook) | ISBN 9781684351992 (hardback) | ISBN 9781684352005 (ebook)
Subjects: LCSH: Kelly, Machine Gun, 1897–1954. | Woolverton, Howard Arthur, 1880–1960. | Kidnapping—United States—History—20th century—Case studies.
Classification: LCC HV6603.W66 M47 2023 (print) | LCC HV6603.W66 (ebook) | DDC 364.15/40973—dc23/eng/20221007
LC record available at https://lccn.loc.gov/2022047977
LC ebook record available at https://lccn.loc.gov/2022047978

In Memoriam

Mary Bowers Jay

March 17, 1920–November 2, 2022

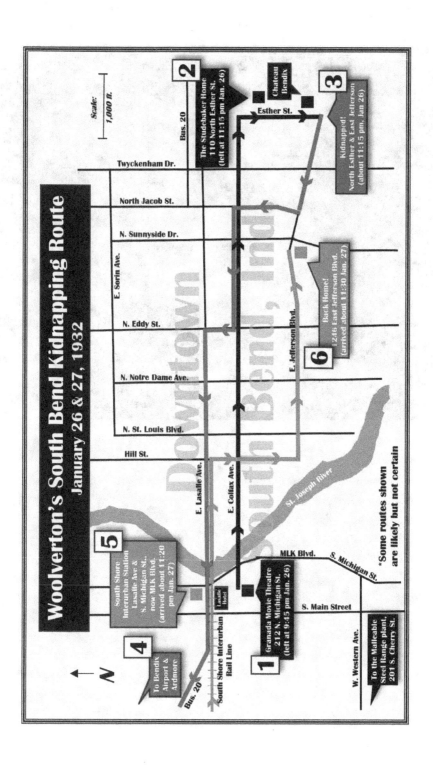

Woolverton's South Bend Kidnapping Route
January 26 & 27, 1932

Scale: 1,000 ft.

N

Downtown

South Bend, Ind.

St. Joseph River

*Some routes shown are likely but not certain

Streets:

Twyckenham Dr.
North Jacob St.
N. Sunnyside Dr.
E. Sorin Ave.
N. Eddy St.
N. Notre Dame Ave.
N. St. Louis Blvd.
Hill St.
E. LaSalle Ave.
E. Colfax Ave.
E. Jefferson Blvd.
Esther St.
MLK Blvd.
S. Michigan St.
S. Main Street
W. Western Ave.

Bus. 20

South Shore Interurban Rail Line

LaSalle Hotel

Chateau Bendix

2 The Studebaker Home 110 North Esther St. (left at 11:15 pm Jan. 26)

3 Kidnapped! North Esther & East Jefferson (about 11:15 pm, Jan 26)

6 Back Home! 1246 East Jefferson Blvd. (arrived about 11:30 Jan. 27)

5 South Shore Interurban Station LaSalle Ave & S. Michigan St., now MLK Blvd. (arrived about 11:20 pm Jan 27)

4 To Bendix Airport & Ardmore

1 Granada Movie Theatre 212 N. Michigan St. (left at 9:45 pm Jan. 26)

To the Malleable Steel Range plant, 201 S. Cherry St.

CONTENTS

PART IV. Who Kidnapped Howard Woolverton?

UNDER **PENALTY** OF **DEATH**

Introduction

AT 8:20 P.M. ON Wednesday, January 27, 1932, a peculiar scene played out among a few desolate blocks in Chicago, not far from the intersection of North and Cicero Avenues: A black sedan pulled up to the curb, its make and model unknown. A man exited the car. He was well dressed, although a bit rumpled, in a three-piece suit and tie and an overcoat he hadn't removed since the previous evening. And he was, at the moment, blind, with painted goggles over his eyes and a scarf wrapped around the goggles.

Had the incident been captured by a security camera—ubiquitous today, virtually nonexistent in 1932—it would have shown the man stepping onto the curb and waiting while a second man exited the car behind him to remove the scarf and goggles. We would have seen the second man mutter something to the first man and return to the car, and the car would have sped away, leaving the first man standing there, staring straight ahead for the most part into a darkened, empty lot. Were the camera particularly close or of high resolution, it might have captured the man turning his head ever so slightly, cutting his eyes discreetly toward the departing vehicle. Only when the car had rumbled away did the man turn right and begin walking, ending the first, terrifying (and occasionally hilarious) chapter of a kidnapping.

It is a story that, until now, has been told only in rumors, incompletely and often inaccurately. But it is an important story, forgotten because of a series of cover-ups that began that very night in Chicago and eventually breached the hallowed halls of the FBI.

Who was the man on the curb? Howard Arthur Woolverton, a wealthy industrialist from South Bend, Indiana.

Of the men who sped away in the car, we cannot be as certain. J. Edgar Hoover, the longtime director of the FBI, asserted multiple times on the radio and in print that the kidnappers were George "Machine Gun" Kelly and Edward Doll, with an assist from Kelly's wife, Kathryn. But there may have been others, new figures emerging only now from the shadows of history, uncovered as this book was researched. They were inconvenient figures, however, and Hoover may have had his reasons for withholding the full truth.

This is the story, then—untold until now except as barely a footnote in the annals of twentieth-century crime—about the snatching of a man, well-to-do but not fabulously wealthy, known and admired in his hometown of South Bend, but no celebrity, a man devoted to his wife and daughter.

Within a decade of Woolverton's abduction, America would sign up to fight a world war, become a global superpower, and drive technologies that changed everything. But first, the country had to contend with a rot from within, a singular crime wave that had the American Dream itself reeling.

And that's why Woolverton's kidnapping was important and remains so to this day.

Thanks to several accidents of timing, the abduction proved a watershed event, a forgotten crime that played a central role in saving the nation from itself.

Howard Woolverton, free and walking along a dark Chicago side street in deep winter, couldn't know the part he was about to play in his nation's history. It was cold, he was tired and surely traumatized as well. He was just looking for Chicago's Loop, where he planned to catch a train to his home in Indiana.

His ordeal was far from over, however. There would be raids and shoot-outs, some fatal. There would be threatening phone calls and letters. A beloved daughter would be sent east to safety. And there would be a federal statement from the victim himself, shedding light on the crime and pointing fingers at new perpetrators—a historically vital document that got buried for ninety years, hidden away in file cabinets and bank vaults, disclosed for the first time in the coming pages.

Only now, nearly a century after Woolverton was dropped off on that Chicago curb, can we relive the man's personal ordeal, the peculiar ways he dealt with it, and the unwitting part he played in restoring his homeland.

"Mr. Woolverton, you are kidnapped . . ."

—from the federal statement of Howard Arthur Woolverton

PART I

The Kidnapping of an Everyman

Howard Arthur
Woolverton, 1932.
*Photographer unknown;
David W. Hendry, Jr.*

Florence Flannery
Woolverton, 1929.
*Photographer unknown;
David W. Hendry, Jr.*

1

"This Is a Stickup"

"WE LEFT THE HOUSE on Tuesday night, January 26, 1932," begins the statement Howard A. Woolverton gave a federal investigator two years after the evening in question. "My wife and I left our home about seven or seven-fifteen to pick up Mrs. George M. Studebaker, Jr., at her residence on Esther Street. I was driving my Pierce-Arrow Five Passenger car."

The statement, dated February 10, 1934, and comprising five and a half single-spaced typed pages, says in its last paragraph that it was delivered by Woolverton to J. T. Hartin, a special agent with the Division of Investigation, US Department of Justice (later known as the FBI), and was transcribed by Kathryn Allen.

The nature of Woolverton's delivery, his method of recounting the most terrifying night and day of his life, remains unknown. One might speculate that Woolverton prepared something in writing, which was subsequently typed up. Given his reliance immediately after the kidnapping on Woolverton family attorney G. A. Farabaugh, there is a good chance he gave his notes to his lawyer, who prepared a report for submission to the feds. Or perhaps he spoke it out loud, with J. T. Hartin listening patiently while Kathryn Allen typed, producing a document

1846 E. Jefferson Blvd.,
South Bend, Indiana.

February 10, 1934.

We left the house on Tuesday night, January 26, 1932. My wife and I
left our home about seven or seven-fifteen to pick up Mrs. George M. Studebaker, Jr., at her residence on Esther Street. I was driving my Pierce-
Arrow Five Passenger car. We then drove to the Granada Movie Theatre. I
parked my car in the lot North of the South Shore station nearest the side-
walk pointed North. Mrs. Woolverton, myself, and Mrs. Studebaker attended
the movie and after the show was over at about 9:45 P. M., we left the
theatre and all walked across the street and down to the parking place,
then proceeded back to Mrs. Studebaker's home in my car taking Colfax Avenue
to Esther Street. I was unconscious of any car that might have been following either going or coming from the theatre; had there been one after leaving
the intersection where 20 turns North, my course being straight East with
very little traffic at night, no car was close enough; in fact, none was
noticed following. We drove in Studebaker's drive, parked in front of Mrs.
Studebaker's house where the car was practically concealed from the street,
a distance of about one hundred feet with about a five foot wall and shrubbery together with gates. The car could have been seen when directly in
front of the gates by passers-by. We visited with Mrs. Studebaker about one
and one-half hours, leaving her at approximately 11:15 P. M. for home. We
drove out on to Esther Street, headed South along the side of Vincent Bendix'
home surrounded by heavy shrubbery, trees and a ten or twelve foot iron fence
and wall. As I approached Jefferson Street, which is a through street and
visibility is poor to the East on account of the fence, shrubbery and trees
and poor lighting, I slowed down before entering Jefferson Blvd.; just as I
was slowing down, I noticed what appeared to me to be a pedestrian about to
cross Esther Street, walking West on the North side and at the same time
another car which appeared to me as if it turned in to the North on Esther
Street which I was about to leave. The pedestrian appeared to me as jumping
to avoid being struck by the other car. The other car squeaked its brakes,
apparently to avoid hitting the pedestrian, but the pedestrian in making his
jump landed on my left running-board and pushed a gun through the window of
my car next to my head. I was not able to estimate the make or type of this
gun but it appeared to me to be an automatic thirty-eight caliber pistol.
My front window was down next to me about four or five inches, I looked
around naturally, at the same time he said "this is a stick-up, look straight
ahead", which I did. He then told me to unlock my back door which I did. He
got in the back seat, rested his arms on the back of my seat and pushed the
gun against my back between the shoulders which I could distinctly feel. He
then said "now you drive where I tell you." We headed West with the other
car following from twenty to thirty feet behind. We drove about two or three
blocks West, then he ordered me to turn right to the North as far as Colfax
Avenue, then about another block West when he asked if there was another
bridge crossing the river farther North. I told him, yes, on LaSalle which
was one block North where we proceeded and turned West again. As we approached the first stop signal at the intersection of LaSalle and Hill Street
he told me to slow down and not stop to wait for the signal but move slowly
until it was green; then as we were crossing the bridge on LaSalle, approaching Michigan Street with the South Shore station on the right, LaSalle
Hotel on the left which was lighted up, he again instructed me to slow down
until a signal was open, then proceed without looking to the right or left
or making any move whatever in passing the hotel and South Shore station,
which is approximately one-half block from the Police Station. These instructions "not to make a move" were under penalty of being killed. We then
proceeded on West and angled off on Route #20 which is Lincoln Highway West.
I was cautioned always to slow down in order not to come to a dead stop at all
traffic lights. We followed Route #20 out of town where he was not familiar
with cross-roads or other roads that might be leading off, away or another to
the North or South, and was trying to find a side road where I supposed I was
to be relieved of my money and valuable. We had driven under the orders to
three or four lanes leading up to houses which were not roads as I knew but
followed his instructions and then when he discovered his mistake, I was

Howard Woolverton's 1934 statement to the FBI. *David W. Hendry, Jr.*

that was promptly locked away in a federal file cabinet and most likely shredded decades later. The statement might never have seen the light of day had Woolverton not kept a copy of it, a copy that eventually made its way into the hands of his grandson, David W. Hendry Jr.

Whether Woolverton spoke or wrote it, the statement is utterly factual, unwaveringly linear, and virtually devoid of emotion. There is not a single flourish in its 5,149 words. If Woolverton cried, philosophized, or despaired while in the clutches of the kidnappers, he chose not to mention it to the federal investigator.

Woolverton continued:

> We then drove to the Granada Movie Theatre.[1] I parked my car in the lot North of the South Shore station nearest the sidewalk pointed North. Mrs. Woolverton, myself, and Mrs. Studebaker attended the movie and after the show was over at about 9:45 P.M., we left the theatre and all walked across the street and down to the parking place, then proceeded back to Mrs. Studebaker's home in my car taking Colfax Avenue to Esther Street. I was unconscious of any car that might have been following either going or coming from the theatre; had there been one after leaving the intersection where 20 turns North, my course being straight East with very little traffic at night, no car was close enough; in fact, none was noticed following.

The Woolvertons, as implied in the statement, were good friends with the Studebakers. And anyone with a passing familiarity with twentieth-century automotive history should recognize the name. Yes, they were *those* Studebakers, scions of the family that made the finest wagons in the nineteenth century before turning their attention to automobiles at the turn of the twentieth, operating from their headquarters in South Bend to manufacture thousands of luxury touring cars, buses, and military vehicles.

George Milburn Studebaker Jr., husband of the Woolvertons' fellow moviegoer (who went by Bess or Bessie), was the grandson of Clement Studebaker, who, with his brother Henry, started out in South Bend as a blacksmith around the middle of the nineteenth century. Clement and Henry began making wagons in 1852, and made them well; the Studebaker product was known for durability and reliability.

The Studebakers turned to making carriages in 1857, an important step in the firm's evolution. Wagons were built to haul things. Carriages

The Woolvertons and Studebakers enjoyed close ties that spanned two centuries. Here are bicycling friends (*from left*) Warren H. Studebaker, Peter E. Studebaker, and a teenaged Howard A. Woolverton, from about 1896–97. *Photographer unknown; David W. Hendry, Jr.*

were built to convey people, and one could not simply throw them together.

Both lines thrived. The Studebakers manufactured tough wagons for the US Army, many of which saw service in the Civil War. One lives on as the iconic Budweiser beer wagon, built in 1900 and drawn by eight Clydesdales. Their carriage line possessed a craftsmanship considered fit for a president. In fact, at least four of them—Abraham Lincoln, Ulysses S. Grant, Benjamin Harrison, and Rutherford B. Hayes—spent time in Studebaker carriages. Lincoln rode in a Studebaker for his fateful trip to Ford's Theatre, where he was assassinated in 1865.

Already wealthy, the family started making electric cars in 1902 and gasoline-powered cars a few years later. The Studebakers made a second fortune off this new industry until, like many grand families before and after, they lost it all. After years of difficulties, the firm went out of business in 1966.

But during their heyday, the Studebakers occupied South Bend's highest social tier, enjoying ties to the Woolvertons and other prominent families that went on for decades. They also built and owned some remarkable homes in South Bend, including Tippecanoe Place, with forty rooms and 24,000 square feet (now a restaurant), and the somewhat more modest home at 110 North Esther Street, where Mr. and Mrs. Woolverton visited just before a pleasant winter's evening devolved into terror.

That home was built in 1928 and comprises 9,897 square feet, with five bedrooms and seven bathrooms. It was valued by Zillow at $1.3 million in July 2019, well over the $104,200 median price for a home in South Bend reported by homes.com in 2020. Today, the building, its exterior virtually unchanged, serves as a center for missionary work sponsored by the People of Praise, a charismatic Christian community whose efforts include running schools and summer camps for hundreds of children, repairing neighborhood homes, and maintaining an urban farm. Amy Coney Barrett was heavily involved in the organization before she joined the US Supreme Court in 2020.

"We drove in Studebaker's drive," Woolverton continued, "parked in front of Mrs. Studebaker's house where the car was practically concealed from the street, a distance of about one hundred feet with about a five-foot wall and shrubbery together with gates. The car could have been

The Studebaker home at 110 N. Esther Street in South Bend, now owned by People of Praise. Moments after leaving the home on the night of January 26, 1932, the Woolvertons were waylaid by kidnappers. *Photograph by Travis Childs.*

seen when directly in front of the gates by passers-by. We visited with Mrs. Studebaker about one and one-half hours, leaving her at approximately 11:15 P.M. for home. We drove out on to Esther Street, headed South along the side of Vincent Bendix's home surrounded by heavy shrubbery, trees and a ten- or twelve-foot iron fence and wall."

Vincent Bendix (1881–1945) was a brilliant engineer who, among other things, invented the first high-quality automobile starter drive, forever supplanting the inconvenient and dangerous hand crank that tormented the first drivers and sometimes snapped a forearm when the crank kicked back. By 1919, almost every car sold featured the Bendix starter drive—about 1.5 million vehicles. He also contributed to early aeronautics, which, along with his donation of land, earned him naming rights to the Bendix Municipal Airport in 1933 (to be mentioned a little later in Woolverton's statement).

In the late 1920s, Bendix bought the home at 107 South Greenlawn Avenue from Clement Studebaker Jr. It was vast, constructed in a U shape around a courtyard and boasting an estimated 26,000 square feet. He christened it Chateau Bendix, rededicated it to lavish living, and hosted wild parties there. Today, it also belongs to the People of Praise and, under the name Trinity School at Greenlawn, serves as an institute of Christian instruction for grades six through twelve.

The backside of the property runs for almost one thousand feet along Esther Street, with the property line marked today as it was in 1932 by an iron fence and thick vegetation.

Woolverton continued:

As I approached Jefferson Street, which is a through street and visibility is poor to the East on account of the fence, shrubbery and trees and poor lighting, I slowed down before entering Jefferson Blvd.; just as I was slowing down, I noticed what appeared to me to be a pedestrian about to cross Esther Street, walking West on the North side and at the same time another car which appeared to me as if it turned in to the North on Esther Street which I was about to leave. The pedestrian appeared to me as jumping to avoid being struck by the other car. The other car squeaked its brakes, apparently to avoid hitting the pedestrian, but the pedestrian in making his jump landed on my left running-board and pushed a gun through the window of my car next to my head. I was not able to estimate the make or type of this gun but it appeared to me to be an automatic thirty-eight caliber pistol. My front window was down next to me about four or five inches, I looked around naturally, at the same time he said "this is a stick-up, look straight ahead," which I did. He then told me to unlock my back door, which I did. He got in the back seat, rested his arms on the back of my seat and pushed the gun against my back between the shoulders which I could distinctly feel. He then said "now you drive where I tell you."

"We headed West with the other car following from twenty to thirty feet behind," Woolverton said in his federal statement, describing streets and an overall itinerary one can still trace on modern-day maps.

We drove about two or three blocks West, then he ordered me to turn right to the North as far as Colfax Avenue, then about another block West and he asked if there was another bridge crossing the river farther North. I told him, yes, on LaSalle which was one block North where we proceeded and turned West again. As we approached the first stop signal at the intersection of LaSalle and Hill Street he told me to slow down and not stop to wait for the signal but move slowly until it was green; then as we were crossing the bridge on LaSalle, approaching Michigan Street with the South Shore station to the right, LaSalle Hotel on the left which was lighted up, he again instructed me to slow down until a signal was open, then proceed without looking to the right or left or making any move whatever in passing the hotel and South Shore station, which is approximately one-half block from the Police Station. The instructions "not to make a move" were under penalty of being killed.

2

War, Flappers, Booze, and the Kidnapping Crescent

NO KIDNAPPING IS AN island, and this was certainly true of the Woolverton kidnapping, a twenty-one-hour ordeal followed by more than a year of terror and pain for the family. In many ways, the Woolverton kidnapping encapsulated in miniature the tumult and confusion of the previous decade.

It all started with the unique and unprecedented horrors of World War I. In the summer of 1914, a billion bullets and bombs were launched by the one-gun assassination of Archduke Franz Ferdinand by a teenaged Yugoslavian nationalist named Gavrilo Princip. The war confirmed that humans, always capable of very bad things, could also perform these things on a grand, mechanized, and mass-produced scale.

Among the new ways to die in World War I were being shot by a plane, being shot in a plane, or being in a plane when it was shot down. Chemical weapons came to the fore during the war, including chlorine, phosgene, and mustard gas. There were flamethrowers, new kinds of grenades and artillery, and submarines. And the war witnessed the debut of fléchettes, metal darts dreamed up by the French that, when dropped from aircraft at a sufficient height, could pass through a man, a horse, or a man on a horse.

But no one involved in World War I had the pleasure of expiring under the barrage of a Thompson submachine gun. The weapon, a favorite of both gangsters and police in the 1920s and 1930s, and the weapon from which Machine Gun Kelly took his name, missed the war to end all wars. Development of the weapon by US general John Thompson began in 1915; it was intended, euphemistically, as a "sweeper" of World War I trenches, but the prototypes didn't ship out for Europe until two days after armistice.

Almost three million Americans went overseas to fight in the Great War. After peace came on November 11, 1918, the nation's soldiers came home from an earth-shaking conflagration abroad to a homeland about to undergo its own maelstrom. Prohibition, the outlawing of the production or sale of alcohol by an amendment to the US Constitution, began on January 17, 1920. Seven months later, on August 26, 1920, American women were granted the right to vote. Throw in a postwar boom, and the decade was off to the races.

Prohibition, which ran for thirteen years, ending in 1933, was not a complete failure, as it did reduce alcohol consumption significantly in one year, 1921. According to Clark Warburton's *The Economic Results of Prohibition*, published in 1932, per capita consumption of alcohol dropped 75 percent, from four-fifths of a gallon in 1919 to a little more than a fifth of a gallon in 1921.

But for the rest of the time, Americans kept drinking. Consumption nearly quadrupled the following year and reached one and a fifth gallons by 1924: 50 percent more than the year before Prohibition.

Among the sources of that liquor, a product known as the wine brick is worth a mention. It was a block of dehydrated, compressed grapes that, to remain legal, was clearly stamped with warnings about what not to do with it. "After dissolving the brick in a gallon of water," one label advised, according to legend, "do not place the liquid in a jug away in the cupboard for twenty days, because then it would turn into wine." The bricks were shipped all over the country, and it is believed that a great many Americans failed to heed those product warnings.

Most Americans didn't want to wait twenty days for homemade liquor, even if it was arguably legal, so libations of more definite illegality continued to flow.

"The big winners from Prohibition were, of course, the nation's gangsters," noted the *Guardian*, a British newspaper, in 2012.[1] "The law had only been in operation for an hour when the police recorded the first attempt to break it, with six armed men stealing some $100,000-worth of 'medicinal' whisky from a train in Chicago. From the very beginning, criminals had recognized that Prohibition represented a marvelous business opportunity."

The war on alcohol was, in some senses, truly a war; the US Coast Guard deployed no fewer than thirty-one destroyers to keep liquor away from US shores. The rumrunners, bootleggers, and moonshiners fought back, of course, usually surreptitiously, sometimes violently. When they chose the latter course, things typically didn't end well for them.

A July 1931 article in the *Standard Union* of Brooklyn, New York, led with this: "One man is in the hospital with bullet wounds and fourteen others are in jail to-day awaiting hearings on several charges as the result of a gun battle between police and gangsters early yesterday which ended in the capture of the men, a seven-ton truck, a 35-foot cabin cruiser, and two passenger automobiles, as well as $10,000 worth of liquor."

The June 13, 1931, *Chicago Tribune* tells the story of the *Bubble*, a benignly named craft carrying $100,000 in devil's drink. When confronted by a Coast Guard cruiser off Coney Island and ordered to stop, the boat's occupants replied with "a derisive yell and a shot."

The cruiser answered with her superior guns, discharging a blast that "ripped a chunk of mahogany out of the bow of the Bubble," followed by "a second savage attack from the [cruiser's] forward rifle," which "found a vital spot in the machinery of the rum runner and stopped her. Simultaneously, a blast from the machine guns of the cruiser smashed every one of her windows. How it was that her crew of three managed to escape that hail of bullets and shell splinters will remain one of the minor mysteries."

Given the superior firepower of the US government, most gangsters chose not to fight back, content instead to find more discreet methods of plying their trade. They secreted casks under their vehicles' floorboards. They deployed second gas tanks that didn't contain gas. Cars sloshed down the highway, their tires pumped full of liquor.

Prohibition proved an utter failure from both a social and a business perspective. America stayed drunk, and gangsters grew rich. What the criminals didn't spend on themselves was invested back into their thriving concerns, enabling a growing list of other violations of law and decency. They bribed public officials, extorted legitimate businesspeople, and bought fast cars and hot guns, committing brazen robberies before they sped away in vehicles the police couldn't follow.

Also in the Roaring Twenties, women were testing out new limits, albeit within the law for the most part, if not within the bounds of decorum or good taste. "Flappers" was a catchall term for these young women who made their first tentative forays into culture earlier in the 1900s but came into their own in both the US and Europe in the early 1920s. Empowered by suffrage and rendered morally ambivalent by the horrors of a war just past, they scandalized the world.

A critical article in the March 26, 1922, edition of the *Baltimore Sun* began by characterizing the flapper as a creature of "jazz, short skirts, bobbed hair and flapping galoshes" before asking, "Is she an innocent fly-by-nighter or is she a public menace?"

Public menace seems to have been the determination of one columnist, writing from New York:

> She wears stockings that are rolled down at the top; her skirts are too short; she paints too much; she uses too much powder; she does not read enough; she smokes cigarettes; she uses slang; she curses and swears; she drinks liquor; she spends too much money; she displays bad taste generally, but particularly in matters of dress . . . she interferes with traffic when she drives automobiles; she attempts to flirt with strangers; she is not domestic and is neglectful of the fine arts of cooking, house-cleaning and sewing; she will not stay at home. Outside of that, she is all right.

It deserves mention that the flappers' prudish detractors rarely stated what was perhaps the women's worst transgression: their penchant for casual sex, a trait confirmed by subsequent, more academic analyses.

If the average flapper was hedonistic but harmless, unconventional but innocent, there were certainly more lethal versions of the class, women who twisted the empowerment of suffrage and the loosening of behavioral standards with a bent toward true mayhem.

There was Ma Barker, for example, who died in a hail of bullets after allegedly organizing her sons' crimes;[2] Bonnie Parker, who went bad after she teamed up with Clyde Barrow and got involved in armed robbery and the murder of several civilians and at least nine police officers; and Cleo Mae Brooks, who changed her name to Kathryn before she married for the first time at fifteen and who very well might have killed her third husband. She took the name Kathryn Kelly when she married for the fourth time, in September 1930, to George Kelly Barnes—the man she single-handedly turned into Machine Gun Kelly.

The 1920s saw the rise of rumrunning gangs and women who were sometimes vapid and sometimes murderous, but much good may be said about the decade.

Six percent of the US populace was illiterate in 1920, a number that dropped to 4.3 percent by 1930, representing two million more people who could read.

Products introduced in the twenties included the hair dryer, cotton swab, and Band-Aid. The traffic light was introduced in that decade, a contrivance already common enough in 1932 that it received several mentions in Woolverton's statement. The world got penicillin as a life-saving medication in 1928. Frozen food and sunglasses arrived in 1929.

Before the world could have radio, television, jets, and the computer, it needed a slew of products both trivial and indispensable. Without the 1920s, we would be forced to surf the internet with damp hair and painstakingly wrapped injuries, devouring cold food, and squinting into the sun.

Less positive, perhaps, was the introduction of a new form of marketing. Advertising had evolved from providing simple product information for things people needed to creating demand for things they didn't.

"By the 1920s," wrote Mansel C. Blackford and K. Austin Kerr in *Business Enterprise in American History* (1986), "advertising executives recognized that theirs was a business to make consumers want products, and they deliberately sought to break down popular attitudes of self-denial and to foster the idea of instant gratification through consumption."

In the 1920s, then, American entrepreneurs set their sights in earnest on creating trifles, and the American Dream took on its current form in that ten-year span, a dream based on the belief that a minor inspiration could become the stuff of life, that a small idea—from initial inspiration to profitable fruition—would receive all the support required from American culture, commerce, law, and politics.

There were, however, some events to get through first, among them a nationwide financial cataclysm. Rampant speculation and irresponsible banking, two other innovations perfected during the decade, brought the Roaring Twenties to an ignominious end in the fall of 1929, which is considered the beginning of the Great Depression. After the stock market crashed, investors recorded roughly $30 billion in losses in 1929 dollars, a sum worth half a trillion in 2020. In 1931, an estimated 133 businesses failed per day.

Survival through the Great Depression was defined in different ways by different people. The flappers, not remotely dissuaded by print condemnation, couldn't survive the deterioration of wealth. They put back on their mother's dresses and set forth on the business of surviving. For the gangsters who found fortune in running rum and robbing banks, it meant business as usual for the most part. The changing economic conditions meant the latter pursuit wasn't quite as profitable, however. Banks were closing, and those still open weren't quite as flush as before. But there were always people, and some of them still had money, leading some gangsters to dabble with the precarious crime of kidnapping.

Kidnappings are relatively rare today, and for good reason. Committing crimes involving alcohol or cash requires the management of an inanimate, if sometimes sloshy, entity. Taking a person, on the other hand, means taking on someone with a will and a personhood, someone who probably doesn't want to be kidnapped and who can make trouble in a variety of ways, both while they are captive and afterward.

Fraught as they were with logistical difficulties, however, kidnappings were becoming part of the American fabric at the time Woolverton was taken. As luck would have it, several reports of kidnapping trends around the nation had come out just months or weeks (or in one case, hours) before the Woolverton crime.

As will be discussed in detail, Woolverton's abduction was timed with near-cosmic precision to amplify the terror-generating impact of these reports. For example, there was the study conducted by St. Louis, Missouri, chief of police Joseph A. Gerk, who sent kidnapping questionnaires to police departments around the nation in 1931. The startling results were published widely in the wake of the Woolverton kidnapping, often as a sidebar to his story.[3]

Between 1929 and 1931, Gerk found, there were 279 kidnappings among cities that responded to the survey. Illinois came out on top, with forty-nine kidnappings during the three years studied, almost double the second-place finisher, California, with twenty-eight. Michigan was third with twenty-five. Indiana held its own at fourth place on the list, with twenty. Missouri had eleven kidnappings. While abduction numbers varied from one report to the next, one study listed more than thirty kidnappings in Ohio.

Among the top states for kidnappings, then, five were contiguous, a Kidnapping Crescent, if you will: five states wrapped around or close to the southern and eastern shores of Lake Michigan: Illinois, Indiana, Michigan, Ohio, and Missouri. Together, these states accounted for about 21 percent of the nation's people, according to the 1930 US Census, but close to half its kidnappings.

If there was an abduction capital in the days of the Woolverton kidnapping, an industrial center, a place where the arts and sciences of abduction were being actively practiced and perfected, this would be it, with Illinois to the west, Michigan and Ohio to the east, Missouri southerly, and Indiana right in the middle.

One strange fact emerged from Gerk's study with direct relevance to the Woolverton kidnapping: victims often didn't want to talk. Among the 279 kidnappings around the nation in Gerk's report, there were 97 known demands for ransom, "but only 28 victims would admit paying, while only seven denied ransom payment," wrote the *Daily Independent*. "In most instances ransom is believed to have been paid but how much or to whom still remains an enigma baffling the police."

Whether or not they got the money, most of the kidnappers got away with the crime. Only sixty-nine people were convicted of kidnapping during the three years of the study. A small but tragic minority of the crimes ended with the worst outcome: in Gerk's study, thirteen kidnapping victims were murdered. Murder can occur even when ransoms are paid. Two cases—one people still talk about and a second, a kidnapping dubbed "the most horrible crime of the 1920s"[4]—are worth mentioning a bit later, as both would have been well known to Woolverton and might help explain some of his post-abduction actions.

3

"Otherwise, I Would Be Killed"

WHEN IT CAME TO killing, Woolverton's kidnappers seem to have had
a good handle on the concept. According to Woolverton's statement, the
gang threatened his life no less than a half dozen times, sometimes in
quite colorful ways. But other aspects of their plot didn't show quite the
same finesse. The crooks, it seems, didn't put as much forethought into
the details of the project as perhaps they should have.

As Woolverton recalled in his statement, the man with the gun at his
back didn't know the difference between a road and a driveway:

> We then proceeded on West and angled off on Route #20 which is Lin-
> coln Highway West. I was cautioned always to slow down in order not
> to come to a dead stop at all traffic lights. We followed Route #20 out
> of town where he was not familiar with cross-roads or other roads that
> might be leading off, away or another to the North or South, and was
> trying to find a side road where I supposed I was to be relieved of my
> money and valuables. We had driven under the orders to three or four
> lanes leading up to houses which were not roads as I knew but followed
> his instructions and then when he discovered his mistake, I was told
> to back out and proceed to a point about three miles from the center of
> town just West of the Bendix Municipal Airport on the right and the
> Wigwam Barbecue on the left, a road leading South where I was told
> to turn in and drove about two hundred or three hundred feet being

concealed by a high hedge fence on the East and no lighted house within view when he ordered me to stop and turn off my lights.

Was Howard Woolverton nervous during this drive? He doesn't say. And what of Florence Woolverton, his wife of twenty-seven years? The statement offers nothing. But we must imagine terror on both sides. Following a pleasant evening with a friend at the movies, Howard Woolverton and his wife found themselves alone with their abductors, miles from the city, on a cold January night on a road empty of homes, with car lights extinguished under orders from the man with the gun.

"The other car which had followed constantly within twenty or thirty feet behind, turned their [lights][1] off at the same time," Woolverton recalled. "He then asked if [I] was Howard A. Woolverton. I answered, 'yes.' He said, 'is this Mrs. Woolverton?' I said 'yes.' He then said 'Mr. Woolverton, you are kidnapped for a ransom of $50,000.00 which will have to be paid before you are released. We are going to give Mrs. Woolverton a letter with instructions which she is to follow and she will be instructed to show it to nobody, particularly the police, under penalty of death to yourself.'"

The next passage of Howard Woolverton's statement, a dry federal document seemingly devoid of humor, fear, or pathos, includes all three if one reads between the lines.

In a section of the statement weighing in at just over one thousand words, Woolverton reveals some touching information about his wife, discusses arguing for his life with his captors (telling what was apparently a blatant lie in the process), describes a clue to the identity of the criminals with a reference to one of their weapons, details their ongoing bumbles as they worked out directions and got their car stuck, and does his best to describe where he was taken despite the almost complete blindness imposed by a pair of painted goggles. Wolverton related:

My wife being slightly deaf, I told them to repeat the instructions distinctly to her so that she understood which they did. He then gave me a pair of goggles, which apparently were heavily lacquered over the lens so that I could not see head lights coming toward us. I could, by turning my eyes to the extreme right or left, get a narrow vision out either side, but I was not at any time able to get a good look at either one of my kidnappers. I was ordered in the front seat of the other car and my wife was ordered in the driving seat of my car with instructions to return to South Bend and follow orders in the letter. She remarked that she had never driven my car which I confirmed and being extremely nervous said that she was not able to do so whereupon they said "she had to." The shorter one of the two who drove the car that followed us from the beginning said that he would back my car out on to Lincoln Highway for her which he did and got out with further instructions for her to proceed and carry out their orders. In trying to start, she choked the motor and did not know how to start it whereupon she tooted the horn three or four times and the man went back and again started the car so that she could proceed. The shorter one of the two got in the back seat and I was warned not to make any move or talk unless spoken to under penalty of being killed. At this time I was in the front seat sitting next to the driver. I was told that they had a machine gun in the back. The taller one who was driving, sitting to my left, transferred his pistol from his right pocket to his left. We proceeded West on Lincoln Highway two or three miles, then took a dirt road to the South where we followed for some distance, then turned right to the West and following a zig-zag course, turning right and left or else South or West until I had lost my bearings. They brought up the subject of ransom demanded in the amount of $50,000.00 whereas I argued it was impossible even if we had the money, to get it out of any South Bend bank because at that time, three in the business district had closed their doors and about five others in the outskirts had closed so that no amount like that which they demanded in cash was available. Furthermore, I told them about depressed conditions of our business since [1929], our struggle to keep our heads above water, my own personal financial condition, at which time, I was heavily in debt and the fact that my father as well as my two brothers were unable to raise any such amount. They told me the amount demanded would have to be paid and that my father, brothers, as well as my wife would be able in some way to dig it up, otherwise, I would be killed. This argument was carried on constantly, but apparently it carried no weight with them. Several times the car was stopped and the driver would refer to a paper about the size of a large letterhead which evidently contained a route or log of the course I was to follow and at one instruction he commented that he had gone wrong which put us into a very rough and muddy road that appeared to be on the Kankakee Marsh. I tried to catch road signs to keep my location as we drove along but the speed made it difficult, being directed not to turn my head one way or another and always being watched, not only by the driver on my left but by the man in the back. I did notice one sign about twenty or twenty-four inches long and about 12 or 15 inches high that read "Kankakee" but could not read the other lettering to know how far it was to that point or what else might have been on the sign. About one-half or three-fourths of an hour before their first stop, we were passing along a paved highway apparently across the river from a town, which road was slightly winding following the river course and considerable elevation above the water level, I could see out the side some sort of plant on the opposite side of the river with Neon lettering extending almost the full length of the plant with white lettering combined with the Neon, but did not dare turn my head to read the name. After following this highway along the river for some little distance, probably a mile or two, we bore to the left on the same highway and we were crossing an intersection of another paved highway and the only building at this intersection which was lighted was on the near right side which was a filling station. As we were crossing the other highway, the man in the back asked the one in the front if he was going to stop and telephone. He checked his speed slightly and replied saying "No, I will come back and telephone." We proceeded possibly a mile or two beyond this intersection then turned abruptly off the paved highway to a one tract narrow side road which was unpaved and quite rough, proceeded approximately one or one-half miles more or less with a deep ditch on the left to a point filled for crossing into a thin grove which was fenced in. The car was stopped, I was ordered to get out and wait with the man in the back until the driver went back to the telephone. I imagine this incident took place about 2:30 or 3:00 A.M. on the morning of the 27th of January. The driver had considerable trouble in turning around because of the road condition and was stuck for a time with one of the front wheels headed down in the ditch. We waited about one-half hour when he returned with the car. I was ordered to put a light colored muffler over the lacquered glasses and my eyes, which one of the men removed from his neck, he being the taller of the two. They remarked that they did not want me to see where I was being taken.

So, in his statement to the feds, Woolverton tells us of a hard-of-hearing wife who couldn't operate the Pierce-Arrow's unique manual transmission and kidnappers who couldn't keep their car out of ditches.

We also have compelling testimony from Howard Woolverton that he was broke and completely unable to get his hands on $50,000 in cash regardless, due to bank failures.

Was any of this true? Three years into the Great Depression, some of it certainly was. Banks all over the nation were going kaput, and very few people in America had $50,000 in cash lying around, an amount equivalent to almost $1 million in 2020 dollars.

But was Woolverton financially insolvent? In 1934, Woolverton told a federal investigator what he'd said to the kidnappers about his desperate financial situation, without qualifying it as a lie. There was no preamble, no "I lied to convince them I had no money" or "Here's the story I told when they asked me for $50,000 cash."

David Hendry Jr., who was born in 1948, sixteen years after his grandfather's kidnapping, feels he knows enough about his forebear's history to insist his grandfather was always wealthy, by the grace of both his own resources and those of his wife and other relatives, and he can state unequivocally that any assertions otherwise were no more than a ploy to save his life and negotiate the ransom down.

Published accounts of Howard Woolverton and his family, of which there were many throughout his life, seem to back up Hendry's claim. Howard Arthur Woolverton was born in South Bend, Indiana, on September 28, 1880, to community pillars Jacob and Alice Rupel Woolverton. In the 1901 *South Bend and the Men Who Have Made It*, the biography of Jacob Woolverton takes up most of a page. Born in 1845, and thus fifty-six at the time of the book's publication, he is listed as president of the St. Joseph County Savings Bank, vice president of the St. Joseph Loan and Trust Company, treasurer of the Malleable Steel Range Manufacturing Company (a company he founded and that lives on today as Southbend, a division of the Middleby Corporation), and a founding member of Kizer & Woolverton, a real estate firm.

"The operations of the firm are most extensive," the book said of Kizer & Woolverton, "and in addition to their important transactions in real estate, the firm loans large amounts of money on property in Indiana, Ohio and Michigan, and have an extensive clientage among the wealthy and influential citizens of this county."

A second piece about Jacob Woolverton—a glowing article from the *South Bend Tribune* dated August 25, 1917—asserts that Jacob Woolverton's "familiarity with real estate and conditions pertaining to it in northern Indiana and southern Michigan is probably unsurpassed."

Howard Woolverton's education speaks to his family's wealth and privilege as well. Though he started in the public schools of South Bend, he later attended the private Lake Forest Academy, north of Chicago in Lake Forest, Illinois, during his high school years. He didn't go to college because, as David Hendry recalls being told, he was needed in the family business and at other enterprises in town.

The young Woolverton also married well. On June 10, 1905, the twenty-five-year-old married Miss Florence Flannery, then twenty-one, at Chicago's Church of the Atonement, a Gothic Revival building

Woolverton family patriarch Jacob Woolverton, circa 1900. *Photographer unknown; David W. Hendry, Jr.*

completed in 1889 that today boasts an ivy-covered facade and occupies a spot on the National Register of Historic Places. "The bride wore an exquisite gown of white liberty satin trimmed with rose point lace and pearls," reported the *South Bend Tribune* of June 12, 1905. "Her veil was of tulle and she carried a shower bouquet of orchids and lilies of the valley."

The article noted that the newlyweds headed straight to "an extended western wedding trip," departing a "brilliant wedding reception . . . at the magnificent residence of Dr. and Mrs. D. Franklin Flannery, uncle and aunt of the bride, 1941 Kenmore avenue."[2]

Money ran in the new family, it might be said. While the groom was descended from the wealth that comes from banking, the manufacture

Howard and Florence Woolverton (*center*) and their wedding court, June 1905.
Photographer unknown; David W. Hendry, Jr.

of high-end cooking ranges, and real estate dealings in three states, Mrs.
Woolverton was no pauper. For thirty-seven years, until the early 1900s,
her father, John L. Flannery, worked his way up through the ranks of
the Wheeler and Wilson Sewing Machine Company, eventually serving
as general manager of the firm's Chicago enterprises.

And a job like that was no small potatoes.

There was a time, before sewing in the household went the way of
the passenger pigeon, when sewing machines were not only big business; they also represented the height of modern consumer technology.
Millions of the machines were sold, enabling people who couldn't afford
to buy fitted fashions—or even get to a store that sold them—to make
their own.

Along with his sewing machine endeavor, Mr. Flannery founded the
Boye Needle Company in 1906 and left it to Florence and her brother
when he died in 1920.

In the annals of two charmed lives becoming one, then, Howard and Florence were exemplars. The *South Bend Tribune* reported, "Both bride and groom are very prominent socially" and declared Mrs. Woolverton to be an "Illinois Belle."

"The bride is well known in the social circles of Wheaton, Chicago, and South Bend. She has visited many times in the latter city and is a great favorite. The groom is one of South Bend's best known young men and is a son of one of the first families of that city."

Given their heritage, the newlyweds lived well, enjoying the upper-class luxuries of corporate ownerships and directorships as the scions of well-to-do families. Howard Woolverton, for example, was driving a Pierce-Arrow Five-Passenger Car, likely a new model, on the night he was kidnapped in 1932.

The Pierce-Arrow company was bought by the Studebakers in 1928, so when Woolverton ordered the vehicle, a favorite of Hollywood stars and flashy tycoons, he was buying local. He was also buying from friends. Pierce-Arrows were big cars, reliable and long-lived, and far more expensive than many cars of the day. A new, perfectly drivable 1932 Pontiac went for $875—less than $20,000 in 2020 dollars. Plymouths were listed at between $445 and $545. The exact model of Woolverton's car isn't known beyond its being a four-door, five-passenger Pierce-Arrow, but prices for the line ranged from $2,385 to close to $4,000, equaling in 2020 dollars an outlay of between $45,000 and $73,000.

Woolverton also wore his wealth more subtly, as was the fashion of the day, often sporting a six-carat, emerald-cut diamond pinkie ring, which Dave Hendry still wears (but not on his pinkie; on his right ring finger).

If there was a blot on the Woolverton marriage, other than the kidnapping, it probably wasn't financial.

It was biological.

A 1932 Pierce-Arrow Five Passenger car, similar to the luxury vehicle Howard Woolverton was driving with his wife on the night he was kidnapped. *Photo by Thomas Schifferli.*

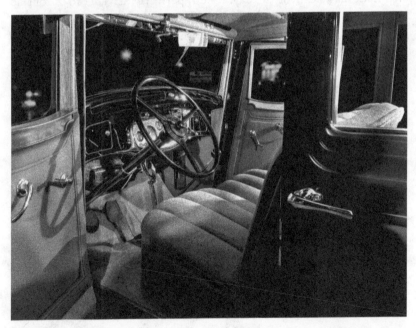

The driver's seat of a 1932 Pierce-Arrow. Unfamiliar with the transmission, Florence Woolverton couldn't get the car out of first gear and killed the engine at the first red light in South Bend. *Photo by Thomas Schifferli.*

4

The Mystery Daughter

IT WAS WELL KNOWN among family members that Florence Flannery Woolverton couldn't bear children. "She had had one miscarriage after another," recalled David Hendry in a 2019 interview, citing knowledge passed down through the generations. Mrs. Woolverton finally gave birth to a live child in November 1919, fourteen years after the couple's glorious wedding.

But it was not to be.

The *South Bend Tribune* offered up these few words on Wednesday, November 26, 1919—the day before Thanksgiving: "May Elizabeth Woolverton, infant daughter of Mr. and Mrs. Howard A. Woolverton, 328 North Lafayette boulevard, died Tuesday night at 11:30 o'clock at Epworth hospital. The child was born Nov. 23. Funeral services were held this afternoon at 2:30 o'clock at Riverview cemetery, where burial took place. Dr. C. A. Lippincott officiated."

According to Hendry, the cause of death was sudden infant death syndrome, known as "crib death" in earlier times, and it left his grandmother devastated. Hendry says the grieving Howard Woolverton, desperate to ease his wife's misery, received some blunt advice. "The doctor told my grandfather, 'Go out and buy her a baby.'" And that's where a

31

second girl comes into the picture. It's not a clear picture, however. The Woolvertons have left us with a century-old mystery.

Eighteen days before May Elizabeth Woolverton began her two-day journey through this world, another girl was born. The names of this girl's biological parents and the circumstances of her birth aren't known, but we can be certain that the girl was adopted, arriving at the Woolverton home in good health and with the name Mary Elizabeth Woolverton, a name just one letter off from that of the baby girl who preceded her in the Woolverton home.

When was she adopted, and how? When did she arrive at the Woolverton household?

Twelve years after her birth, the girl would become, briefly, the most famous preteen in Indiana, her picture splashed in gray on newsprint around the region. She would also be remembered as one of the very few American adolescents ever threatened publicly with death. Her origins, however, will likely remain shrouded.

According to a book with gilt roses and the words "OUR BABY" on the cover, a book handed down through the family until it reached the safekeeping of David Hendry, Mary Elizabeth Woolverton was born at Epworth Hospital in South Bend on November 5, 1919. Perhaps her birth was difficult or premature, for the book states that two physicians were required to bring her forth—Drs. Dugdale and S. S. Clark—with assistance from two nurses, Marietta Stewart and Ulga Fraid.[1]

Although the rest of the book is dedicated to the girl who lived, on the first page of the Woolvertons' baby book appears a nod to the deceased child, in the form of a poem by Violet Alleyn Storey. The poem had been cut from a magazine, apparently, and pasted down.[2]

In "Prayer for a Very New Angel," a desolate mother asks God to treat the girl she has lost, for just one night and the next morning, as the mother had treated her in her short life. The mother notes that she left a light on in the hall when the child slept in the crib beside her bed and asks God to honor the practice by lighting a star for her, just once, on her first night in heaven.

"I always kissed her on her left cheek where / The dimple was," the mother notes, and this is a thing she wants God to do for her lost child when she wakes for the first time above. "And, oh, I wet the brush. / It made it easier to curl her hair. / Just, just tomorrow morning, God, I pray, / When she wakes up, do things for her my way!"

Howard Woolverton and his infant daughter, Mary Elizabeth, in 1920. The girl went by "Betty" all her life. *Photographer unknown; David W. Hendry, Jr.*

The Woolvertons' baby book serves as a tribute to two lives, one of just two days and the other far longer, for this second infant was a beloved daughter who went on to be a mother of four and, for a time, was the famous object of terrifying threats, a girl who needed a police escort just to get to school.

According to the book, Mary Woolverton was weighed for the first time on November 25, 1919, coming in at just five and three-fourths pounds twenty days after her birth. Her weight was next recorded three months later, on February 5, and then on March 5, and so forth, with all records put down in Florence Woolverton's nearly illegible cursive.

Her low weights—about two-thirds of the weight of an average child at those ages—were consistent with her petite stature all her life. Her adult height was recorded in her passport as a little under five feet.

What is perplexing is the first date Mary was weighed—November, 25—for that was the same date May Woolverton died. Was Mary weighed on that date because the Woolvertons had expressed interest in her on the very date they lost May? Is it possible she went home with the Woolvertons on that day, the day of May's death, the day before May's funeral?

Hendry does not discount the possibility that his grandparents dealt with a devastating loss with remarkable speed, losing one child at the hospital and leaving with another a few hours later.

But Hendry considers it more likely that, while the November 25 weighing might have been done on his grandparents' behalf, the adoption happened days or weeks later. Or the date might be a simple coincidence.

Either way, by Christmas 1919, Mary Elizabeth was firmly ensconced in the Woolverton household. Mary Elizabeth Woolverton, the tiny girl who wasn't wanted on November 5, 1919, was, on Christmas morning fifty days later, showered with gifts.

According to the first few pages of her baby book, she received two checks from her grandfather, Jacob Woolverton, for $25 each, or $725 total in 2020 dollars. She received a silk carriage robe, a gold bracelet (still in Dave Hendry's possession), and a pair of Cinderella slippers, states the book, which listed more than two dozen family and friends as benefactors. And the girl who was decidedly not born with a silver spoon in her mouth more than made up for it by her first Christmas, receiving a silver set, a silver cup, and not one but two silver spoons.

Regardless of what scenario elapsed, the conventional adoption through the usual channels or parents who dealt with shattering grief by almost immediately taking home another little girl, Mrs. Woolverton's numerous entries in her "OUR BABY" book indicate their daughter was loved, doted on, and perhaps a bit indulged.

In the infant's first few months of life, we know that she held a blue rattle; played with Mary, her (presumably stuffed) lamb; drank orange juice; wore her first short dress "and looked like a little doll"; and "played with her toes when 6 months old." In those months, she "kissed her daddy for first time" and "kicked her little feet & kept time to music."

She also conducted official visits now and then. "Made her first call upon Mrs. J. M. Studebaker Sr.," wrote Mrs. Woolverton in an entry dated February 12, 1920.

Jacob Woolverton and granddaughter Betty, 1920.
Photographer unknown; David W. Hendry, Jr.

Was Betty, as Mary Elizabeth was nicknamed from her first days, impressed by the widow of John Mohler Studebaker, one of the five brothers who founded the Studebaker Corporation, the brother who served as its president from 1868 until his death in 1917 (the last years in an honorary capacity), and whose name has been enshrined forever in the Automotive Hall of Fame?

Apparently not.

"Fell asleep," the entry concludes.

But Mrs. Studebaker was smitten, it seems. An entry a few days later reads, "Mrs. J. M. Studebaker Sr. wrote Betty her very first letter."

Within a year of her birth, Betty Woolverton had moved with her parents into their new home, at 1246 East Jefferson Boulevard.

The home, an elegant dwelling, beautiful but not pretentious, still stands on a large corner lot guarded by shrubs and heavy vegetation at the front and side.

According to Zillow, consulted in fall 2020, the home was built in 1890, comprises 3,651 square feet, and was valued at the time at $836,000.

Betty Woolverton celebrated her first birthday there, an event duly recorded in Betty's baby book. Attendees at the event included someone interesting: Ulga Fraid, the nurse who assisted at her birth.

Indeed, the woman who witnessed Betty's arrival and who undoubtedly saw Betty's biological mother was a presence in Betty's life for seven years after her adoption, tending to her and even traveling to Mississippi with her and Mrs. Woolverton when Betty was five.

Ms. Fraid took her leave of the girl in February 1927 when she moved to Michigan, according to the baby book. Did she ever, in the seven years before she left, share with the Woolvertons the name of the biological mother or the conditions of Betty's birth? As David Hendry recalls, his mother expressed no interest in knowing about her birth mother, and her adoptive parents probably felt the same way. Who were the birth parents? The nurse was most likely never asked.

We know from the baby book that Betty started studying French and dancing when she was five and began performing more public roles at that age as well.

"Betty was the little flower girl at Mary McKibbon Sheppard's wedding," Mrs. Woolverton wrote in June 1925. "We were very proud of her for she was so dignified and sweet during the ceremony." She was not

The Woolvertons moved to 1246 East Jefferson Blvd., South Bend, in 1920. The home still bears the reinforcements installed after 1932 to protect Betty. *Photo by Tonya Hardisty.*

This Victorian-era silver snuff box named Wiggly entranced Betty as a child. *David W. Hendry, Jr.*

Florence Woolverton and Betty, from the mid-1920s. *Photographer unknown; David W. Hendry, Jr.*

always perfect, however, in the era before unconditional parental love had been invented.

As Mrs. Woolverton wrote, "When 28 months old she could say sentences perfectly. She was naughty at the table one day and her daddy said 'Betty when you are naughty your daddy does not love you.' She looked at me and said 'Mummy loves her naughty baby.'"

And then, there was this incident: "When three years & ten months old she saw a slouchy, unattractive man standing in a door way down town and she said to her nurse, 'Is that a bootlegger?' and I said 'Where did you ever hear of a bootlegger?' and she said 'from Daddy.'"

Betty Woolverton might have been endearingly cute, and she was certainly beloved, but she struggled academically as well as possibly with her health as a child. According to her third-grade report card for January through June of 1928, when she was eight, Betty missed twenty-seven days of school.

The only A's were for Personal Neatness, Health Habits, and Courtesy. She earned B's in English, Spelling, Reliability, and Geography. All the rest of the grades were C's: Reading, Writing, Arithmetic, Music, Art and Industrial Arts, Conduct, Application and Neatness of Work.

The Leadership column of her report card was left blank. Perhaps only boys received scores in that category?

Mrs. Woolverton's observations of her daughter tapered off through the twenties, with just a word or two in 1927, followed by five years without any history at all.

The events of her life during that time are not lost altogether, however.

There was an item in the January 20, 1930, edition of the *South Bend Tribune*. A few months after the advent of the Great Depression, the paper had started a "Quick Relief Fund" to buy food, clothing, and heating fuel for the local poor and had collected $140 to date. "One contribution of $5 came from Betty Woolverton," the paper said, "daughter of Mr. and Mrs. Howard A. Woolverton, 1246 East Jefferson boulevard." The money came with a note from the girl: "I am 10 years old and giving the $5 bill that I earned all by myself." Concluded the *Tribune*: "Would there were more little girls in South Bend like her."

Some of the blanks in this part of Betty's life were filled in by Betty's best friend, Mary Jay, formerly Mary Frances Bowers, interviewed by email and in person several times in 2019 and 2020.

The two girls lived near each other and first met in 1929, when both were about ten, as they walked to the elementary school on Colfax Avenue. Martha, the Woolvertons' nanny, escorted Betty on those walks, and Mary was accompanied by her older sister, Virginia.

The friendship was cemented when Charlie Bowers, Mary's father, was building an airplane for Betty's uncle, Hugh Woolverton. The girls occasionally went to the airport to watch and sometimes help with a small task here and there. Charlie Bowers was no casual hobbyist; he won enough fame as an aviationist to earn a whimsical profile in the May 29, 1929, *South Bend Tribune*. The article began:

Betty Woolverton enjoying one of the pursuits of the wealthy in 1928.
Photographer unknown; David W. Hendry, Jr.

Betty Woolverton, *left*, with Mary Bower in South Bend, about 1929. The two were lifelong friends, and two decades later Mary Jay (her married name) became godmother to Betty's first child, David W. Hendry, Jr.
Photographer unknown; David W. Hendry, Jr.

A lad of 14 lay dreaming under the shadow of a tree on a farm near St. Joseph, Ill., 26 years ago. A stiff odor of burning corn silk floated from his crude cigarette. To all onlookers he was just a farmer boy stealing a few puffs out of sight of his father. To him the smoke wove fantastic patterns and shaped future things.

The boy was Charlie Bowers, now known to thousands as Capt. Charles R. Bowers, manager of the local office and aviation school of the Shockley Flying Service.

Mary sometimes called her best friend "Betty Boopy," the ninety-nine-year-old Mary recalled in one of her 2019 interviews. Betty returned the favor with the nickname "Mary Pany." The girls played with a doll they christened "Long-Legged, Knock-Kneed, Pigeon-Toed, Beverly Jean No Last Name."

Mary remembered Betty as "very sociable, outgoing, fun and generally happy. She did not like to study or do anything like crafts or projects and certainly did not like to work. She did very much enjoy boys and parties."

An interest in boys coupled with a less-than-stellar school record were not standard fare for a young girl's baby book, which might explain why Mrs. Woolverton went silent on her daughter's progress from 1927 until this entry, dated January 27, 1932, when Betty was twelve: "Daddys father was kidnapped and held for ransom. He was released within 24 hours unharmed"

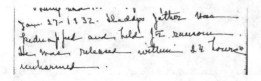

One of Florence Woolverton's last entries in Betty's baby book, about the kidnapping. *David W. Hendry, Jr.*

Of course, there is an error in the note. "Daddys father" was Jacob Woolverton, who was still alive at the time of the kidnapping but was certainly not kidnapped. Mrs. Woolverton must have meant to write either "Daddy" or "Betty's father," but she lost her place in the words and combined the two, the way people sometimes do when under great stress.

The terse account of the kidnapping is one of the last notes to appear in the pages. The book was set aside forever after, as if the daughter's childhood had come to an end on that day.

And, in some ways, it had.

Betty Woolverton around the age of 5. Seven years later, she would become one of no more than a handful of 12-year-old Hoosier girls ever publicly threatened with death. *Photographer unknown; David W. Hendry, Jr.*

5

Unsatisfactory Lodging

"I WAS THEN ORDERED back in the car in front with the driver, the other man in the back," Howard Woolverton recalled in his statement to the feds, "and they proceeded on this same road possibly another mile more or less to a point where they turned abruptly to the left and drove but a short distance bearing to the left, either into an open garage or one with the doors open, and then I was instructed to get out through the left side under the wheel."

Before Woolverton described his makeshift prison and the intriguing voice of a third kidnapper, a recap of Woolverton's statement up to this point might be helpful.

On the evening of January 26, 1932, Howard and Florence Woolverton took Bessie Irene Studebaker to a movie at the Granada Movie Theatre in South Bend, Indiana. Howard Woolverton was driving his Pierce-Arrow Five-Passenger Car, and after the movie, he brought Mrs. Studebaker back to the mansion she shared with her husband, George M. Studebaker Jr.

The couple visited there for about an hour and a half and departed about 11:15 p.m. On the short drive to their home, the Woolvertons were waylaid by a man jumping on their car's running board, pushing a handgun through Woolverton's slightly opened window, and demanding to be let in the back seat. Once seated there, the man pressed his gun against Woolverton's back and ordered him to drive west while another car followed. After they got lost once or twice, they pulled onto a desolate road where Mr. Woolverton was told he was being kidnapped for $50,000.

The kidnappers gave Mrs. Woolverton a note and told her to drive back to town and collect the money from family members. If she went to the police, she was assured, Mr. Woolverton would be killed.

While blinded with goggles and a scarf, Mr. Woolverton argued with the kidnappers about his ability to pay the ransom. They drove west, toward Kankakee and parts beyond before the kidnappers pulled into a garage, where Woolverton was ordered out.

> As I crawled out, it was a dirt floor and my right hand struck another car fender next to it. The two men, one on either side, took my arms and led me a short distance to the entrance of the basement apparently in an old farm house. I had to step up one step then down about five or six steps and was told to stoop down to avoid bumping my head when entering the basement. My reason for believing this to be a farm house was because of the surrounding country and the outside basement and the condition of the road. I did see that it was approximately 50 to 100 feet distant from the garage or shed to the basement entrance. I was then led in to a basement room, still blindfolded with lacquered goggles and muffler and there was a cot for me to lie on and was ordered not to remove my muffler or goggles until I was told to.

Now, before we proceed, it must be acknowledged that Woolverton's narrative is laden with peculiarities specific to what he could and could not see.

Perhaps his reports of his on-again, off-again blindness were due to the way stress interferes with forming memories or the fact that more than two years had passed between the kidnapping and his statement to the federal investigator. Or we might blame the notorious unreliability of eyewitness accounts, even when considerable time hasn't passed and the eyewitness hasn't repeatedly been threatened with death. Or we might label these discrepancies something else altogether: the first of several places in the statement where Woolverton apparently chose to be less than entirely forthcoming with the feds.

For when it came to the physics of vision, Woolverton's statement, to be blunt, didn't hold water. Just before his wife was dispatched with the $50,000 ransom note, Woolverton's eyes were covered with a pair of paint-covered goggles, which impaired his vision but did not leave him completely blind.

Recall that Woolverton had reported: "I could, by turning my eyes to the extreme right or left, get a narrow vision out either side, but I was not at any time able to get a good look at either one of my kidnappers."

This assertion seems off. Woolverton's eyes remained uncovered for the first stages of the kidnapping. Did he not look at his abductors then? And after he put the goggles on, he says he was sitting in the front seat with one of them while they drove. Could he not, by turning his eyes to the extreme left, take a good, long look, even if it was a bit dark? The car presumably featured a lit instrument panel, and there were surely the lights of oncoming headlights to illuminate Woolverton's captor. The moon, at 81 percent full that night, would have provided a little illumination as well under weather described by the *South Bend Tribune* as cold but "fair" and possibly cloudless.

But the assertion of blindness is even odder if one considers the things Woolverton did claim he could see while wearing the goggles and, later on, the scarf.

Goggled, Woolverton says he saw the driver move his pistol from his right pocket to his left. In his statement, he says he saw the driver refer to "a paper about the size of a large letterhead." He says they got stuck on a road "that appeared to be on the Kankakee Marsh." He says he "tried to catch road signs" but couldn't, not because of his goggles but because the car was moving too fast. He did see a small sign that said "Kankakee," but when they drove past a neon sign with letters as large as a building, he couldn't read those for some reason and "did not dare turn my head to read the name." But if he could see only out of a small gap to the extreme left or right, why would he need to turn his head to get a better look?

At one point, he noticed they were driving beside and high above a river. At another, he saw a filling station.

Soon thereafter, according to his statement, one of the kidnappers took off his scarf (which Woolverton called a "muffler") and ordered Woolverton to put it around his face to keep him from seeing where they were going. Did the captors realize Woolverton was conducting a veritable travelogue with only the goggles to blind him?

But the scarf, once it was on him, was no more opaque than the lacquered goggles they covered. Even in the dark of night, Woolverton was able to see that he was being driven into a garage, and he also made note of "the surrounding country and the outside basement and the condition of the road. I did see that it was approximately 50 to 100 feet distant from the garage or shed to the basement entrance."

Possibly, the goggles and scarf had come off at some point before he arrived at the basement, but Woolverton, trying to dredge up two-year-old memories from almost twenty-four hours of terror (we haven't gotten to the scariest parts yet), thought he'd worn one or both throughout.

It is only in the next passage of Woolverton's recollections that the scarf and goggles do officially come off. He's confined to a makeshift prison, and we're treated to unintended comedy involving a trapdoor. We are also given one tantalizing hint at the identity of a third captor:

> They then locked the door to the room, both men leaving and went to the first floor where I would hear them walking directly above me and I could hear them talking with others and I thought once I heard a woman's voice but I am not positive and did not hear any women talking from then on. I could then hear something tearing like linoleum or carpet with considerable noise, moving chairs or some other furniture around them, finally they tore open a trap door above during which operation, considerable litter and other particles dropped down striking what proved to be several empty glass fruit jars and gallon glass jugs on an old table immediately under the trap door. After this operation I was instructed through the trap door to remove the muffler and if I cared to the goggles, but not to touch anything in the basement or examine anything under penalty of death. Immediately at my left near the door there proved to be an old fashioned oil lamp sitting on the dirt floor, lighted dimly. Further on at the left was a double hanging shelf extending lengthwise with the room, containing the empty fruit jars, pints, quarts, etc., one or two or more, I believe contained fruit or something. In the far left hand corner from the door was piled four or five of what appeared to be empty five gallon alcohol cans. It was a dirt floor with old fashioned stone foundation around the room, the ceiling was at least eight to nine feet high and a folding cot with a couple of blankets stood on the floor close to the hanging shelves running lengthwise with the shelves. The atmosphere was cold and damp and when breathing, I could see my breath from my nostrils.

Howard A. Woolverton, born to wealth and privilege, united by marriage to another wealthy family, close friend of the Studebakers, doting husband and father, and driver of *the* car of the era, had descended—literally and figuratively—to a very low place in a matter of hours.

He'd been imprisoned in a cold basement jail, a rude space where debris fell from the ceiling, a subterranean cell stacked with forgotten cans and jars of food, gas, and alcohol. A single lamp lit this new world, where looking around or touching anything was considered a capital crime. And his hoteliers were a ruthless band of gangsters, one quite possibly a woman.

And there was no one to complain to, which must have been the insult to top the injuries for Howard A. Woolverton.

A smattering of Woolverton's letters and memos remain in the files of grandson David Hendry, and they reveal an economically fastidious man who, regardless of how much money he had, would carefully pursue redress for any disappointment in service or billing.

"Your boy failed to leave our Chicago Tribune . . . for at least three Sundays out of the past month," Mr. Woolverton complained in an August 2, 1929, letter to the City News Agency of South Bend. "One of the three I called for personally at your place around noon."

Woolverton's letter accompanied his payment in full of $1.50 to renew his newspaper subscription, but he implied that he was due a refund of some portion of the payment.

Two months before the Great Depression kicked off, he complained about other inconveniences in that letter: "For several days your morning paper has not been delivered either at all or later in the forenoon. Would like to have you instruct your boy to make his delivery not later than 7:00 or 7:30, otherwise I do not get to look the paper over until evening. We have called your office repeatedly making a report but usually some small boy or girl answers the phone and we get no satisfaction."

Twenty-six years after the thugs threatened to kill him, Woolverton was still following that playbook, sending precisely written letters to the firms he'd done business with to resolve matters he felt were important. These letters typically bore, at the bottom below his full name and signature line, his initials "HAW," followed by a forward slash and the initials of the typist.

In a February 4, 1958, letter about being overcharged for oyster stew at the St. Francis Hotel in San Francisco, "HAW/hl" appears at the bottom of the page.

That letter, carefully preserved in Hendry's files, is presumably a copy of what he sent the hotel. It's unsigned and bears no folds. The person with the initials "HL" most likely created two copies at Woolverton's dictation, perhaps typing it again, perhaps using carbon paper, then sending one and filing the other. In 1960, two years before the photocopier became commercially viable, having duplicates created mechanically was Woolverton's best option.

So that's what he did, sending letters, having duplicates made and meticulously filed, passing the records down until today, where they remain in the careful guardianship of his grandson, Dave Hendry.

"My daughter and I had lunch at your marvelous hotel about three weeks ago today," Woolverton wrote in that 1958 letter. "We each ordered oyster stew with the small oysters . . . and was [sic] charged $7.00 for the two oyster stews."

Oyster stew, Woolverton went on to note, costs just $.85 at his "best club," making $7.00 "way out of reason."

Of course, the St. Francis Hotel was no flophouse, its attendant restaurants no greasy spoons. Built as a luxury hotel, it opened on San Francisco's Union Square in 1904, survived the 1906 earthquake with no structural damage, and remains one of the city's most admired establishments today, doing business as the Westin St. Francis.

But still, luxury or not, $7 in 1958 was the equivalent of $62 in 2020 dollars, a bit much for two bowls of small oysters, regardless of the address.

Woolverton notes in his letter that he voiced his displeasure immediately on seeing the bill at the end of the meal.

"I complained to the waitress as well as the hostess and finally to the manager of the commissary on the Mezzanine floor," Woolverton claims, eventually getting the promise of a refund check of $1.25 for each of the oyster stews.

After three weeks of waiting for his $2.50, however, and several more complaints sent via mail, no check was forthcoming, Woolverton asserted in his letter.

That February 4 letter did the trick. The matter was resolved soon thereafter with a check for the full $7.00, which Woolverton graciously acknowledged in another missive.

"It was more than I expected," he wrote, "and I want you to know it was much appreciated and will make me continue as a faithful patron of the St. Francis, where I have stayed for more than 20 years."

The timeline in Woolverton's letter puts his first visit to the St. Francis no later than 1938, six years after his kidnapping.

The differences between his San Francisco lodging and those afforded by his abductors were, in as few words as possible, stark.

According to the *South Bend Tribune*'s daily temperature report (which drew its data from a "self-recording thermometer"), readings were at or just below 40 degrees Fahrenheit during the wee hours of January 27, 1932.

We may assume that Woolverton's unheated basement prison was no warmer.

Woolverton continued in his statement:

> I asked them for some more blankets, because I was told to lie on the cot at all times unless instructed otherwise. All conversation between me and the kidnappers was carried on through the crack in the trapdoor. The gap in the trapdoor was covered with some loose material, similar to loose woven burlap so that I could see a dim light, evidently an oil lamp above and at times could see shadows when the men above were walking around. I was told upon inquiring the time that it was 3:00 or 3:30 A.M., January 27th, having attended the movies the night before I had removed my bifocal glasses and was wearing distance glasses which made it impossible for me in this dim lighted room to read the time on my own watch.

Not being able to see his watch would soon become one of the least of Woolverton's worries. In the next portion of Howard A. Woolverton's federal statement, we are treated to what is perhaps the oddest part of the narrative, where Woolverton, whose apparently faulty memory recalled impossible feats of vision earlier on, now arises for a precise retelling of his meals.

And his captors, meanwhile, are revealed to have improved in the fine art of hospitality while, almost simultaneously, growing apoplectic with murderous rage.

It is early morning, January 27, 1932. Perhaps Woolverton has gotten a few hours of sleep, but he does not say so. It is breakfast time, and his kidnappers—here, at least—do not disappoint.

> I was given some coffee and a ham sandwich and a piece of boughten cake, then I was again instructed to lie on the couch [*sic*: meant cot] and stay there until further orders. I could hear an automobile going and coming at frequent intervals and I also heard a dog bark sounding like a good sized dog, possibly a Shepherd, frequently, when cars were moving. There was a window in the wall from the opposite side of the door,

also one on the side next to the hanging shelf which evidently had been covered up with dirt from the outside or covered so that no light could shine in. The only way I could tell it was day light was by a narrow streak of light on the wall from one side of the trap door. I was fed again (in) the morning and at noon. I had breakfast and dinner and was always guarded by one man on the above floor and I knew that some of them were sleeping part of the time. Whenever a car passed I could hear them walk to one side or the other of the house and comment: "Who the hell could that be?" During the day I heard at least eight to ten airplanes pass and I also heard what must have been a small tractor. Later on I was told through the trap door that we would eat in about an hour, then leave this place after it got dark. I took it from that that it must be about four P.M. I was anxious to know if they had any word from my family but was afraid to ask. Finally after finishing a small thin tough steak with chunks of partly fried potatoes, two pieces of bakery bread cut thick, covered with a thin gravy, a cup of coffee and a piece of cake, all of which was passed down through the trapdoor, the only part I could see of the man was his arm, I inquired if any word had been received from my family. The same man who jumped on my running board and had done most of the talking, answered my question saying, "Yes your god-damn wife went right straight to the police station with the letter, turned it over to them, and made a hell of a mess of the whole job, and you are going to pay for it." They said "your picture as well as your wife and daughter is on the front page of all Chicago papers, all of the police are searching as well as all of the Indiana Highway police, so we are going to move from here and you are going to pay the penalty."

As throughout his statement, Woolverton recounts none of the emotion he felt with this latest turn of events. But we have to imagine that these words began one of the darkest episodes of his life.

The kidnapper's meaning was clear. Because Florence Woolverton had decided—for reasons her husband could only guess at—to go to the police and the press, Woolverton was going to die. The fact that he would die a celebrity was surely no consolation; his fifteen minutes of fame would be a bitter pill.

We might imagine Woolverton's mind went to all the places minds stumble through when a death sentence is handed down.

How will it be done? When and where? Will it hurt?

How will I be remembered?

And then, because people seek meaning even when there is none, why? How does anything else in this life comport with its strange conclusion? The wealthy son of wealth; the corporate director; "one of South Bend's best known young men," as his wedding announcement put it; the man who lost one daughter and gained another almost immediately thereafter; the driver of a Pierce-Arrow Five-Passenger car was about to be executed by thugs who held him mortally accountable for a kidnapping they'd botched.

Did Woolverton wax philosophical as the day progressed in that cold basement? Or did he ponder more temporal matters?

Why, he surely asked himself, did Florence go to the police, when she was specifically told not to, when she was told her husband would die if she did?

Where would his body be left, and would it ever be found? What, specifically, are the papers saying?

His mind must have turned often to his daughter, Betty, now just twelve years old, growing up to become a woman he would never know.

She already had two strikes against her, abandoned by her mother and her father immediately after she was born.

And now, the man who had adopted her and loved her (except when she was naughty) and made her his own would soon be dead, utterly lost to her. She would be heartbroken, no doubt. But would she also be forever terrorized, perpetually scarred by what had been done to her dad?

And how would his wife fare, without Howard A. Woolverton to provide for her? Was there life insurance? A solid bank account? Family who would be willing to provide? The Boye Needle Company was part of her portfolio, and household sewing implements are the kinds of things people should in theory buy more of during a depression, so she should have been doing well in that regard. And between her family and her husband's, there was probably all the money and support needed to ensure Betty's well-being.

But still, the mind must wander when one faces existential questions. Might Florence, without her husband's income, and with the nation two years into sweeping financial dissolution, find the support of the families and the wealth at her disposal not quite as robust as she might have expected? Might she be forced to sell the house and a slightly used Pierce-Arrow Five-Passenger car, the latter at a premium if she was fortunate enough to find a buyer who preferred possessions tinged with morbidity?

And if so, where would widow and daughter live next? With her parents? With his? Or in some private but less assured domicile?

An apartment or a small home in one of South Bend's less exclusive neighborhoods?

Perhaps Mrs. Woolverton could learn a trade. She had done considerable work with the Gray Ladies, a volunteer Red Cross organization dedicated to helping the sick and injured, where she no doubt had learned a variety of marketable skills.

Or perhaps, at the age of forty-eight, she could find another man to share her life and her home with. Many men would be glad to take a bride at that age if the package included a beautiful home and a Pierce-Arrow Five-Passenger automobile. And in time, perhaps, this new husband might even find the room in his heart to love his new stepdaughter.

That he would soon be dead, Woolverton likely had no doubt. We must assume he believed his captors on that matter. He read the papers. He liked getting them first thing in the morning, in fact. He didn't like to be kept waiting. And he clearly didn't skip past the stories from that other world, where criminals and gangs ran rampant, robbing, kidnapping, and murdering.

Before her fourth birthday, Betty Woolverton had received her first lessons in that realm, courtesy of her father, who taught her not only the word *bootlegger* but a bootlegger's demeanor as well. Show her "a slouchy, unattractive man standing in a door way down town," and Betty, at three years and ten months old, thought about bootleggers.

We know Woolverton read the *Chicago Tribune* because we have that letter complaining about its delayed delivery. We can be certain he also read the *South Bend Tribune* to keep up with family if nothing else; South Bend's paper of record mentioned the Woolvertons hundreds of times throughout the twenties and thirties, maintaining a running account of their parties, their visits, their cruises, and their vacations.

The *South Bend Tribune* also featured murder, and lots of it.

Along with the steady drumbeat of fatalities in smaller quantities, we may assume Mr. Woolverton saw the nationally syndicated story in the March 20, 1927, *South Bend Tribune*, authored by Nell Ray Clarke and titled "Perplexing Riddle of the Very Many Unsolved Crimes."

Among the statistics presented in the article that a man like Woolverton might find terrifying: 237 homicides were reported in Manhattan in 1924, 112 of which resulted in indictment, and only 35 concluded with conviction.

"What became of the other 202 murderers of that single year in that single borough?" Ms. Clarke asked her readers. "A good guess is that they are wandering at liberty about the city and that you and I might meet several of them. . . . Daily throughout the country the number of unsolved murder mysteries is augmenting our national disgrace—our crime record."

Closer to home, the article continued, in Chicago, "whose criminal record is notorious"—a city less than one hundred miles west of South Bend—225 defendants were apprehended in murder cases during 1922. It goes on to state, "More than three-fourths of them paid no penalty and only six were executed. Only one out of every hundred murderers in 1922 paid the death penalty."

In 1925, the article continued, Chicago suffered another 509 homicides, with comparable prosecutorial results, and that "it has been estimated that in the country as a whole in 1923 there were about 10,000 homicides, and in 1924 11,000—a rate which has almost doubled in twenty-five years."

The article extensively quoted Louis Howe of the National Crime Commission.

"The greatest single contributing element is the automobile," Howe asserted as he sought a reason for the current crime wave. "In crimes roughly defined as banditry, involving murder as a sort of byproduct of robbers, the ability of the criminal to dash up from some unknown place, commit the crime and lose himself in the traffic or in the maze of country roads at great distances from the scene of the crime in a car . . . presents a problem to the police which has, as yet, no effective solution."

We might assume that the new phenomenon of the automobile caught the authorities by surprise. Introduced toward the end of the nineteenth century, some thirty million cars and trucks were sold through the 1920s, with an estimated one in five people owning a vehicle by 1930. What had begun as a fad popular among a tiny minority was a few short decades later a new American institution that cried out for control and regulation.

By 1918, all states were issuing license plates, often requiring drivers to register for new plates annually, with a new color each year so the cops could immediately spot the scofflaws.

Cars were a concern, but a lack of law enforcement coordination in the sprawling nation was another significant problem.

"The way of the criminal is made easy," Howe continued, "by the fact that there is no one central bureau in the country for the identification of criminals and no one agency through which criminals can be apprehended."

Further, in America, he wrote, there was "no standardized method of exchanging information among the States. Each State has its own method of criminal procedure, and as soon as a criminal steps across the borderline from one State to another he has an advantage that is not easily surmountable."

It was a recurring complaint of those distressed by crime and the absence of punishment: America had no real federal investigative or law enforcement agency and too few laws to define, prevent, and prosecute interstate crime, kidnapping or otherwise.

"Give me your tired, your poor, your huddled masses yearning to breathe free," begins the poem on the Statue of Liberty's great copper tablet. "The wretched refuse of your teeming shore; Send these, the homeless, tempest-tost to me."

The statue, installed in 1886 and welcoming those arriving by ship from Europe, was intended to serve as a beacon of hope for the world.

Instead, in the first decades of her life, the Statue of Liberty summoned the world's most desperate citizens to a place no better than what they'd left behind, a lawless land where murders went unpunished and kidnappers plied and perfected their trade, a nation of criminals little troubled by the short arms of the law, arms no longer than the nearest state border.

Surely, even before his kidnapping, Woolverton knew of all the crime and corruption lurking just beyond his threshold. The distressing news came thick and fast, and he doubtless read it all, including the *South Bend Tribune* on February 14, 1929—less than three years before his kidnapping—when the top of the front page bore a series of headlines describing what became known as the Saint Valentine's Day Massacre: "Seven Chicago Gangsters Killed by Rival Band; Riddled Bodies Found Huddled Against Wall; Victims are Lined Up and Executed With Machine and Shot Guns; Cold-Blooded Wholesale Murder Called New in Battles of Bootleggers."

The killers showed up dressed like police, the article noted. The victims were mostly members of the George "Bugs" Moran gang.

> Seven of the bodies, all in grotesque positions, just as they had fallen, were found by the police, ranged along the bullet marked and blood-spattered wall. On the floor in an outer room two others were found

still living but probably fatally wounded. Every body, including those of
the wounded men, bore six to 10 bullet wounds.

The assassins pulled up before the Moran gang headquarters in two
large automobiles . . . displaying stars and ordering the eight occupants
to raise their hands.

The article listed the names of most of the seven deceased men and
their roles, which included "Moran henchman" and "west side hoodlum."
The injured man, Frank Gusenberg, refused to speak to police as he lay
dying.

"To-day's slayings, in the form of a massacre, was something new in
Chicago gang warfare," the article noted. "Heretofore the gangsters took
their victims for a 'ride,' luring them into automobiles and killing them,
or else swept past in automobiles and raked their victims with gunfire.
Never before, however, has one gang invaded the stronghold of another,
rounded up the victims and calmly shot them to death."

No one was prosecuted for the massacre, but it is widely believed to
have been ordered by Al Capone, and it cemented his control over Chicago's bootlegging, prostitution, and gambling industries.

Chicagoans enjoyed Capone's services, incidentally. His net worth at
the peak of his operations has been estimated at $100 million, or a stag-
gering $1.3 billion in 2020 dollars. Capone's reign lasted just a few years,
however. He was convicted of tax evasion in October 1931, spent the next
eight years in prison, and died a syphilitic recluse in 1947.

The times were grim, the people knew it, and they wanted their news
to say as much, particularly the news that came into their homes every
day on paper.

According to a media survey conducted in 1939, newspapers—with
their ability to both depict and graphically describe the events of the
day, good and bad—were the first source of news for 63.8 percent of
Americans.[1]

Radio was coming into its own by then, however. Forty percent of US
households owned a radio in 1930, a number that jumped to 82.8 percent
by 1940. But radio remained a distant second to newspapers as a news
source in the 1930s, with 25.4 percent of respondents getting their news
primarily from that resource. Other sources of news cited by the survey
included magazines and the word of friends, but newsreels—the short
summaries of entertainment and current events that preceded movies
and served as the forerunner of television news—weren't mentioned as

a primary news source in the survey, perhaps because they were seen only when one went to the cinema.

Television wasn't mentioned in the 1939 survey, being several years away from its general introduction.

While the Great Depression brought a dramatic increase in radio ownership throughout the 1930s, American newspapers remained king of the news in that difficult decade, the principal means by which the people of this nation remained informed, forewarned, and terrified.

The process by which the news was brought day by day into people's homes and lives was perhaps just as terrifying, a Sisyphean task that involved not merely rolling a stone up a hill but also laboring against even more difficult things: acid, molten lead, and the truth.

6

Manufacturing the Truth

ON JANUARY 27, 1932, the great, clattering printing presses of American media turned their attention to Howard Arthur Woolverton.

The story was important.

The story of how the newspapers brought the news to their readers is important too.

People have always wanted to know. Sometimes, it's morbid curiosity. Sometimes, it's knowledge of a danger relevant to themselves. Often, they just want to learn more about something strange, interesting, or useful.

Whatever drives it, we have not yet satisfied the urgency of the human desire to find things out.

Today, every face before a computer screen, a tablet, a phone; every ear listening to an electronic speaker; every fingertip reading braille is another manifestation of that urge.

Paper—light, flat, and foldable—was the medium of choice for conveying information throughout most of modern human history. First fabricated around 100 ce in China from bark, rags, and bamboo, paper has played a central role in human knowledge ever since.

Making marks on paper has always been easy, of course. A blackened stick will do.

a solid majority of the city's residents lived in a home where at least one local paper showed up.

Usually, like Howard Woolverton, they were reading about other people.

But on January 27, 1932, the typewriters, the Linotypes, the hot lead, the paper, the acid, and the vast spinning presses were brought together to tell the world about Howard Woolverton himself.

Because on that day, he was the news.

Reduced to the terms an average newspaper editor would understand, here's where the Woolverton kidnapping stood on the morning of January 27, 1932:

Who: Howard Arthur Woolverton, fifty-two, wealthy Indiana industrialist; his wife, Florence Woolverton; and at least two hoodlums, identities unknown

What: A kidnapping

When: Beginning a little after 11:00 p.m. on January 26, 1932, and not over yet

Where: South Bend, Indiana, and unknown wilderness west of the city

Why: For a $50,000 cash ransom

How: With a gun, at night, using the element of surprise, along with a ransom note and the threat of murder

This was the kind of story the average American newspaper editor lived to publish because it was the kind of story the average newspaper subscriber loved to read.

The Woolverton story offered something for everyone—crime, fear, wealth, guns, a distraught wife, a twelve-year-old daughter.

Most importantly, it was a story with a victim anyone could relate to. Howard Woolverton was a family man, a working man, a regular Joe. An everyman. While he was wealthy, he was no celebrity. He went to his job every day, like most people. He came home to his family, like most people. He wasn't an actor, a tycoon, a notorious playboy, an aristocrat. He was the secretary-treasurer of the Malleable Steel Range Manufacturing Company. He maintained notes and records, handled the money, and balanced the books—all honest work—for a company that made things.

If Howard Woolverton could be kidnapped, anyone well-to-do or even solidly middle class was at risk. If the criminals were going after the likes of Howard Woolverton now, who would be next? Would abduction be the fate of anyone who reached a comfortable degree of wealth? If a man like Howard Woolverton could be kidnapped, so could anyone else who'd made it.

The American Dream was dead.

Furthering the power of the event, the story of Woolverton's abduction came with a built-in cliffhanger: As of the morning of January 27, 1932, Howard Woolverton, whereabouts and condition uncertain, remained in the clutches of murderous hoodlums, his life dangling by a thread, the impossible sum of $50,000 all that stood between him and the hereafter.

It was a riveting story, the kind the newspapers existed to tell.

Before the reporters could report, however, they needed to get the story, and that's a story unto itself.

On that desolate road in the wilderness west of South Bend, Florence Woolverton had been given clear instructions, spoken at least twice to make sure the hard-of-hearing woman clearly knew the conditions under which she would not become a widow.

In his statement, Howard Woolverton had recalled the kidnappers telling him, "We are going to give Mrs. Woolverton a letter with instructions which she is to follow and she will be instructed to show it to nobody, particularly the police, under penalty of death to yourself."

By the next afternoon, however, Howard Woolverton—imprisoned in a cold farmhouse basement—had received the grim news that his wife had violated the simple terms of that agreement, and done so spectacularly. Not only did Florence Woolverton go "right straight to the police station with the letter," as the kidnappers put it, but things had deteriorated further: "Your picture as well as your wife and daughter is on the front page of all Chicago papers."

What happened?

Well, as instructed, Mrs. Woolverton had headed back to South Bend—slowly—as she presumably had no idea how to shift from first into any higher gear.

Nor did she know how to get the car moving from a stop. So at the first red light she reached in town, she choked the engine.

"As she neared the downtown section the motor of her car stalled," reported the *South Bend Tribune* in its afternoon edition of January 27. "Police Sergt. Nicholas Laskowski stood near the intersection and she called to him, explaining excitedly that her husband had been kidnaped.[2] The officer took her to police headquarters immediately. It was about 12:10 o'clock then."

In retelling this portion of the story, the *Garrett (Indiana) Clipper*— which repeatedly stood alone in the journalistic universe for the odd things it wrote about the Woolverton case—stated that Mrs. Woolverton "managed to drive into the city but became confused in traffic and a traffic officer jumped to the running board of the car when she lost control of the auto."

Depending on whom you believe, Mrs. Woolverton either hit the city limits of South Bend in a wildly careening Pierce-Arrow or simply killed the engine because she didn't know how to drive it, but it also should not be said that Mrs. Woolverton failed anything that winter night.

The kidnappers were in charge; Mr. and Mrs. Woolverton were merely unwilling employees of the enterprise.

In fact, along with the fact that the central player in a kidnapping project—the person kidnapped—doesn't want the role, kidnappings generally lack the team spirit one looks for when launching a bold new enterprise. Even if the long arm of the law can be kept in check, many on the team—in particular, the people being snatched and those gathering up and delivering the cash to free them—are decidedly opposed to the success of the venture and are wholly unqualified to participate even if they do decide to give things the old college try.

Mrs. Woolverton, daughter of wealth, upper-class housewife and mother, Red Cross volunteer, an "Illinois Belle" popular during her younger years in the social circles of Wheaton, Illinois, and a certified "great favorite" in South Bend to boot (if we can believe that 1905 marriage item from the *South Bend Tribune*), would not be anyone's first choice for doing what had to be done when a kidnapping team needed her to buck up and take charge.

This was the play she'd been brought on to quarterback: Take this note back to town, Florence Flannery Woolverton. Don't get the police involved. Just show it to your rich relatives, gather the cash and drop it off as instructed, and you'll get your husband back.

Do it for the Gipper, they might have added.

But Mrs. Woolverton was given the wrong equipment: a car she couldn't drive. The woman who'd miscarried more than once, whose only known live birth ended in crib death two days later, who turned around and adopted an abandoned baby weeks after that, if not hours—thus

tough as she might have been in the face of certain kinds of disappointment—was not cut out for this work.

When a well-to-do woman is threatened at gunpoint, forcibly separated from her husband, and told to drive a car with an unfamiliar
transmission at night, discretion is most likely not at the forefront of
her mind.

And then, stuck in a dead car in the dead of night in winter at a red
light in downtown South Bend, we might imagine that turning in panic
to the first police officer she saw and blurting out the whole sordid story
was most likely something like reflex.

Of course she talked to the police.

But then, the police talked to the press.

Why?

Secrecy was, most likely, never an option for the cops. The Woolvertons' twelve-year-old daughter was going to find out what had happened
to her daddy, and she'd blab. The household staff would surely talk.
And, as we'll see in the coming pages, the state of Indiana was about to
get involved in very noticeable ways. So the South Bend police had the
choice of issuing an official statement or tamping down a rumor-fueled
uprising of frightened citizens.

Thus, the police went to the press. And the press, as the press is wont
to do, went to the people.

When one searches "Howard Woolverton" with the date of January
27, 1932, on Newspapers.com, which has compiled full-page, optical-
character scans of original newspaper editions from the last two centuries, 242 matches are returned, linking to papers across the country.
In Indiana, at least twenty-one papers picked up the story. In neighboring Illinois and Ohio, the story was covered by a dozen papers. Comparable numbers of papers in Pennsylvania and New York published
news of Woolverton's abduction, including the New York Times, where
it ran on page two. It was picked up by several papers in Brooklyn and
New York City's Daily News, founded in 1919 as the nation's first tabloid.
The Austin-American Statesman was one of at least five newspapers in
Texas to publish the tale, dedicating half a column of its eight-column
front page to details of the crime. At least eight California papers helped
spread the news. As far away as Alaska, which would not become a US
state for another twenty-seven years, people were talking about Howard

Woolverton. "Manufacturer Kidnapped" read the headline at the bottom of the front page of the *Fairbanks Daily News-Miner*.

The most thorough coverage, however, fell to the two dailies in Woolverton's hometown, the *South Bend Tribune* and the *South Bend News-Times*, both of which published numerous front-page stories and pictures, including a range of terrifying allegations.

"A band of seven criminals," the *News-Times* confidently announced, "graduated from machine gun bank holdups to kidnaping for ransom, is the gang holding Howard A. Woolverton, secretary-treasurer of the Malleable Steel Range Mfg. Co., for $50,000 ransom."

Who shared these allegations with the *News-Times*? That's a story in itself, to be told later, an element of the perfect storm of factors that gave Woolverton's kidnapping its unique significance in American history.

"The Woolverton abduction," the article continued, "is another in the long series of abductions which the band has engineered in the last two years in Illinois, Indiana, Iowa, Wisconsin, Missouri and Michigan. The wealth the desperadoes have exacted from victims by torture and terrorism is estimated at more than $1,000,000. Last year they got $500,000."[3]

That version of the abduction was picked up by the United Press and distributed to its subscribing newspapers around the nation, some of which embellished it further. The *Oakland Tribune* in California, for example, promoted the kidnappers from merely "seven criminals" to a "band of seven *super*-criminals," a variation other papers published as well. Sensationalism sold then, as it does today, and America's primary wire services were happy to try to outdo each other on that score.

The United Press was one of two major news associations active in the twentieth century. Founded in 1907, it competed fiercely with its bigger, older rival, the Associated Press, whose birth dates to 1846. Together, they still provide thousands of newspapers and other media outlets with a barrage of daily news, features, fashion updates, and analyses.

While more distant publications relied on the wires for the Woolverton story, many of the papers closer by sent their own staff to cover the kidnapping, especially the papers that could establish a local angle. The *Chicago Tribune*, for example, sent a reporter and gave the story top billing, with this headline across the top of the front page on January 27: "Rich Man Held for $50,000."

Pursuing local angles, the article noted that Mrs. Woolverton was the daughter of a Wheaton, Illinois, man, married her husband in Chicago, and was part-owner, with her brother, of the Boye Needle Company in Chicago.

The story went on to mention Betty Woolverton, declaring that she "was at home with three maids when the kidnaping occurred."

It also presaged the birth of a new national fear, rippling outward from South Bend, Indiana.

"Carl L. Hibberd, president of the South Bend Chamber of Commerce," the *Chicago Tribune* article stated, "declared that no one was safe while such crimes were possible."

Hibberd, who we must imagine shook his fist above his head as he spoke, added, "All the resources of South Bend should be mobilized to bring the perpetrators of this crime to justice."

Given the urgency of the crime and the necessity of telling many aspects of the story quickly, errors and contradictions were inevitable, and once something was published inaccurately, it would roll out along the wires and get picked up by every subscribing publication.

One of the day's most glaring errata originally appeared in the *South Bend News-Times*: Immediately after announcing, "This is a stickup" and getting into the Woolvertons' car, the bandit "removed Mr. Woolverton's glasses and gave him a pair of smoked spectacles to wear."

The next paragraphs describe the course through South Bend Woolverton was forced to drive.

Most kidnappers, no matter how bold or desperate, do not remove spectacles or cover the eyes of men who are driving said kidnappers through a city, something that apparently escaped the notice of both the reporter and the paper's front-page editors.

The *Chicago Tribune*, which billed itself in 1932 as "The World's Greatest Newspaper," not only republished the mistake; it also repackaged it, adding drama and making the transition from being blinded to being ordered to drive even more pronounced.

"From this car stepped a man with a pistol," recounted the article. "He threw open the rear door of the Woolvertons' car and stepped in, menacing the couple with his gun. Then he leaned over into the front seat, drew off Woolverton's spectacles, and replaced them with a pair of smoked glasses. Then he told Woolverton to obey orders strictly, and commanded that he drive through the city."

The award for most unforced errors, however, goes to the *Garrett Clipper* of Garrett, Indiana, which packed them in thick, including two inaccuracies (number of cars and scene of abduction) into a single sentence: "The kidnapers, traveling in two automobiles, trailed the Woolvertons to their home, abducted them in front, and took them to an isolated section two miles east of the city."

The article further alleged that Mrs. Woolverton "had to walk most of the way back to South Bend" instead of driving the Pierce-Arrow.

Perhaps the greatest faux pas in the article, at least from a social perspective, had to do with where the Woolvertons went between the movie and their abduction. According to the *Garrett Clipper*, they did not enjoy a nightcap at the stately Studebaker mansion; rather, as Mrs. Woolverton was quoted as claiming, "It was late when the show was over and we stopped at a little lunchroom for a bite to eat."

The paper also quoted Mrs. Woolverton as recalling, "Two young men jumped out. They had revolvers in their hands. One got into our car. He sat in the front seat with my husband and pressed the revolver against him." This directly contradicts the account of a single pedestrian who climbed into the back seat after brandishing a gun

The number of people involved in actually taking Woolverton remained fluid throughout that day's coverage, in the *South Bend News-Times* and other publications. One front-page *News-Times* story said it was "two men," while another article several columns away claimed that "Mr. Woolverton was kidnaped late Tuesday night by three armed abductors."

The *News-Times* also offered a second, competing theory of who had orchestrated the crime.

While the paper had declared confidently on the front page that the kidnapping was the work of "a band of seven criminals" who had made a career of kidnapping from their base in Chicago, an article on page two of that day's paper offered compelling evidence that the abduction had been planned from the other end of the Kidnapping Crescent, in Detroit, by a gang of drug dealers.

"Members of the Detroit underworld have been investigating the habits of wealthy South Bend men during the past year," the article alleged. "Members of a dope ring in the Michigan city were in South Bend for some time, endeavoring to learn the names and relative financial standing of the city's industrial and financial leaders."

This information came from an unnamed local man, who claimed that a "woman companion" told him she'd been tasked by her "chief" in Detroit with gathering the data on South Bend's leading lights.

Among the many discrepancies of the day's newspaper coverage, the kidnappers' note generated its share.

Each paper with local reporters on hand presented a variation of the note, different from the others in various respects, and all presented as the one true version.

The *South Bend Tribune* presented one of the longest versions of the note and detailed its appearance—twice, in two separate articles, with contradictions. One article described the note as "printed in large, coarse, penciled letters on four sheets of ruled tablet paper." A second said it had been "printed in pencil on three sheets of ruled tablet paper," adding, "Although the printing was coarse and uneven in an attempt to disguise the handwriting the instructions were in good grammar."

The *Tribune*'s version of the note read this way:

> Do not notify police. Your husband has been "kidnaped" for ransom. We want $50,000. Failure to comply with commands means you will never see him again: Now, here is what to do. Wrap the money—good—in heavy paper. Get in the four-passenger Packard with the trunk on it that stays at the plant. Indiana license No. 20. Go to Chicago Heights at 8 p.m., Wednesday night. Start out on highway No. 1. Do not drive over 25 miles an hour. When you see a car behind you flash the lights 10 times, drop the package on the pavement. If you do not get the signal by the time you get to Danville, turn around and come back the same way, not over 25 miles an hour. This is your final instructions—no others. Do this, you and some of the family will get hurt—bad.

For starters, it should be acknowledged that the last sentence of the ransom note includes a typo. It's missing some words; indeed, an important phrase, as the note as published suggested that following the instructions of the ransom note would result in further harm to multiple family members.

What did the note really say?

As luck would have it, images of the original note in its entirety were published by the *South Bend Tribune* on April 23, 1932—almost three months after the kidnapping. One could speculate at length on the why and the how of its publication. Perhaps the *Tribune* pestered the police

The first page of the January 26, 1932, ransom note. *South Bend Tribune*, April 23, 1932.

for months for the okay to publish the actual note. Perhaps the police finally relented, either to shut up the *Tribune* or to see if putting prime evidence of the crime out there for public consumption might turn up a new lead or two.

The five-page note (not three or four pages) got prominent coverage in the *Tribune* that day, plastered across the bottom of the newspaper's front page beside the following preamble: "Photostatic copies of the $50,000 ransom note given Mrs. Howard A. Woolverton by the kidnapers of her husband a few minutes after both were seized the night of Jan. 27 [*sic*; should have said Jan. 26] are shown here for the first time."

It turns out that the *Tribune* did a fairly good job of transcribing the note on that first frantic day after the kidnapping—except for that one typo that ended up in virtually every newspaper's coverage.

The letters on the note were big and blocky, most of them capitalized, with random dashes and other punctuation, a horizontal line here and there, and Roman numerals I through V circled at the top of each page to indicate order.

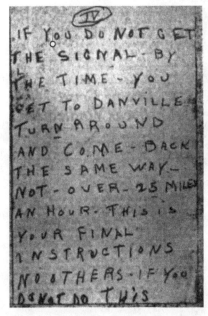

The last two pages of the January 26, 1932, ransom note. "IF YOU DO NOT,"
plainly visible at the bottom of page IV, was dropped in virtually all newspaper
reporting. *South Bend Tribune*, April 23, 1932.

The first page featured these words: "Do Not Notify Police" followed by several black lines, and then this: "Your husband has been
'Kidnapped' for ransom. We want $50,000—Failure to comply with our
command..."

One must turn to the second page for the ominous consequences:
"means you will never see him again."

After two more horizontal lines across the sheet, the kidnappers got
down to business: "Now here is what to do—wrap the money—good—in
heav [sic] paper—get in the four passenger Packard with the trunk on
it—that stays at the plant."

The next line is illegible, but, based on reporting by numerous papers
at the time, it most likely read "Indiana license No. 20."

The third sheet says, "Go to Chicago Heights (at 8 PM Wednesday
night start out on Highway #1—Do not drive over 25 miles an hour
When you see a car behind you flash the lights ten times—drop the
package on the pavement."

Pages four and five outline the rest of the steps, as previously re-ported, and page five ends with that grim warning: "This is your final instructions no others—If you do not do this you and some of the family will get hurt—bad."

Publication of the note in pictures confirmed that it ended with a logical threat. Do what the note says, or people are going to get hurt. But in the journalistic frenzy of the first day's reporting, "If you do not" got dropped from the message, so the version published in virtually all papers read "Do this, you and some of the family will get hurt—bad."

Which made no sense.

Somewhere along the trail of steps required to bring information to the daily newspaper page, someone left off four crucial words. The fault may have been the reporter's, or the error might have occurred at the printing press. Remember, the kidnapping occurred well before the days of photocopiers, instant cameras, or cell phones that took pictures. Most likely, every reporter tasked with learning the contents of the note had to copy it down by hand or, worse yet, hear it spoken aloud by whatever official was responsible for keeping it safe. Maybe that's where the er-ror occurred, with its official reading by a police official who left off the words. The note—a key piece of evidence, written by hand, establishing a clear motive and making threats against multiple lives—was probably not passed around a room full of reporters.

So, with the note out of reach, each scribe assigned to the story had to do their best to capture or manufacture the message, and the errors and fabulations cascaded.

For example, in the version of the note published in the *Indianapolis News*, no mention was made of dropping the bundle of cash. According to that version, the kidnappers would be entirely satisfied with things as long as the $50,000 was packed up tight and given a ride back and forth to Danville by way of Chicago Heights.

This was no minor errand the kidnappers were demanding, inciden-tally. Chicago Heights, Illinois, is a drive of some eighty miles west of South Bend. And once the person with the ransom reached Chicago Heights, they were looking at another 119-mile trek, due south to Dan-ville, Illinois, all of which was to be driven at twenty-five miles per hour—a five-hour trip. And if the kidnappers had not flashed their lights before the driver of the tightly wrapped cash reached Danville, back they must go at the same snail's pace. It would take all night and well into the next morning to complete the round-trip journey.

The version of the note published in the *Indianapolis News* included the Chicago Heights–to–Danville itinerary but ended with this sentence, a complete fabrication: "If there is any slip up in this plan your husband may be killed."

More amusing still, the *South Bend Tribune*, in another article on the front page of that day's paper, claimed, "A note given to Mrs. Woolverton by the kidnapers when she was released demanded that the money be paid over to them at 8 o'clock tonight or 'your husband may be killed.'"

That passage did not appear at all in the actual note.

So, to follow the journalistic thread, the *South Bend Tribune* offered up what it claimed was a complete, verbatim copy of the ransom note in one article in that day's paper, but cribbed another paper's erroneous version of the note elsewhere in the same edition.

One must wonder if the kidnappers were at least a little miffed by the inaccurate representations of their note, even while they raged most vociferously about the fact that word had gotten out at all.

Looking back through the filter of nearly a century of hindsight, we can agree with the *South Bend Tribune* that the note was a marvel of good grammar, as well as a concise, well-written document that featured more than its share of drama. And its author was afraid to think outside the box when it came to punctuation, capitalization, and creative underlining.

Fail to do what the note said, the highly literate hoodlum had written, clearly channeling the muse who inspires criminals, and "you and some of the family will get hurt—bad."

It is with the dash and that final word that our bootlegger-cum-Shakespeare really worked to bring life to his (or her) prose.

Getting threatened with being hurt is all in a day's work for some people. But getting hurt "—bad" is an attention-grabber for even the most nonchalant. And "bad" preceded by a dash adds the additional element of uncertainty that "bad" alone cannot.

How bad is "—bad," after all?

Did the gang's master of prose read the various versions of the note in that day's papers with a sense of professional pride? And was it disappointing for him or her to read that last sentence in the *South Bend Tribune* and other papers and lament the dropped words?

The dramatic conclusory flourish, the grand finale of the handwritten ransom note, must have been meant to prompt awe, fear, and perhaps a little literary respect. Instead, the subscribers with the sharpest eyes must have finished reading with a sense of disappointment.

Regardless of which version of the note one reads as they were published in that day's newspapers, and despite the typos, the note's intent was clear: if the police are notified, Howard Arthur Woolverton will die.

Keeping the abduction of Woolverton out of the newspapers was not an option, so John Kuespert, chief of the South Bend Police Department, did the next best thing. He talked to the kidnappers.

7

A Message for the Kidnappers

THE PEOPLE WHO KIDNAPPED Howard A. Woolverton might have
been ruthless criminals, and they did know how to wave guns around
and talk tough, but South Bend police chief John Kuespert knew they
were beholden to the same rational calculations as any other human
being.

Yes, Kuespert knew, the kidnappers wanted $50,000 in cash. How-
ever, the chief surely understood that walking away with $50,000 was,
while the best outcome, not the only result the kidnappers imagined.

Should the plot fall apart, the kidnappers would move to plan B: don't
get killed and don't get caught; or, if we do get caught, don't get charged
with murder.

By bringing in the press, announcing far and wide that a kidnapping
had occurred, and letting the newspapers and their subscribers in on all
the details, Chief Kuespert was notifying the kidnappers in no uncertain
terms that their little scheme had not gone according to plan.

The wheels had come off. The whole thing was a smoking wreck.

Sharing the full contents of the ransom note was part of the plan,
most likely. By letting the papers have at it, Kuespert was letting the
kidnappers know that there would be no payment happening that night,

and they wouldn't want to try for it even if the drop was still on. After all, once the note had been published, complete with the time and the route of the ransom delivery, who in South Bend with a car wouldn't have headed out at the appointed hour? People might have gone in the hopes of catching the kidnappers themselves, or witnessing the whole thing going down (a viable form of entertainment years before the widespread arrival of the television), or flashing their lights ten times behind every car in the vicinity in the hopes one might disgorge $50,000 in well-wrapped cash.

Had the kidnappers headed out that night on the designated route, they would have known what to expect, courtesy of Chief Kuespert: a parade of thrill-seekers, detective wannabes, and the morbidly curious, along with enough flashing headlights to match a firefly infestation of biblical proportions.

But, along with throwing a spanner into the kidnapping logistics, Kuespert also needed to convey the most important part of the message to the kidnappers: the money wasn't there.

At a noontime press conference, Kuespert's central message was clear, and it was dutifully passed on in an article that received above-the-fold treatment on the *South Bend Tribune*'s front page: "Chief Kuespert notified the abductors through a statement to newspaper men at noon that it is impossible for Mrs. Woolverton to comply with their ransom demands."

The reasons given were both financial and emotional: "'Mrs. Woolverton cannot raise any such sum of money or any amount near it,' Kuespert said, 'and furthermore, the condition under which the money was to be delivered cannot be met because of Mrs. Woolverton's physical condition. She is in a state of nervous breakdown and cannot drive a car.'"

To make sure the financial point was conveyed clearly, Mrs. Woolverton—likely with the approval of Chief Kuespert—made herself available to the press, during those moments when she was not an emotional basket case (if she ever was—we'll have more to say about this brave woman in the coming pages).

"Wife Says She Cannot Meet Ransom Offer" declared one front-page headline in the *Tribune*.

"He told them their demand was preposterous," Mrs. Woolverton recalled of her husband's reaction to the ransom amount.

The article followed with another version of what Woolverton said in his statement that he told the kidnappers—that he was on the verge of going broke: "'Mr. Woolverton told them that it was impossible for him to give them any large amount of money,' Mrs. Woolverton added. 'He told them that the business of the Malleable Steel Range Manufacturing company had been bad and that he had very little cash.'"

But pleading relative poverty was only the first helping of Kuespert's communications plan. A second objective: notify the kidnappers that the police were already on their trail.

The kidnappers probably thought their ransom note of block letters and random punctuation was very clever, but they'd revealed something in it, and in their statements to Mr. and Mrs. Woolverton, that Kuespert used to his full advantage.

"Get in the four passenger Packard with the trunk on it—that stays at the plant," they'd written. "Indiana license No. 20."

So, they'd been watching. One of the kidnappers had been stalking the Malleable Steel Range plant, paying attention to the cars parked there, how long they were left and who drove them, even noting license plate numbers.[1]

They weren't just watching the plant, either, as indicated by a chilling exchange reported in the *Tribune*: "Mrs. Woolverton was instructed to drive the Woolverton car back to South Bend," the paper reported.

> "But I can't drive this car," she protested.
> "Oh yes you can," one of the bandits said with a laugh. "You drive a car all right."

The implication? When it came to who drove what when, the kidnappers had done their job, cruising South Bend, observing, waiting, and watching Mrs. Woolverton as she went about her day.

As the *South Bend News-Times* put it, "Mrs. Woolverton said she believed the terrorists had planned the crime for some time and had become familiar with her family." One man, the paper reported, "called her husband by name, she said, and asked personal questions."

It is the inconvenient nature of physics that watching puts one at risk of being watched, and this was a point Kuespert worked hard to drive home on the day after Woolverton was snatched: We've seen you.

Did Chief Kuespert really have any leads on who the spies were? Most likely, he was bluffing, but the chief wanted to plant seeds of doubt, and he got the *South Bend Tribune* to cooperate.

The Woolverton kidnapping was front-page news across the nation and dominated the evening edition of the *South Bend Tribune*. *South Bend Tribune*, January 27, 1932.

In fact, the biggest headline in the January 27, 1932, evening edition of the *Tribune*, the headline that ran across the top of the front page, each letter some two inches tall, featured three words in all caps, clearly meant to sow fear and uncertainty in the kidnappers' hearts:

"HUNT WOOLVERTON 'SPOTTER'"

The subheadline elaborated on the point: "Police Work on Tips Kuespert Got."

The article led this way: "Police this afternoon were working on clews which they hope will lead them to the local 'spotter' of the gang that kidnaped Howard A. Woolverton."

Later in the story, that line of reasoning resumed:

The search for the local "spotter" got under way immediately on the heels of the kidnaping when Chief Kuespert told members of the Woolverton family that he was convinced that the kidnapers were professionals from another city and that they operated in league with a local man who tipped them off as to the movements of the Woolvertons. . . . Chief Kuespert said that he has certain definite information concerning the man believed to have been the "spotter" but declined to discuss these facts.

"This man may have been watching Mr. and Mrs. Woolverton for several weeks, even trailing their car, until conditions were right for staging the kidnaping," Chief Kuespert said.

We know you've been watching, Kuespert was telling the kidnappers. Your note and your words to the Woolvertons made that clear. But while you were watching, you got watched.

You're not invisible, after all.

Before they saw that headline and the words beneath it, each kidnapper's thoughts were perhaps focused on how best to spend his or her share of $50,000.

After they'd read the paper that day, a new set of more serious concerns would have set in: How many trips did one or more of us make to scope out the Malleable Steel Range plant and the Packard parked there? How many times did we trail Mrs. Woolverton? How much of this work was done in daylight? Could anyone have seen our spotter well enough to identify him or her, or the car they drove?

And, most importantly, the kidnappers must have thought, let's just say, hypothetically, that Kuespert isn't bluffing, that they really do have some clues about who was surveilling the Woolvertons, and those clues eventually lead them to our spotter and thereby back to us, who have, again, hypothetically, just happened to have murdered Howard Woolverton in the meantime . . . what are the chances we'll all hang?

When day broke on January 27, 1932, Chief Kuespert had a kidnapped man, a distraught wife, and his work cut out for him.

With the release of the afternoon dailies, in particular the *South Bend Tribune*, he had gotten the ransom note published, making it null and void; he had told the kidnappers that the Woolvertons and their kin didn't have anything close to $50,000, making their little enterprise hopeless; and he had warned them that one of them had been seen, making murder a really bad idea.

But there may have been a fourth to-do involving the media, drawn up by Kuespert or other members of his ad hoc committee of Woolverton rescuers. The objective: control the emotional narrative.

In the first years of the Great Depression, the public was just as likely to sympathize with the hoodlums as the authorities. It was the authorities that had gotten everyone into this fix, recall, while the hoods were doing their best to redistribute the wealth downward. A rich man who lost $50,000 would still be richer than most people, and some of that

Woolverton dosh would surely have made its way through the kidnappers' fingers and into the hands of the little people soon enough.

So, Godspeed, kidnappers. It's been a pleasure doing business with you. Come on back soon.

But no, this was not just a business transaction between adults, one a rich man and the rest poor men with guns. There was a girl involved, a twelve-year-old, and the cowards who took her dad were threatening her life as well, promising in their ham-fisted ransom note to hurt unnamed members of the family "—bad."

So how do you play up that angle for the people of South Bend who might be inclined to see things from the kidnappers' perspective?

Here's an idea: Don't keep Betty cowering at home. Send her to school. But not alone. Assign a cop to protect her all the way there and back.

And tell the press.

She could have stayed home, of course. Why take the chance? How important were classes that day? Surely they'd invented makeup assignments by 1932?

But a girl going to school under police guard would elicit far more sympathy than a girl hiding in her mansion, and the newspapers were glad to cooperate.

"Under Guard," read the headline on page two of the *South Bend Tribune*. In the photo beneath it, Betty Woolverton smiles enigmatically, dressed casually and looking a little boyish, hands tucked into trouser pockets. The date of the photo isn't provided, but her short sleeves suggested it was a summer shot, not an image captured that day. Nor was that trip to school really much of an occasion for smiles.

The one-sentence caption under the picture read, "An armed policeman escorted Betty Woolverton, 12-year-old daughter of the kidnapped manufacturer, Howard A. Woolverton, to and from the Jefferson school today while police sought the whereabouts of her father, for whose return $50,000 is demanded. Betty Woolverton is the only child of Mr. and Mrs. Woolverton."

The threat would not cease when the girl got home, either; her home had become an armed camp.

As the *South Bend Tribune* reported, "A police guard was thrown about the Woolverton home by Chief Kuespert a few minutes after he received the report of the kidnaping from Mrs. Woolverton shortly after midnight."

Woolverton Reward Fund Near $10,000

UNDER GUARD.

BETTY WOOLVERTON

A picture and story in the *South Bend News Times* of January 27, 1932, concerning the kidnappers' implied threats against Betty Woolverton, appeared next to news of a reward fund established by the *South Bend News-Times*. *South Bend Tribune*, January 27, 1932.

So there you go, folks. These are no heroes of the poor and downtrodden. They've grabbed a working man, driven his wife into "a state of nervous breakdown," and scared his little girl to boot. If you know something that you've decided to keep to yourself, you're not protecting Robin Hood and his Merry Men. You're protecting thugs for whom even little girls are a target when there's lucre at stake.

One must wonder if the kidnappers themselves looked into the mirror with a little more introspection.

An odd footnote to the story of that day's coverage: the job of notifying the Woolverton family of the kidnapping was left to the press, if the *South Bend News-Times* is to be believed.

John Woolverton, Howard's brother and president and general manager of the Malleable Steel Range company, "read the details of the kidnaping in the News-Times extra edition," that paper announced. And then, on reading the story, he immediately notified Jacob Woolverton, the father of both men.

"Betty, 12-year old daughter of the Woolvertons," the article continued, "and the servants in the household did not learn of the affair until informed by The News-Times early Wednesday morning."

How exactly a reporter for the *News-Times* was the first to get word of the kidnapping to Betty Woolverton, waking up in her home, was not explained. Nor was the necessity of informing her made clear, given the commotion around the dwelling immediately after Mrs. Woolverton met with the chief of police.

These small mysteries aside, it is no wonder the kidnappers were irate as they read that day's newspapers. What was intended to be a private business matter between themselves and one South Bend family had not just the whole city up in arms, but—as shall be detailed in coming chapters—the whole region as well, including multiple state police forces.

In fact, the first thing that morning, phones were ringing all over the Kidnapping Crescent, and not just to government officials in state capitals.

At least one call was placed to the Chicago headquarters of a team of shadowy vigilantes. These once-famous amateur sleuths were about to be disbanded in infamy, but not before they helped elevate the Woolverton case to its pivotal place in history.

Before we discuss the extraordinary response the Woolverton kidnapping generated, however, we need to remember that all of it was reported by one woman: Florence Flannery Woolverton.

Three times on the front page of the *South Bend Tribune* of January 27, 1932, Mrs. Woolverton's emotional state was described in the starkest of terms.

"Early this morning," reported one article, "she had suffered a hysterical, nervous collapse as a group of curious onlookers gathered in front of the home."

Where Mrs. Woolverton's picture appeared, at the top of the front page beside her husband's, the caption read: "Unable to raise $50,000 demanded as ransom by kidnapers who abducted her husband and terrorized her late Tuesday night, Mrs. Howard A. Woolverton to-day was reported near a nervous breakdown."

A third article on the front page also mentioned her "state of nervous breakdown," and the point is made one more time on page two: "'These kidnapers evidently are out-of-town men and are old hands at the game,'

Chief Kuespert said after talking with Mrs. Woolverton, who left his office on the verge of hysteria."

Remember, this was an upper-class woman in her late forties enjoying an evening at the theater, followed by a pleasant nightcap at the Studebaker mansion, when her world was abruptly turned upside down by armed thugs.

She should have been asleep by midnight. Instead, as January 27 began, she was sitting in a stalled car in downtown South Bend, frantically flagging down a police officer moments after she'd been separated at gunpoint from her husband of twenty-seven years, sent off with warnings and a note that made clear she must produce an impossible sum in less than twenty-four hours or lose her beloved for eternity.

Surely, as the hours wore on, her mind worked through a parallel of what Howard Woolverton pondered when he was told his wife had gone to the police and he must therefore die.

If my husband is killed today, how and where will it be done? Will it hurt? Will we ever find his body? How shall I explain this to Betty? Will she be forever scarred? How will the two of us make our way without him?

The importance of Mrs. Woolverton's pulling herself together cannot be overstated, however.

We know that after Mrs. Woolverton arrived at South Bend police headquarters, Police Chief John Kuespert was roused from his bed to hear her story. And, with one of South Bend's pillars in the hands of murderous extortionists, his family under threat as well, and no citizen of middling or better means safe from abduction if this first gambit succeeded, Kuespert needed answers.

Mrs. Woolverton might have been exhausted, hysterical, or on the verge of a nervous breakdown, but Kuespert had to get information only she could provide, and he needed it immediately.

We can guess at that extraordinary, wee-hours meeting between a distraught wife and mother and the chief of police, a chief who had to balance comforting her with the safety of his city.

Surely, Kuespert knew, at any moment as he sat in conference with Mrs. Woolverton at police headquarters, an officer might pull up to the station to report that the bullet-riddled body of a well-dressed man in his early fifties had been found dumped along a highway west of town.

Identifying the remains would have been a mere formality at that point.

But Kuespert, despite professional stress and lack of sleep, seems to have worked as well with Mrs. Woolverton as he would the next day with the press.

And Mrs. Woolverton showed a profound grace under pressure, despite the fear of impending widowhood, the lack of sleep, the knowledge that her home must now be surrounded by cops, and her twelve-year-old daughter requiring a police guard to go to school.

The evidence of her stoic resolve lies no further away than the same *South Bend Tribune* that painted her as a shrinking violet, a quivering basket case of hysteria and broken nerves.

"Mrs. Woolverton," the *Tribune* reported on that day's front page, "surrounded by a police guard in her home at 1246 East Jefferson boulevard, was calm and collected as she talked with a representative of The Tribune."

The *Chicago Tribune* also captured the dichotomy of the woman's condition, writing that she "was hysterical and under a physician's care most of the day" before adding, "Mrs. Woolverton gave a coherent account of the kidnaping during the morning before her collapse."

Truly, if there was a lead reporter in that day's coverage, it was Mrs. Woolverton herself, who was probably no more deserving of being called "hysterical" than any upset man ever was.[2]

Details of the kidnapping appear throughout the paper and the hundreds of others that picked up the story nationwide, all of which came only from her.

Indeed, what Mrs. Woolverton gave the press that day was a report thorough enough to constitute a second statement, an alternative narrative to her husband's that sometimes matched it closely, sometimes offered additional information, and sometimes disagreed with his.

History has handed down a half dozen versions of the Howard Woolverton kidnapping: one shared with the police and the newspapers by his wife the day after the kidnapping, another told by Woolverton through his lawyer that evening, a third compiled by snooping reporters in the days and weeks after the crime, one presented as truth by a team of shadowy Chicago vigilantes, FBI director J. Edgar Hoover's tale told years later in books and magazines, and a sixth asserted by Howard in his 1934 federal statement. This book, of course, represents the seventh take, a narrative culled from all those other tales and presented for the first time here.

None of them agree with each other, not even the accounts told by Howard and Florence Woolverton.

For example, husband and wife described the start of the kidnapping in distinctly different ways.

While Mr. Woolverton recalled a pedestrian who was crossing the street as Woolverton pulled up to an intersection and who jumped onto Woolverton's running board after another car almost hit him, Mrs. Woolverton's version of things read this way in the *South Bend Tribune*:

> As they approached the Jefferson boulevard intersection on Esther street a five passenger, black sedan bore down on them from the east. A collision seemed unavoidable and Mr. Woolverton slammed on his brakes, shouting at the occupants of the other car.
>
> The Woolverton car was forced to the northwest curb of the intersection and one of the occupants of the dark sedan jumped onto the running board of the Pierce-Arrow.
>
> "This is a stickup," he explained tersely, producing a revolver and leveling it on Mr. Woolverton.

While Mr. and Mrs. Woolverton remembered differently how the gunman arrived on the running board, their accounts matched immediately after that event. As stated in the *Tribune*: "He opened the rear door of the car, got in and pointing the gun at the couple instructed them to start the car and follow his direction, proceeding west on Jefferson boulevard toward the business district."

As her husband also recalled, Mrs. Woolverton said that the man ordered that the car be slowed as it approached red lights so it would never come to a complete stop. She also remembered, as her husband had, that the kidnapper got confused about the South Bend layout. After driving on Jefferson Boulevard and Sunnyside Avenue,

> the man ordered Mr. Woolverton to turn north.
>
> "Go this way a block and turn toward town again," he commanded.
>
> At Washington Avenue Mr. Woolverton started to turn west but was halted by the man with the gun.
>
> "This isn't the street," he said. "Isn't there another street with a bridge as you go into town?"

They eventually found their way, the *Tribune* reported, passing through downtown and continuing west of the city, the kidnapper menacing them all the while.

There were, it must be noted, various internal contradictions in Mrs. Woolverton's retelling of things, as there were in her husband's statement two years later. Just as he claimed to be able to see rivers, factories, and signs in the dead of night but couldn't get a good look at the villain sitting right beside him, she also seemed to suffer from selective visual impairment where the kidnappers were concerned, claiming an inability to see them in one breath before describing them in the next.

According to the *South Bend Tribune*, "She said that she is able to give only a meager description of the pair because they held a revolver at her back throughout the ride and told her several times to 'keep your eyes ahead.'"

At another point in the article, however, the *Tribune* quoted her thusly: "'I couldn't get a good look at the man in back because every time I tried to turn around he would poke the gun at me and tell me to keep looking ahead,' she said. 'But later I got a good look at him and his confederate and both appeared to be well dressed and about 30 or 35 years old.'"

In the *Chicago Tribune* of January 28, she said that "the one who rode with us was clean shaven, dark complexioned and soft spoken."

Elsewhere in that day's *South Bend Tribune*, Mrs. Woolverton described her kidnappers in additional detail, comparing one to Rudolph Valentino, the Italian American heartthrob who starred in silent films between 1914 and his death in 1926: "'I might describe one of them, however, as a sort of Valentino movie type, sleek and well-dressed,' she said. 'They appeared exceedingly polite.'"

The same internal disagreement appeared in the *South Bend News-Times*'s account of Mrs. Woolverton's memory:

> "I don't know if I would know one of the men or not. A gun was pressed against my face, and I was ordered not to turn my head.
> "The man who spoke, though, had a pleasant voice. I saw him only while he stood in the dark, but I could observe he was tall and clean-cut. He impressed me as being of the Valentino type."

Why the discrepancy? Why contradict yourself before the press, claiming not to have seen anyone before describing them thoroughly?

We can only speculate, but the simplest guess is that Mrs. Woolverton's memory was restored under the guidance of Chief Kuespert.

Mrs. Woolverton undoubtedly knew that claiming she'd seen the kidnappers increased the chances they'd target her in future reprisals, as threatened explicitly in the note. Dead men tell no tales, after all. Neither do dead Illinois belles. But after Kuespert, who presumably sat in on all the press interviews, heard her deny she'd seen the kidnappers, perhaps he took her aside and encouraged her to admit she'd gotten a good look at the thugs.

If that's how things unfolded, we may guess that, once again, his goal was communicating with the kidnappers.

Mrs. Woolverton, he might have said to her in private, yes, admitting you got a good look at the men who took your husband might make you a target. But put yourself in the shoes of the thugs, and you'll see that the good outweighs the bad. Letting them know, through the newspapers, that you saw them well enough to point them out in a courtroom provides them a powerful incentive not just to spare your husband's life but to be done with the whole thing, to cut their losses in South Bend, to go to other towns and terrorize other people who don't know what they look like.

And so, we might imagine, after her conference with Kuespert, Mrs. Woolverton returned to the interview and took the plunge, admitting what she'd really seen.

The reporters for the two papers took it all down and reported both sides of her recollection, too hurried or too polite to point out the inconsistencies.

Other aspects of Mrs. Woolverton's newspaper narrative added more color to Mr. Woolverton's account, or details he didn't bother relating to the federal investigator.

For example, Ardmore receives a mention in the newspaper accounts but not in Mr. Woolverton's statement. The area west of South Bend remains an unincorporated community, as it was in Woolverton's day, and the key elements of the story Mrs. Woolverton told the *Tribune*—both about where they were ordered to drive and what happened next—began there:

> As the Woolverton car proceeded along the highway and through the hamlet of Ardmore, about four miles west of South Bend, the man in the rear seat appeared to be looking for a side road. A short distance

beyond the village he ordered: "Turn off here and stop, and put out your lights."

As they turned off the road the other kidnaper approached in the sedan and Mr. Woolverton was ordered out of his car. Mrs. Woolverton remained in the front seat. The second kidnaper came up to them.

"You're Howard Woolverton, aren't you?" he demanded.

Mr. Woolverton answered that he was and they turned to Mrs. Woolverton in the car.

"And you're his wife, aren't you?" they asked.

Then, to Mr. Woolverton: "Your father is Jacob Woolverton, president of the St. Joseph County Savings bank, isn't he?"

Mr. and Mrs. Woolverton realized then that they were the victims of kidnapers.

Mr. Woolverton was asked, how much money he could produce and took about $100 in bills from his pocket.

This was an amount worth almost $1,800 in 2020 dollars, but the bandits were not impressed, according to the *Tribune*'s account.

Both of the kidnapers laughed at his display of what they called "loose change."

"Then one of them asked Mr. Woolverton if he had a blank check and he searched his pockets and informed them that he had not," Mrs. Woolverton continued. "Believe me, I'll always carry a blank check the next time I go out riding."

Mrs. Woolverton said that she pleaded with the pair to let her and her husband go and promised that a reasonable amount of money would be turned over to them today.

"And I meant it, too," she said. "But of course they wouldn't listen to that."

As the brief encounter by the roadside came to a close, the *Tribune* reported, Woolverton received his goggles. He was done driving, so the timing made far more sense than it did in the other accounts of the day: "One of the pair removed Mr. Woolverton's spectacles and gave him a pair of dark smoked glasses, ordering him to place them over his eyes."

Mrs. Woolverton also shared this peculiar vignette through the *Tribune*, which occurred after Mr. Woolverton had been blinded and she'd been ordered to drive the Pierce-Arrow back to South Bend. Husband and wife both insisted she didn't know how to drive it, so "the kidnaper thought a moment, climbed into the driver's seat beside her and backed the car out onto the highway, heading it in the direction of South Bend. When she asked him to explain the gear shift to her he politely commanded her to place her hands over her eyes in order that she would not be able to identify him."

When one is instructing someone about how to operate an unfamiliar car transmission, one usually wants them to take a good look at things, not block their vision. And it seems his request came a little late, as he had just driven her back to the highway without making any demand relating to the covering of eyes. Maybe Mrs. Woolverton experienced a rare moment of confusion as she told this part of the story, or the *Tribune* misquoted her. We can only wonder.

Despite all the detail supplied by Mrs. Woolverton, the day's most important question remained unanswered: Where was Howard Woolverton?

But a second question had also begun to emerge: How do we fight back?

8

The Secret Six

FLORENCE WOOLVERTON, ON THE day after her husband was kidnapped, recalled being forced by the thugs to travel west of South Bend, through Ardmore, so that's where unnamed sources placed the captive Howard Woolverton that day. The *South Bend Tribune* couldn't get that detail officially confirmed, however, most likely because Chief John Kuespert didn't want the kidnappers to know where the authorities were looking.

"Although police were silent on the subject," wrote the *Tribune*, "it is believed the search for the hideout of the kidnapers and Mr. Woolverton's place of imprisonment is being directed toward LaPorte county, particularly the small town of Wanatah, about 10 miles southwest of LaPorte."

LaPorte County, Indiana, lying adjacent to and west of St. Joseph County, seems to have provided a good home for bad people.

The paper continued:

According to Chicago police, the territory around Wanatah, which is on U.S. highway No. 30, is known as the hideout of a syndicate of kidnapers operating in Chicago and southern and central Illinois.

The gang, which kidnaped a wealthy LaPorte merchant two months ago and later released him unharmed without receiving the money they demanded, had its headquarters in that vicinity, the Chicago police said. The gang also is known to frequent resorts in Chicago Heights and Whiting.

While the area was apparently plagued with a veritable kidnapping corporation, headed up and staffed by people wealthy enough to enjoy a little leisure between abductions, Kuespert told the *Tribune* this was the first kidnapping for ransom recorded in South Bend.

There had been kidnappings before, in other cities, each receiving attention in the South Bend press commensurate with their significance, notoriety, or horror. More kidnappings would follow Woolverton's abduction.

But the taking of Howard Woolverton from South Bend seems to have struck a particular nerve among the populace, not just locally but elsewhere, including in the big city to the west.

"Feeling ran high in South Bend," reported the *Call-Leader* of Elwood, Indiana, on January 29, 1932, "as it did in Chicago, over the fact that organized kidnaping had reached a point where the field of underworld victims is exhausted and business men are subject to abduction."

It was a theme that would repeat itself many times in the days and weeks to come: This was new. Woolverton's abduction was evidence of something much bigger than one man in South Bend. The criminals used to restrict themselves to snatching each other; now, they're coming for the rest of us.

This unprecedented threat to respectable, law-abiding businesspeople was immediately felt—and amplified—in the halls of power in Indianapolis. A concerned governor promised resources. South Bend man and close Woolverton friend, Frank Mayr Jr., who served as Indiana's secretary of state, sped home.

"Search Joined by State Police," announced a headline in the middle of the *South Bend Tribune*'s front page, one of ten articles or photo features about the kidnapping on the first and second pages of that day's paper. The *Tribune* reported, "Gov. Harry G. Leslie, in a telephone communication to [South Bend] Mayor W. R. Hinkle, announced that 75 state officers would be put at the disposal of local authorities if necessary."

The article announced that "Mayr, himself, rushed to the city from his Indianapolis office . . . to offer the aid of state police in the search for Howard A. Woolverton (and) to offer his personal aid to the shocked family of his friend and neighbor."

The *South Bend Tribune* numbered the contingency ordered to South Bend by Mayr at more than a dozen officers. Also racing to northern Indiana to do what they could were E. L. Osborne, head of the state criminal bureau, and Charles F. Bolte, an investigator for that bureau.

Outside Indiana, in Chicago, a city that might be called the nation's capital of kidnapping, the crime was the day's top news, heralded across the top of the *Chicago Tribune's* front page.

Indeed, the abduction of Howard Arthur Woolverton put the entire Kidnapping Crescent on a veritable war footing, as if Woolverton's kidnapping was the work not of a couple of crooks in a black sedan but of foreign invaders with terrifying powers.

"Police of three states were mobilized and deployed at strategic points between South Bend and Chicago," announced the *South Bend News-Times*. "The mobilization of armed forces to combat the kidnaping terror took on the aspect of a major movement in the Chicago district."

The article continued, "Illinois state police were deployed along the Indiana line prepared for any emergency. Michigan state police, likewise, were centering their attention along the Indiana line to the north, waiting for the command to go into action."

Describing efforts in Woolverton's home state, the article added, "Over the 100 mile course between South Bend and Chicago Heights the Indiana state police were dispatched late Wednesday morning."

The *Belvidere (Illinois) Daily Republican* described the search for Woolverton as "one of the most feverish man-hunts ever conducted in Indiana. Throughout yesterday machine gun details and heavily armed state highway police scoured every highway in northern Indiana in search of the big sedan in which the kidnapers had spirited Woolverton away."

On February 5, the *South Bend News-Times* described the activation of the preceding week this way: "The kidnaping received wide publicity and the city police staffs of Chicago and South Bend together with the state police of Indiana and Illinois launched a scouring manhunt a few hours after Mrs. Florence Woolverton, the victim's wife, informed police here that he had been abducted."

News coverage at the time also provided inklings of things to come, of new law enforcement scrutiny being directed toward the shadier elements operating in the region—a trend that would soon become another critical repercussion of the Woolverton kidnapping.

"Police at Chicago Heights," reported the *South Bend News-Times*, "were detailed over that district through the underworld haunts of gangsters and racketeers."

And the *Belvidere Daily Republican* noted a similar trend: "The hunt extended into Illinois where roads and gang hideouts were combed by state authorities and Chicago police."

Government authorities weren't the only ones looking into the crime, however. The kidnapping of Howard Woolverton had also captured the attention of a famous but mysterious band of Chicago vigilantes who inserted themselves into the case in a desperate, and ultimately futile, bid for relevance.

On the morning after Howard Woolverton's kidnapping, South Bend had become a magnet for all sorts of crime stoppers, both official and less so. This peculiar passage in one of the *South Bend Tribune*'s front-page stories served as evidence of the latter: "The 'secret six' crime investigating group of the Chicago association of commerce spread its net at noon for the kidnapers when its director, Alexander Jamie, described the crime as engineered by a national ring. . . . Jamie sent detectives to vantage points in Illinois and Indiana to-day in hopes of finding Mr. Woolverton."

Besides being an organization any preteen boy would join on the strength of name alone, who were they?

The Secret Six were a half dozen or so (the exact number was also a secret) wealthy, anonymous Chicagoans fed up with the corruption and lawlessness of their city, and they pooled their resources and their talents to go after the criminals the police weren't bothering with.

"In the last three years the organization has been active in the probing of kidnapings, bank robberies and gangland atrocities," reported the *Times* of Streator, Illinois, in December 1932. "It was given credit for solving many important crimes in the middlewest."

The group helped build the tax evasion case that sent Al Capone to prison, ending his reign of terror over Chicago. Forgotten today, they were a big enough deal at the start of the Great Depression that they got a movie loosely based on their exploits, 1931's *The Secret 6*, starring Wallace Beery and featuring Clark Gable in his last minor role before he became a household name. The Secret Six even operated their own speakeasy in Chicago, breaking the small law of liquor distribution to catch the violators of much bigger laws.

But the Secret Six got perhaps a little full of themselves around the time of Woolverton's abduction. Eleven months after swooping in for an attempted rescue of the man, the group dabbled in irresponsibility and went from there straight to rank absurdity.

Its members laid the groundwork for dissolution by lodging baseless charges against politician and private citizen alike. For example, it publicly accused a young man, on scant evidence, of sending extortion letters to the daughter of a wealthy steel executive. The young man sued and prevailed in December 1932, and the Secret Six were ordered, along with other defendants, to pay a very public $30,000, worth more than half a million in 2020 dollars.[1]

And then there was this, less than a year after Woolverton's kidnapping, as reported by the *Chicago Tribune* in mid-January of 1933: "The Secret Six detectives planted a bomb on Dec. 30 in an effort to trap an extortionist who has been sending threatening letters to Solomon A. Smith, Chicago banker. . . . Their quarry entered the trap and set off the bomb on New Year's eve, but made his escape before the detectives who were concealed some distance away, arrived on the scene."

In another January 1933 article about the would-be trap, published in the *Chicago Tribune*, this stratagem of the crime-busting amateurs received a scathing review:

> The Secret Six executives decided that super-detective methods would be necessary and accordingly consulted the officials of the crime detection laboratory of Northwestern University.
>
> The supertrap was laid according to a plan concocted by the Secret Six in conjunction with the laboratory. A decoy package was stuffed into the stump. Attached to the package was a string. Attached to the other end of the string was the "trigger" of the mousetrap. Under the spring of the trap was an explosive cap.
>
> When the package was lifted the string sprung the mousetrap. Its spring set off the cap. The cap exploded a large can of flashlight powder. The explosion of the flashlight powder lighted a short fuse attached to a couple of sticks of dynamite.
>
> The theory behind these intricate preparations was this: Jamie [Jamie Alexander, chief investigator for the Secret Six] was assured by the crime detection specialists that the brilliant explosion of the flashlight powder would dilate the suspect's eyes, blinding him for 20 seconds or more. The dynamite, it was explained, would serve the double purpose of giving him a mild case of shell shock and convincing him that he was

surrounded by the Japanese army. The minions of the Secret Six would then sweep out of their ambush, presumably to find their quarry with hands upraised screaming.

Things didn't go quite as expected, however.

As the *Chicago Tribune* reported, "There had been but one slip in their careful plan. The suspect, divining from the flash and roar of explosives that there was probably some unfriendly scheme afoot, had gone away in a great hurry, climbed into an automobile, and been driven off to safety."

Local authorities, including the managers of the forest where the explosion occurred, were incensed, complaining to the *Chicago Tribune* that "the bomb, which contained a large quantity of explosive flashlight powder and two sticks of dynamite, was placed only a few hundred yards from the Riverside-Brookfield High school."

In response to the outrage, the *Tribune* noted, County Commissioner Frank Kaspar "introduced a resolution instructing forest preserve executives to oversee any future bomb planting activities by the Secret Six."

The Secret Six was disbanded within a few months of the incident, as waning confidence in the organization resulted in the loss of both private donations and the cooperation of Chicago law enforcement authorities.[2]

But eleven months before the bomb fiasco, the Secret Six were still riding high, their involvement in the Woolverton kidnapping front-page news, other law enforcement officials perhaps granting them a begrudging respect.

In fact, we might be able to detect the group's fingerprints on one of the stories that ran the day after Woolverton was kidnapped.

In their ransom note, the kidnappers had instructed Mrs. Woolverton to drive her car to Chicago Heights and then to Danville, traveling no faster than twenty-five miles per hour and waiting until a car behind her flashed its headlights ten times, at which point she was to toss her bundle of cash out the window and continue on her way.

"Officials to-day," stated the *South Bend Tribune*, "pointed out that it would be almost impossible to trap the kidnapers by a 'plant' of ransom money under the directions contained in their note to Mrs. Woolverton. The stretch of road which they designated is about 125 miles in length and it would be impossible to hide any officers in ambush along it effectively."

Why say that to the media? Why admit that the kidnappers' plan for getting the cash was airtight, impenetrable, too advanced for even the most creative detective to crack?

Because it wasn't.

We know that the Secret Six enjoyed laying out elaborate schemes for the apprehension of evildoers. Eleven months after the Woolverton kidnapping, they would tell an extortionist to come to the woods for his money, where he would instead discover a hollow tree stump, a pot of flash powder, and two sticks of dynamite.

Surely, as soon as they'd read the ransom note, the minds of the Secret Six began whirring.

If the kidnappers don't get their money tonight, they might kill Howard Woolverton, or they might send another ransom note (which they in fact did, the original of which has been carefully guarded for almost a century, but let's hold off on that for a bit).

If they send that second note, the Secret Six might have been thinking, we want them to provide the same or similar instructions—drive down a certain road at night and wait for flashing lights.

And we're gonna get 'em, you see, because we have a plan.

But first, we have to make the kidnappers think we consider their ransom drop idea foolproof. Brilliant, even.

And then, we set our trap.

What might the Secret Six have been plotting?

It was probably not flash powder and dynamite, but surely it included an element of surprise, if not high drama.

Perhaps an agent of the Secret Six would hide in the trunk of Mrs. Woolverton's car and leap out as soon as she dropped the money. Or they would run a convoy along that length of highway, blocking the path of any car that seemed to hold a suddenly flush band of toughs.

No telling. The plan was never executed, the trap never sprung. As brazen as the kidnapping of Howard Arthur Woolverton had been, and as public as it had become, neither the police nor the Secret Six had much to work with on those most important questions: Who's got Howard Woolverton, and where?

The dearth of information about one of their own also left South Bend's citizenry up in arms, and they responded to the crisis with a variety of behaviors, from the merely curious, to the would-be heroic, to something akin to madness.

9

Pandemonium in South Bend

THE PEOPLE OF SOUTH Bend, for whom a kidnapping for ransom was either a terrifying or exciting new distraction, responded in various ways to Howard Woolverton's abduction, depending on social position and personal decorum.

We know, courtesy of the January 27, 1932, edition of the *South Bend Tribune*, that a gaggle of curiosity seekers parked themselves in front of the Woolverton home at some point that morning, in quantities large enough to provoke—in the newspaper's words—a "hysterical, nervous collapse" on Mrs. Woolverton's part.

And the arrival of a morning message at the Woolverton home prompted widespread speculation in South Bend, according to the *Tribune*: "A rumor spread about the city shortly before noon that a telegram had been received at the Woolverton home from the kidnapers but Mr. Farabaugh[1] explained that the telegram was a message of condolence from a friend in Illinois."

A technology failure triggered more concern, the *Tribune* announced: "Police to-day were investigating what may or may not have been a coincidence in connection with the kidnaping last night of Howard A. Woolverton. At the time Mrs. Woolverton was closeted with Chief of Police John B. Kuespert relating the events of the kidnaping the telephone

96

lines in the city hall and police department were 'jammed' and it was impossible to put through any calls."

No correlation between jammed lines and the kidnapping was ever established; the telephone failure was apparently just another example of technology that gives out at the worst possible time.

The mood of the city was most succinctly summed up by the *South Bend News-Times*: "The sensational kidnaping threw this city into pandemonium today."

The good citizens of South Bend weren't just gawking and gossiping and getting scared, however. They were also giving money, in a big way, to a fund started by the *South Bend News-Times*.

"News-Times Begins Fund With $1,000" crowed the paper in an article at the top of the front page. "Studebaker Adds $2,000 to Pool for Capture of Kidnapers."

The fund, described by the *News-Times* as a "reward for information leading to the arrest and conviction of the kidnapers of Howard A. Woolverton," had reached $10,000 by that afternoon, a fact that probably didn't escape the notice of our newspaper-reading kidnappers and probably added to their headaches, of which there were plenty to go around.

Remember, the chief of police said their spotter was spotted; South Bend and its outlying realms were crawling with city and state cops; Indiana state officials, from the governor on down, were focused on saving Woolverton's hide; the illustrious Secret Six, archnemeses of powerful gang chieftains, were on the case; Woolverton's picture had been published far and wide; and now the citizens themselves were getting into the act, raising $10,000 in less than a day—the equivalent of $180,000 in 2020 dollars—with the express purpose of putting the abductors of Howard A. Woolverton behind bars—or at the end of a noose, if need be.

So important was this effort considered that the *South Bend Tribune*—in an act of cooperation unusual for journalistic competitors—acknowledged the *News-Times* fund in its own pages: "Woolverton Reward Fund Near $10,000," announced the *Tribune* headline, over a story that gave credit by name to the other paper for getting the effort rolling.

While competing publications, particularly two daily newspapers serving the same city, are typically loath to mention each other in any but the most negative contexts, rivalries must take a back seat when a respected citizen's life is at stake.

The *South Bend Tribune* won the war, however, even if it lost that day's public relations battle. While the *Tribune* continues to publish to this day, the *South Bend News-Times* turned off the presses for good in 1938, ending a run that began with the merger of two older papers in 1913. Its final edition included the confession that the paper had been losing money for the previous seven years, making its commitment of $1,000 (worth close to $17,000 in 2020 dollars) to rescue Woolverton all the more noble (or strategic, if one is cynical enough to assume the charity was primarily a move to boost subscriptions and advertising revenue).

The *News-Times*'s fund article included something of a who's who of South Bend's leading lights.

"The News-Times started this fund Wednesday morning with $1,000," the article declared. "This amount was promptly matched by the Bendix Aviation corporation, the St. Joseph Loan & Trust company, and J. D. Oliver."

The St. Joseph Loan and Trust Company, it should be noted, was founded by Jacob Woolverton, father of Howard Woolverton.

J. D. Oliver, like Howard Woolverton, was a South Bend child of wealth who went on to distinguish himself in his own right. He was the son of James Oliver, a South Bend inventor whose farm plows—for which he registered forty-five patents—made him rich and dominated the farming industry during the late nineteenth century. J. D. inherited his father's company when the elder Oliver died in 1908. He sponsored a girls' softball team and had a park named after himself.

Other donors listed in the article included the Studebaker corporation, which pledged $2,000, while Studebaker executives A. R. Erskine and Harold S. Vance each pledged $500.

News of the kidnapping and its accompanying reward fund spread far and wide at remarkable speed that morning. The *News-Times* reported that day that Thomas English, vice president and general manager of the Indiana and Michigan Electric Company, "telegraphed $500 from New York City where he is on business."

Would someone who knew something spill the beans, sing like a canary, rat out the kidnappers—despite the attendant risks of doing so—for enough cash to buy a modest home or a matching set of Pierce-Arrow Five-Passenger automobiles?

The gang holding Woolverton had to wonder.

Of less concern to the kidnappers, we might imagine, was the news that civic organizations were also getting into the act.

As reported by the *South Bend Tribune*, "The Rotary club, meeting in the Oliver hotel[2] at noon, appointed a committee to take whatever action it deems necessary for Mr. Woolverton's safe return."

Unless this committee (which included South Bend mayor William Riley Hinkle) intended to become South Bend's answer to Chicago's Secret Six, one might wonder how exactly they planned to rescue the man.

With plenty else to keep the kidnappers quaking in their boots, we might safely speculate that their boots registered no more than an additional tremble or two when they learned the Rotary Club was hot on their trail.

But surely, once he learned of all that had been done on his behalf in two states, from the highest echelons of law enforcement to the humble rungs of the civic-minded, Howard Woolverton would be grateful.

One advantage of being very publicly kidnapped—if one is fortunate enough to survive the ordeal—is discovering who one's true friends are, who will stand up and take action, pledge money, form committees.

A second advantage is that one might read a facsimile of one's obituary in the resulting news coverage.

And so it was for Howard Woolverton.

Among the other stories in the *South Bend Tribune* on January 27, 1932—rumors of spotters and gangs, a wife in the throes of a nervous breakdown, a twelve-year-old daughter being escorted to school by the police, and all the things Chief Kuespert wanted the kidnappers to know—there appeared a tidy summation of Howard Woolverton's life to date, the sort of thing not normally published until one has died: "Mr. Woolverton," one article read, "as secretary and treasurer of the Malleable Steel Range Manufacturing company, of this city, has offices at 201 South Cherry street."

The address, two and a half miles from the Woolverton home and perhaps prime real estate in its day for those getting business done, is now occupied by a great brick hulk of a building, three stories high and as long as a city block, weeds growing through the cracks around its foundation, most of its windows broken, some askew, some gone altogether. Debris litters the fenced space on its right, but trees have reclaimed some of the land immediately surrounding it, and modest homes lie farther on.

"He is a native of this city," the article continued, "being the second son of Jacob Woolverton, president of the St. Joseph Savings bank and vice president of the St. Joseph Loan and Trust company. He was educated in the public schools of this city and also at Wheaton, Ill., where he won some distinction scholastically and as a golfer. He has always taken an interest in the affairs of South Bend, and with his wife, has served in many capacities in connection with community work."

An impressive array of Woolverton's memberships was listed next, from the stolid to the esoteric. The South Bend Country Club, the Indiana Club, the Chamber of Commerce, and the Citizens' Committee of 100 got mention, all civic organizations dedicated to furthering business and/or social concerns in the city and state.

"Mr. Woolverton is well known in the Masonic fraternity," the article continued, listing affiliations "with Portage lodge, no 675, F. & A. M.; South Bend chapter, No. 29, R. A. M.; South Bend council, No. 62, R. & S. M.; South Bend Lodge of Perfection, Zerubabbel council, Princes of Jerusalem, John Hazen White chapter of Rose Croix and South Bend Consistory, A. A. S. R."

As mystical as some of its lodges and chapters might sound, the Masons were a mainstream group in Woolverton's day, a centuries-old, secretive, worldwide body of mostly men (although women have been allowed in or formed their own chapters on occasion). There are rituals, handshakes, and doctrines, but the general focus is on Christian principles, doing good works and raising funds for charity.

"Although having taken membership therein in recent years," the article noted, "he has advanced to the 32d degree and in the campaign for the refinancing of the St. Joseph Valley Temple association last summer, he was among those most active."

Howard Woolverton, son of wealth, already a man of significant promise on his wedding day in 1905, might in happier times have perused the public summation of his life with a little well-earned pride.

But as the sun set on January 27, 1932, the people of South Bend—like anyone reading the hundreds of papers that covered Woolverton's kidnapping—held their collective breath, nothing but threats and rumors to ponder as Woolverton's life hung in the balance.

In South Bend, the potential loss must have cut particularly deep. He was one of their own, after all—a family man who worked a steady job and kept regular hours, a volunteer dedicated to state and local causes. If he could be taken, so could any of them who had rich relatives, a thriving business, or a few dollars to rub together.

Chief Kuespert had done all he could that day, notifying the kidnappers through strategic use of the media that the details of their secret plot were known far and wide, that $50,000 in cash was certainly not available, that they had driven Mrs. Woolverton to a nervous breakdown, that the couple's blameless twelve-year-old daughter required a police guard to go to school, and that a virtual army of law enforcement officials, both professional and amateur, were on the case, some looking for Woolverton's place of captivity, some collecting the funds to reward informants, others poring over the bevy of alleged "clews" that would lead them to the gang's spotter and, from there, to the gang itself.

But perhaps the essence of the situation appeared, in picture form, at the top of page two of that day's *South Bend Tribune.*

Left to right are Woolverton's brother Hugh; Woolverton's good friend, Indiana secretary of state Frank Mayr Jr.; and Woolverton's father, Jacob.

The caption says the picture was taken in Chief Kuespert's office, where the three had gathered to discuss the kidnapper's demands. Hugh is looking grimly at Mayr, who is peering off to his right. Jacob Woolverton, in glasses and a goatee, seems to be gazing into the middle distance, looking spry and dignified at the ripe age of eighty-six, but with a current disposition conveyed by his mouth, lips pursed with what appears to be helpless concern. He's wearing what looks like a hearing aid, perhaps the newfangled vacuum tube-based model only the rich could afford, with a black band over his head holding a black speaker against his left ear, his right ear turned away from the camera but perhaps similarly accoutered.

The men are seated. Their mouths are closed. No one seems to be speaking or, judging from the varied direction of their gazes, listening to anyone else speak.

Three men of wealth and power are, in short, doing nothing, because there is nothing to be done. Each could only ponder the unknown fate of a brother, a friend, a son who was out there somewhere, perhaps a few miles west of South Bend, perhaps somewhere farther away, utterly alone, facing the gravest danger of his life.

This image from the *South Bend Tribune*'s kidnapping coverage of January 27, 1932, sums up the helplessness of those closest to Howard Woolverton as he remained in the kidnappers' clutches. *South Bend Tribune*, January 27, 1932.

10

A Series of Odd Decisions

WHILE THE TOWNSFOLK OF South Bend fretted, gossiped, raised money, and formed committees, Howard Arthur Woolverton merely lingered in his cold basement prison, lying on a cot, begging for blankets, and receiving food now and then.

Waiting for death.

In late afternoon, it was time for the kidnappers to carry out their sentence, to fulfill their idea of justice regarding the wealthy industrialist, the man whose capital crime was marrying a woman who blabbed to the police and the press when she was supposed to go to her family and the bank.

Woolverton recalled in his statement:

I was instructed to put on the glasses with the same muffler over them so that they could come down which I did. One of the men came down, unlocked the door and frisked me and asked me if I had touched or picked anything up whereupon I said nothing had been touched or picked anything up. The one who had jumped on my running board, from up stairs through the trap door called down to the other one, asking if he had searched me for anything I might have picked up. His answer was yes, although he had not gone through my pockets, simply frisked me as he would looking for a gun on the outside. I forgot to mention in the trip the night before, the man driving asked if I had any money on my person. I said 'Yes'. He said, 'how much?' I said, I didn't know exactly, around $150.00. He said, let me have it. I handed him my wallet which he put in his pocket. I told him it contained some memorandums and other data of no value to anyone else and if agreeable, after removing the money would like to have it back which he agreed to do, and returned it the next day intact all except the money. We then left the basement with one man ahold of either arm, the same two who had taken me from South Bend. I was placed in the back of the car with one of the men while the other drove leaving the yard. We proceeded I think back to the same paved road that we had come in on. This was about 5 or possibly 5:15 P.M. January 27th. Conversation was started about what was going to happen. I was told they were going to drill a hole in me, dump me in the ditch where I would be found.

Were these words any consolation to Woolverton? Did the knowledge of how he would die (presumably by gun and not an actual drill) and the assurance that his mortal remains would be left for someone to find ease his grief at all?

There are worse places to be dumped than a ditch, of course. Deep woods, a forgotten field, a sucking swamp, an abandoned basement.

Rivers come to mind, of which there were a few in the South Bend area and which tend to transport a body unpredictably, submerging it or depositing it in forgotten eddies while it decomposes, rolling it with the currents until the bloated form is discovered by the hapless fisherman or the strolling couple or the children at play by the bank.

Howard Woolverton, being driven to his death, given the scant comfort of knowing how his final moments were going to play out, and knowing that his remains would likely at least be found would have been entitled to despair, to beg for mercy, to babble about his wife and daughter.

But no, Howard Arthur Woolverton rolled up his sleeves, figuratively at least, and went to work.

From his statement: "I argued the point that inasmuch as I had no idea where I was held and being blindfolded was unable to identify anyone it would be more serious if ever caught to kill me. This conversation continued for an hour or more when the subject was changed to the amount of ransom demanded."

These five words—"when the subject was changed"—serve as the climax of Woolverton's narrative, the turning point, the moment at which the fate of the manufacturer transitioned from a death sentence to a financial negotiation.

Something Howard Woolverton had said during that hour-long argument turned the kidnappers away from exacting murderous retribution to something more constructive, as well as closer to Woolverton's comfort zone—letting him live and salvaging the kidnapping plot for whatever cash arrangement they might find mutually agreeable.

But his life still hung in the balance. If he couldn't arrive at a satisfactory sum, death was imminent.

While this was likely the only bargaining Woolverton ever conducted where not being killed was one of the terms, he applied an essential technique to the discussions: let the other party know you can walk away from the table, that you don't absolutely have to have what they're offering.

How is that done when one's life is at stake?

"And I again told them," Woolverton continued in his statement, "it was impossible to raise the amount and if my life depended upon their demand it was too bad for me."

Too bad for me, Woolverton told his kidnappers. Too bad for me.

Too bad for you kidnappers too, of course. Because you're going to add capital murder to your list of misdeeds, and all for naught.

Here, then, we see Howard Woolverton playing a few hands from the deck of South Bend Chief of Police John Kuespert: if you kill me and you get caught, it's going to be serious, especially in an age when cold-blooded killers (and leaving Howard Woolverton's bullet-riddled body in a ditch would certainly qualify) were routinely hung or electrocuted.

And besides, the money just wasn't there.

Mr. Woolverton, working blindly to anyone else's efforts, had managed to parallel the claims of his wife, Chief Kuespert, and the local newspapers. Some combination of his words and the messages from others had turned his captors away from retributive murder and back to business. Now it was time to horse trade.

Woolverton recalled:

Finally they asked what amount could be raised. I again repeated our bank conditions, the impossibility if we had the money to get it out in cash. I told them if my release depended upon ransom being paid to tell me the minimum amount they would be satisfied with and I would do everything within my power to carry it out. They finally stated that

$10,000.00 would have to be reached and I said that was just as bad as the other. After arguing the point sometime, I was told that the very best they would do was $8,000.00 in cash in small denominations, that they were going to release me with the understanding that the full amount would have [to] be paid in accordance with instructions contained in a letter that would follow within three days addressed to my brother, John J. Woolverton.

And there you have it. Some array of forces, not the least of which was an hour of jawboning by one Howard Arthur Woolverton, put a new deal on the table, one the Indiana industrialist could, quite literally, live by.

Woolverton would go free in exchange for the promise to pay $8,000 in accordance with a second note, to be mailed to Woolverton's brother John in a few days.

All of which raises the question: Why?

Woolverton was being offered his life and his freedom, a chance to return to his wife of twenty-seven years, to watch his twelve-year-old daughter grow up, to continue his duties at the firm his father founded. All he had to do was make a promise.

Instead, Howard Woolverton quibbled.

He could have named any amount. He could have guaranteed the full $50,000 in small, unmarked bills, triple wrapped in parchment. But no, when they cut their price by 80 percent, to $10,000, he refused. Cut it another $2,000, to an even eight grand, he insisted, or kill me now.

What was going on? Why not make any promise to go free, and then renege?

Was Woolverton that afraid of losing his honor? Did he fear—more than death itself—the opprobrium that accrues to those who stiff their contractual counterparts, even if said counterparts have made an art of being dishonorable?

Or was the concern more practical? Did Woolverton know that if he didn't pay up, the kidnapers would have no trouble exacting murderous vengeance?

We must guess it was the latter. Whether the kidnappers spelled everything out or it all was simply understood, it seems that Woolverton knew that if he didn't produce the cash, his freedom would be short-lived, and would end unpleasantly.

But this understanding raises another question that goes to the heart of the Woolverton kidnapping, and to a peculiar strain of crime in that era.

If gangsters could collect ransom money from people who were free, why even bother with the kidnapping part? Why not just inform the victim you'd be killing him or her if they didn't deliver a wad of cash within some reasonable deadline, and dispense with inconveniences like having to jump on running boards and wave guns around, convoy out to the Kankakee swamp, stash someone in a subterranean prison where you have to feed them three squares a day, all the while running the risk of being caught with the goods, so to speak?

And how could society possibly function this way, where the richest people were those who were most prolific at sending threatening notes to the soon-to-be-not-so rich?

But no, the extortion game in Howard Woolverton's day was not so simple.

You didn't have to maintain physical possession of a person to shake the money loose, but you couldn't just send a letter and wait for the cash to roll in either.

You had to establish credibility. You had to prove that you had the gumption, the wherewithal, the technology—yes, the technology—to back up your threats of murder.

How was that done? In Howard Woolverton's case, the cred came thick and fast. They'd snatched him once; they could do it again. They knew where he lived, who his wife was and what she drove, what his daughter looked like and where she went to school, who his friends and family were. They had a car, guns, and a secret hideout. If he didn't produce the cash, he was as good as dead, sooner or later. The kidnappers had proved themselves.

But there were other avenues to establishing credibility that didn't require body-snatching, and the press of Woolverton's day had enough examples to go around.

For example, there was the enterprising individual who sent identical notes to a dozen homes in Chicago's fashionable Gold Coast district, demanding that $50,000 be mailed forthwith to East Chicago, Indiana.

"The writer," reported the *Chicago Tribune* on April 12, 1931, "who appears to have worked alone, gave his victims five days to produce the money. In any case where his demands were ignored beyond Friday night, he warned, the victim had best not venture on the street. A kidnaping or acid throwing would be the penalty, he threatened."

Acid, then. Not just a boring gun or knife.

Acid.

In the golden age of kidnapping and extortion, the award for most impressive technology might go to the extortionist seeking money from Marion Wright, the eighteen-year-old daughter of steel executive William Wright of Chicago.

The contents of his (he was presumably male) nefarious missives earned international coverage: "My associates have perfected a wonderful but deadly dart," wrote the extortionist, as quoted in a United Press wire story that ran, among other places, in the *Windsor Star* of Ontario, Canada, on December 11, 1930. "With the use of powerful but silent springs this weapon is capable of striking an object at 3,000 feet. Imagine this dart dipped in a very deadly poison."

Demanding that "a small sum of $25,000" be paid by mail on November 30, the writer also implied a familiarity with his victim that added base creepiness to his team's technological prowess.

"Honestly, Miss Wright, I hope it won't be my choice to commit the deed, because, darn it, I fell in love with your photo, which shows the power of your personality."

The extortionist, in a bid to make sure the teenaged socialite was bringing her full attention to the potential unpleasantries, even claimed in a subsequent letter to have been in her presence: "Have seen you in person last night, and may I compliment you on your good looks."

A sense of community combined with grand ambition and meticulous organizational skills marked the efforts of another extortionist, who turned his attention to the underworld in St. Louis, Missouri.

According to the *St. Louis Globe-Democrat* of May 13, 1930, at least two, and possibly closer to a dozen, wealthy men engaged in dubious enterprises in that city received via regular mail a letter that "appears to have been written in longhand, but it is believed it was prepared on a machine which prints script." The letter read, "The Lawbreakers Protective Association of Chicago is being extended to all leading cities of importance. Law and society being unable to tax those who work beyond the law causes us to place you or your place of business upon our books for one year, with dues of $20,000, payable in hundred-dollar bills to whom and as directed at a later date."

While the first paragraph of the letter conveyed a businesslike preamble, the second got down to brass tacks, outlining what would happen if the men didn't pay: a choice between "complete subjugation or elimination." The letters, signed "RED TERROR," also threatened, vaguely, "unpleasant tactics" for those who failed to deliver.

In all three cases—acid, poison dart, and the Lawbreakers Protective Association—victims went straight to the police. It's safe to say the extortionists, although possessed of solid communication skills and armed with innovative approaches for scaring people away from their cash, didn't come off as adequately credible.

The would-be extortionist of Chicago bank president Solomon A. Smith tried a good bit harder.

On November 9, 1932, according to the December 2, 1932, *Chicago Tribune*, a small bomb was sent to the Smith home, disguised in "an imitation leather box that had been used as a card index file." Powder and bird shot, a battery and copper wire completed the device, which detonated when Mrs. Smith opened it, thinking it might be a present for her granddaughter.

"(T)he force of the explosion threw her against a wall," the *Tribune* reported. The durable woman was not injured, however.

Inside the bomb's remains was a terse note: "This is just a warning. Wait. Say nothing. Do nothing."

The second shoe, so to speak, dropped a few weeks later, on November 19, when Mr. Smith received the following letter, as detailed in that *Chicago Tribune* story: "Just a line to let you know we haven't forgotten. How did you like our little present [*sic*—the extortionist, regrettably, neglected to include a question mark]. There are more where that came from. We want $4,000 from you and intend to get it. You can see that we have means of enforcing our demands and if you don't want any bloodshed you will follow further instructions closely."

The letter warned Mr. Smith that he was being watched, included the obligatory demand that he "not get the police into this," and told him to post an advertisement in the *Chicago Tribune* to indicate his willingness to pay up.

"Your life will be penalty for failure to comply with our demands, attempts to capture us or notification to the police."

Mr. Smith did go to the police, and nothing more of significance came of the matter.

A month before the Woolverton kidnapping, a similar but much more destructive strategy was employed in Cleveland, Ohio, against the home of wealthy real estate dealer Samuel A. Cowan.

In October 1931, Cowan received a letter demanding that $5,000 be dropped off near a lumberyard. If he didn't fork over the cash, the letter promised, they'd take his son Joseph as collateral (press reports put Joseph's age at both eight and eleven).

Cowan notified police, they set up a sting with a fake money package and an undercover cop, but no one showed. Two months later, the frustrated extortionists registered their disappointment noisily. As the *South Bend Tribune* reported on December 21, 1931, the home was bombed. The blast didn't injure anyone but "wrecked the porch of the house, damaged the front and showered plaster and wreckage through some of the front rooms."

According to the *Newark Advocate*, "The detonation was heard for miles around and hundreds of spectators gathered at the house."

Tales of extortionists facing justice were distressingly rare in the 1930s press, but one front-page story of apprehension, from the November 16, 1932, *Chicago Tribune*, stands out. In November 1932, J. E. Halligan of Evanston, Illinois, received a letter demanding that $100 be deposited in the bushes at the corner of Colfax Street and McDaniel Avenue. "You have the choice of having your home bombed, or probably a few kids killed," the letter warned, "or paying a paltry $100." The letter demanded that the money be dropped off at 9 p.m. November 15, so at the appointed hour, six police officers staked out the drop point. They were duly surprised when the criminal turned out to be Parker Kaehler, a thirteen-year-old neighbor of the victim. Young Parker "admitted writing the letter and said he didn't know why he wanted $100. Police sent him home after an appropriate lecture."

Howard Woolverton read the papers. He knew that threats were, often enough, followed up with tangible harm. And he might have guessed that for every extortion plot that went public, there was another that never earned a headline, the victim believing the threats and quietly paying to have them lifted.

Like the many others who parted with money to save life and limb, Woolverton surely knew there were no depths to which these hoodlums wouldn't descend to get their lucre.

He might be about to be set free, but he would remain their captive.

And, as twilight turned to night, Woolverton had something else to worry about while still trapped in the kidnappers' car. As he recalled in his federal statement:

When I found out I was to be released my one thought was to avoid meeting any police cars who might be searching and being killed in a shooting affray or by being killed in an automobile accident trying to get away from the police so suggested that they drop me immediately giving me my location and sufficient money to get home. My excuse to them was the danger that they were running if all of the police were running [sic] of being picked up. I was told that they [would] drop me when they got ready in Chicago. I mentioned the subject two or three times later about letting me out because of my fear and each time was given the same answer.

Woolverton's suggestion seems like a sound one. The longer his kidnappers drove him around, the greater the risk that someone would identify him from his picture in the papers, notify the police, and let them sort it out. And Woolverton likely didn't know it, but an additional threat was posed by the Secret Six, whose increasingly ham-handed methods might have involved firearms, explosives, and a posse of unpredictable irregulars giving chase behind the thugs' black sedan.

Woolverton's abductors didn't share his concerns, however. Inexplicably, instead of dropping him off a half mile from South Bend civilization—where he could flag down a car or find an open business with a telephone—they went north to Chicago, adding some three hours to his ordeal and their inconvenience, not to mention everyone's mortal risk.

Why? Reduced chance of apprehension, we might speculate.

The press made clear that the search for Woolverton was underway in and around South Bend, particularly to the west of town. We know the South Bend police owned ten roadsters and a gaggle of motorbikes, surely most or all of which were on patrol that evening. The city was, further, host to its share of state authorities, those unbadged operatives of the Secret Six, a full-fledged committee of determined Rotarians, and probably more than a few individual citizens on the lookout for the stolen industrialist, motivated either by the desire to do good or to earn a piece of that $10,000 in reward money.

If we pull up to a South Bend curb, the kidnappers might have thought, disgorge the man of the hour and speed off, we'll have to pray that some authority doesn't zip by in the next minute, see Woolverton by the road, pick him up, and give chase.

So yes, the kidnappers went farther west, and then they turned north.

Chicago, with a population in 1932 of 3.4 million people, provided the same benefit as any teeming metropolis: the ability to hide in plain sight. Drop Woolverton off somewhere there and hit the gas, and the man on the curb would be just another well-dressed civilian, the kidnappers' black sedan one of thousands.

Even if Howard Woolverton had on his liberation stood on the curb waving his arms frantically and screaming about the gun-toting villains who were getting away, he would have most likely fit right in among the denizens of the Windy City.

Woolverton recalled in his statement's next passage:

> Finally at 8:20 P.M., the car stopped. I was ordered out and told to stand with my back to the car and remain in that position until they were out of hearing distance. One of them got out and removed the muffler as well as the goggles and I was told to look straight ahead and not turn my head in either direction under penalty of being killed until they were far enough away. From the time that I left the farm house, it was approximately 5 or 5:15 P.M. until they let me out at 8:20 in Chicago. They were driving fast over good roads all of the time with very few turns except what appeared to be towns because I was told several times to swing the upper part of my body to the left and lie across the lap of the other man with me which I figured was to avoid having anyone see me pass in the light blindfolded. After they drove away I looked around and walked to the first corner to my right surrounded by vacant property for a distance of 200 feet in all four directions.

Howard Arthur Woolverton was free.

Or was he?

Blinded, imprisoned in a cold basement, with guns leveled at his head and body as a matter of course, and told twice in no uncertain terms he was going to die, Howard Arthur Woolverton found himself quite alive—sight restored, the thugs and their guns gone—standing on a desolate side street in wintry downtown Chicago.

The temperature at 8:00 p.m. in the city, according to the *Chicago Tribune* of that date, was a brisk but not arctic 37. The skies were clear.

Where in the city was he?

Woolverton recalled: "I looked at the street sign on the lamp-post which was not familiar and inquired of two women one considerably older than the other, the quickest way to met [sic] down to the loop. One of them pointed to North Avenue which was about two or three blocks away where she said I could get a car or cross over to Cicero Avenue about the same distance to the East."

From this portion of the narrative, we can pinpoint with fair precision where Woolverton found his freedom.

And it wasn't where one would expect.

North Avenue runs east and west through Chicago, terminating on the eastern side on the shore of Lake Michigan. Cicero runs north and south. We know from his statement that Woolverton was dropped off a few blocks from the intersection of the two streets—east of Cicero and either north or south of North Avenue. Today, row houses share space there with a Walmart, a junkyard, railroad tracks, an auto repair shop, and other small businesses.

Strangely, the intersection was four miles east of Chicago's western city limits in 1932 and eighteen miles north of Chicago's southern edge.

Think like a kidnapper for a moment: your black sedan is conveying a man who had become an overnight sensation, an industrialist whose picture had been plastered all over the news, a man famous not because of who he was but because of who he was with: a band of murderous kidnappers.

Bootleggers hid liquor under the floorboards or in their tires. But Howard A. Woolverton, the possession of whom represented the apex of ruthless crime, was virtually unconcealed in the back seat of a car, in goggles and a scarf, being driven for miles over the teeming avenues of Chicago.

Dropping Howard Woolverton in the middle of a populous city seems like the worst decision of many poor choices the band of scoundrels had made in the preceding twenty-four hours.

We can assume the city was adequately lit. Even in the relatively desolate area where Woolverton was dropped off, he reports seeing a lamppost. Surely there were more pedestrians on the streets of the city than the two he encountered as soon as he was freed. What if one of them took note of a car idling at a stop sign or a red light, two men illuminated in the back seat, one with his head wrapped in a scarf, apparently hiding or sleeping in the other's lap?

Or maybe, in a city of millions ruled by gangs and corrupt politicians, such a sight was hardly worth a second glance.

Woolverton's narrative, in which he claims the kidnappers "were driving fast over good roads all of the time with very few turns" only serves to deepen the mystery. Surely they weren't driving fast through miles of Chicago cross streets. The stop sign was invented in Detroit in 1914 to cut down on the new epidemic of horseless carriage fatalities; Chicago must have had plenty of stop signs by 1932, as well as a good number of those stoplights invented in the 1920s.

We may forgive Woolverton's memory, two years after the fact, about how fast they drove once they'd arrived within Chicago proper. The kidnappers' decision to take him there must remain a mystery.

But a greater mystery, and one of many in Woolverton's statement to the feds, concerns what he did after he was let go.

His first act was to ask two women how to get to Chicago's Loop, which made sense, as it was and remains a hub of activity and transportation in the city, and was no doubt a district he was familiar with. They pointed to North Avenue, then to Cicero, both main thoroughfares beside which ran the streetcars that formed a transportation network in Chicago in Woolverton's era (but that even then were being choked out by the increasingly ubiquitous private automobile).

Given the choice of North and Cicero Avenues, Woolverton states, still sensibly,

> I chose the latter after thanking them, and walking across, I met another man and asked him the same questions. After catching the Cicero Avenue car I asked the conductor the quickest way down to the loop and was told to transfer at Lake Street where I got off. I caught the Lake Street car and crossed to the loop turning South off of Lake on to State where I got off at Randolph Street and the corner of State, crossing to the corner I noticed at the news-stand all of the papers spread out with my picture and that of my wife and daughter in some of them and my name in the headlines so I proceeded to the corner of Wabash and Randolph where I purchased a package of cigarettes and picked up four or five copies of the various newspapers at another stand and went on to the Randolph Station of the South Shore line arriving there at approximately 8:45.

So.

We have pondered the psychologies of our kidnappers. We have studied the various states of hysteria and coherence attributed to Florence Woolverton. We have speculated regarding the motives and machinations of South Bend Police Chief John Kuespert.

Now we must wonder at the decisions made by Howard Arthur Woolverton because most of them don't exactly make sense.

Surely, had he approached a Chicago police officer or introduced himself at any business with a phone, he could have gotten word to his wife and daughter immediately that he was alive and free, and then arranged a trip home (a motorcade with flashing blue lights is probably not too far-fetched).

Instead, the man who spent almost twenty-four hours facing imminent death chose on his release to . . . saunter.

Dropped off at 8:20 p.m., he spent the next twenty-five minutes buying cigarettes and newspapers. He rode streetcars and asked people for directions, content to be an anonymous face in the crowd while his family, his town, and three contiguous states held their collective breath.

Over the distance of roughly eight miles from the point where he was dropped off near Cicero and North Avenues to Randolph Station (now known as Millennium Station), he must have passed a dozen pay phones and a score of police officers, availing himself of neither.

Why?

Woolverton gives us very little to go on in his statement, but he does make a rare emotional confession in the first words of the next passage: "Through fear of being followed and wanting to communicate with my family in South Bend immediately, decided to phone a close friend of our family in Chicago to in turn telephone my family and ask that she relay the message by telephone to my family in South Bend whereupon I proceeded to buy a ticket and catch the 9 o'clock South Shore interurban."

Howard Woolverton was fearful of being followed.

The sentence is oddly worded, however. What exactly did "fear of being followed" have to do with calling a friend instead of his family directly?

Perhaps Woolverton was more than afraid. After all, he'd just been through a sleepless kidnapping, complete with what qualified as a mock execution, a form of psychological torture in which the victim is led to believe they are about to be killed.

Mock executions sometimes involve being paraded before a firing squad where the guns never discharge or set in a noose above a trap door that does not open, but they don't have to. Any viable threat of imminent death can cause trauma and all that attends it—insomnia, depression, posttraumatic stress disorder. The practice is considered so cruel it is forbidden, even in a military context. The US Uniform Code of Military Justice prohibits the practice.

Over several hours, Woolverton was told at least twice that he would die—"I was told they were going to drill a hole in me," he had recalled—and until the very moment the black sedan sped away from the curb, he had no reason to believe otherwise.

In Woolverton's narrative, he doesn't offer up any reflections on this fear beyond stating he felt it, but two years had passed since the incident, a period in which Woolverton's trauma might have eased considerably, and he might have forgotten that his first moments of freedom were marked by sheer terror, his first movements lurching steps, his eyes wide, his voice so shaky and tentative he could do no more than ask directions from strangers and certainly couldn't speak calmly to the Illinois belle he'd been married to for twenty-seven years.

We can only speculate. Until one is kidnapped for a night and a day, one should probably not question Howard Woolverton's behavior or judge him too harshly.

We are left with other unanswered questions, of course. Whom did Woolverton call, and why did he call her and not his home?

We might guess that Woolverton used a pay phone, commonly used by then—there were twenty-five thousand in New York City alone by 1925, positioned near public transportation and other high-traffic areas. Maybe he was too upset to speak to his wife, the phone couldn't reach the South Bend network, or he couldn't afford the long-distance toll of a call to another state, while his unnamed female friend was glad to incur the charge. Collect calling had been invented by then, and perhaps Woolverton could have had the charges reversed to call home, but that would have required interaction with an operator and potentially a wait of some time, and perhaps he chose to avoid the hassle.

What was said between Woolverton and the mystery woman? Owning a phone in 1932 was something reserved for the well-to-do, so his friend might have been at least upper-middle class, subscribing to the papers, knowing full well of his abduction. She probably owned a car or at least knew someone who did.

"Howard, don't be a fool," she might have said. "Let me come pick you up or at least send the police to find you!"

We might guess that Howard Woolverton politely declined her offer of assistance, hung up, and bought his tickets for South Bend on the South Shore Interurban, one of the nation's most venerable of train lines.

Built between 1901 and 1908, the line originated in Chicago, at the intersection of Randolph Street and Michigan Avenue, where Woolverton bought his tickets, and it ran all the way to South Bend, a trip of some ninety miles, covered with impressive speed.

"South Shore Line trains run from Chicago to South Bend in an hour and fifty-three minutes," declared the *Chicago Tribune* in March of 1932.

"Seven years ago three hours was required for the same run," the article added, asserting that Chicago's interurban lines were the fastest in the nation: "No other interurban line in the country has been able to touch them for several years."

Speed was critical for these lines, which were in fierce competition with the automobile for passengers.

It still runs, albeit a bit slower than in Woolverton's day, most likely because of additional stops on the line. Today, the one-way $14.25 ticket for departure at 7:10 p.m. from Chicago won't get you to South Bend until 10:45 that evening, a three-and-a-half-hour trip.

The train took a little more than two hours for Howard Woolverton, it seems. Starting out at 9:00 p.m. in Chicago, Woolverton didn't reach his home city until after 11:00 p.m.

"I arrived in South Bend," Woolverton continued in his statement, "I believe at 11:15 P.M. January 27th and was met at the station by a Chicago friend who had come to South Bend who took me in his car to my home which I found was surrounded by many cars and police motorcycles who were in and out of the house."

And now we have another mystery.

Who was the male friend from Chicago? Possibly the husband or an acquaintance of our nameless Chicago woman? Someone associated with Woolverton's wife's firm, Chicago-based Boye Needle Company? A Malleable Steel Range employee? But how did the man know to meet Woolverton at the South Bend train station? The only call Woolverton recounts making after he was freed was to that woman. Either he made an unreported second call at some point on his journey, or he told the woman to pass his itinerary on to the male friend with the car.

Perhaps that was the compromise: No, Woolverton told the woman on the phone, I won't let you come get me or send the police, but if you must help, notify whatever man seems handiest that I should be arriving at South Bend on the South Shore Interurban around eleven, and he may get me the rest of the way home.

Yes, maybe it all happened that way.

Or maybe not.

There might be another explanation for several postliberation mysteries.

Staring death in the face, we know that Woolverton told what were most likely lies about his finances. After he'd already pushed the kidnappers' cash price down from $50,000 to $10,000, he insisted on a further reduction to $8,000 and professed himself ready to die if they wouldn't agree.

And then, there was this tidbit about Woolverton's surreptitious managing of his cash at the start of the abduction, published in the *Indianapolis News*, a vignette attributed to Woolverton family attorney G. A. Farabaugh: "Mr. Woolverton had $96 in a purse in his hip pocket and $25 in bills in another pocket. The $25 he managed to slip into his watch pocket, and had this amount when he returned home. The kidnappers took the $96, but returned $10 to him for car fare."

There is ample evidence, then, that Howard Woolverton had no trouble keeping his wits about him while under duress. He lied to armed thugs, hid money from them, and drove a hard bargain with his life in the balance.

The caricature of a shell-shocked Howard Woolverton, staggering his way down the street to the Chicago Loop, so traumatized after his release that he could complete only a few strange and random tasks—buying newspapers and cigarettes, calling a friend instead of his family, getting on a train instead of summoning the police—might be entirely false.

Discard the dazed and confused Howard Woolverton and replace him with a man still plotting and planning—and lying—to navigate the terrible moral dilemma confronting him.

Released from the black sedan, Woolverton needed time and some space to think.

He needed a plan.

What happened over the next ten days—the chaos of competing claims, bizarre assertions, lies exposed and investigations mysteriously quashed—suggests he did indeed arrive at a workable scheme.

A good one, in fact.

As Woolverton sauntered, just another anonymous face in the Chicago crowd, he hatched a plot to protect his honor, save his skin, and keep his wife and daughter alive.

Most likely, as a wealth of evidence suggests, Howard Woolverton didn't call that woman in Chicago, didn't try to get word directly to his wife that he was alive, didn't reach out to that Chicago man to come give him a one-mile ride home.

No, Howard Woolverton didn't do any of those things.

Howard Woolverton called his lawyer.

"I'm not going to talk."

—Howard Woolverton, *South Bend Tribune*, January 28, 1932

PART II

Anatomy of a Cover-Up

11

Howard Woolverton, Reluctant Kidnapper

WE KNOW THAT THE press got things wrong when it came to Howard Woolverton's abduction. There were the multiple versions of the ransom note, each presented as the one true copy. The *South Bend News-Times* had Woolverton blinded by the painted goggles *before* he was forced to drive through downtown South Bend and into the wilderness west of town. A second *South Bend News-Times* story, carried cross-country by the United Press, declared with admirable drama but no clear attribution or evidence that Woolverton had been kidnapped by "a band of seven criminals" who used "torture and terrorism" to score a million dollars in a few short years.

And the *Garrett Clipper*—that rag of the wrong, that missive of misapprehension, that bungling bugle—outdid all the other papers in publishing its unique version of things, adding a second kidnapper's car, a second gunman at the start of the abduction, and the Woolvertons' Pierce-Arrow Five-Passenger automobile careening wildly through the streets of South Bend, the city and its people saved from ruin only by the courageous policeman who jumped on the running board and, presumably, took the wheel forcibly from the insensible Mrs. Woolverton.

But what of Howard Woolverton? What was he doing to set the story straight?

Nothing. Indeed, the opposite of nothing. He was doing all he could to make the story go away.

A gentleman, it has been said, should appear in the newspapers three times: when he is born, when he is married, and when he dies.

On January 27, 1932, the newspapers blew that idea to smithereens when it came to Howard Arthur Woolverton.

By the evening of that date, however, even before he made it home, Woolverton seems to have been working industriously to contain the damage.

The first stages of his plan were conducted clumsily. Lies were told that had to be walked back. Inconvenient truths were told that had to be awkwardly retracted as well. Sensing deception and cover-up from the outset, the reporters on his front porch staged a near-riot.

But now, on the strength of Woolverton's statement, a comprehensive survey of newspaper accounts, and an eyewitness interview, we can piece together what Woolverton and those around him did, how they lied, and how it all played into the larger narrative of a terrorized nation and a terrifying new kind of crime.

Woolverton never wanted this story told, but can we blame him?

At some point, as the winter light faded in the early evening of January 27, 1932, Howard Arthur Woolverton—industrialist, husband, father, scion of wealth—added a new position to his resume: kidnapper.

Yes, Howard Arthur Woolverton himself was the latest inductee into that desperate band of human beings who steal other human beings for money.

No, he never jumped into someone's back seat and waved a gun, never hid someone in a farmhouse, never wrote a ransom note in big block letters or told someone he was going to die because his wife had talked.

But on January 27, 1932, Woolverton was playing a vital role in an ongoing abduction enterprise.

First, he was about to cover the gang's expenses and pay their salaries, to the tune of $8,000.

That kind of money, worth about $150,000 in 2020 dollars, would go a long way toward keeping the business of his new associates profitable and growing. In those days, one could get a new black sedan—ideal for kidnapping—for less than $1,000. A machine gun went for about $200, pistols for far less. A double-breasted suit, for the kidnapper who wanted to look their best while they people-snatched, went for under $20 in New York City. A deluxe silk-lined hat, with a brim one could pull low over one's eyes, sold for a mere $2.85.

With $8,000, the gang could completely outfit a second kidnapping team, apply their winning approach to new states and regions, and double the number of people they stole.

With that kind of cash, they could cover lodging, per diem and abduction incidentals, and have enough left over for end-of-year bonuses and a Christmas party.

Other people were carrying out the skullduggery, of course, but Howard Woolverton was going to bankroll it.

Just as important as the money, Woolverton also kept the business of taking people against their will safe by going quiet, clamming up, refusing to talk.

But before we explore the lengths to which Woolverton and his friends in high places went to ensure the kidnappers were able to keep doing business beyond the law's reach, we must ask ourselves, briefly, if any of us would have behaved any differently.

Ripped from a half-century of pleasant living, Howard Arthur Woolverton had been brought in a matter of hours to, surely, the depths of once-in-a-lifetime despair. Stowed in a cold basement, promised death for the indiscretions of his wife, forced to imagine his body bleeding out and growing cold in some roadside ditch, his subsequent decisions are entirely understandable and most likely not so different from what any of us would do.

It wasn't just trauma or fear for himself that drove him, we can be certain. We know Woolverton negotiated for at least an hour with his kidnappers, and we may guess that they reiterated—frequently and graphically—the terms of the deal: pay up or die. Or worse, lose a loved one.

As the first ransom note warned, "If you do not do this you and some of the family will get hurt—bad."

Unite with the kidnappers, in other words, or look perpetually over your shoulder. And if harm comes to your wife or child, the blame will be on you.

So, when Howard Woolverton joined the kidnappers in common cause, he also joined a long line of other kidnap victims who refused to provide critical details of their ordeals to the authorities.

Remember, in that study of kidnappings by St. Louis Police Chief Joseph Gerk, there were ninety-seven instances where the police were aware of a ransom demand, but "only 28 victims would admit paying, while only seven denied ransom payment."

More than half, then, of those who got away refused to say how they'd orchestrated their liberation. They might have been sworn to secrecy and threatened with more unpleasantness if they blabbed, often enough, but surely a few went silent out of shame, recognizing the bright line that ran from their payment of ransom to the next victim.

For Howard Woolverton, the moral dilemma must have been particularly acute.

A day after citizen and official alike in South Bend had mobilized to save a favored son—searching the hinterlands, forming rescue committees, donating to a reward fund—Howard Woolverton was doing all he could to pave the way for the next abduction.

Whom might they next take from South Bend? One of the Rotarians on that rescue committee? Someone he'd dined with at the South Bend Country Club or rubbed elbows with at the Chamber of Commerce? A fellow member of the Indiana Club or the Citizens' Committee of 100? Another 32nd degree Mason?

Or one of his dear friends?

Mr. or Mrs. Studebaker, perhaps?

Or might the gang decide to work through the rest of the Woolverton family first? His brother Earl had died in 1915, at the age of thirty-one, of pneumonia, but Howard had two siblings left. John might go next, then Hugh, and then the grand finale: the patriarch, the founder of two banks and a large manufacturing concern, Jacob Woolverton himself.

And what sort of reunion could Woolverton expect with those future victims, assuming they survived the ordeal, knowing as he embraced them and welcomed them home that his silence had kept their abductors free, that he might have paid for the car they were tossed into, the guns pressed against their spines, the meals, like the one he described in his statement, of "small thin tough steak with chunks of partly fried potatoes," while they sat in a cold basement waiting for freedom or death?

For Howard Woolverton, the calculus must have been bitter, but it must have been clear: pay off the kidnappers, save your hide, protect your wife and your daughter.

Betray your community.

And take the shameful secret to your grave.

Secrecy attends abduction. It is the nature of the business, for both the perpetrators and the victims. It's not just that the criminals don't want to be caught. They might also, quite justifiably, not want their trade secrets aired. If they've found a winning formula, a recipe for success in the exciting new field of kidnapping, they should prefer to keep their competition out of the loop. America in the 1930s was rich with potential kidnap victims, but the supplies—of bodies and ransom money—weren't infinite.

And it's not just that the victims were ashamed of colluding with the kidnappers, or that they kept their peace in response to threats of death. Surely, for some, including Howard Woolverton, perhaps, there was that very real humiliation of having been under the complete control of terrible people, of having been rendered so frightened that parting with one's fortune, the precious fruits of one's labor, was an acceptable compromise.

But how does one make private that which is already out of the bag, a nationwide story, complete with pictures and a $10,000 reward fund and the police of three states gearing up as if preparing for a foreign invasion?

Howard Woolverton found a way.

Indeed, the man stands out as a singularity.

Few kidnappings, particularly of adults, got more attention than his when it happened.

And few kidnap victims—if any—had the precise combination of connections, luck, and moxie to accomplish what he did next, a series of actions that—while they provoked vigorous counteractions—satisfied his objectives.

A series of actions that, ultimately, changed the course of history.

12

The Mystery of the Phone Call

IN 1934, TWO YEARS after his kidnapping, Howard Woolverton told the feds that soon after he was freed, he called a Chicago lady friend from a pay phone in that city with the understanding that she would call Mrs. Woolverton, waiting desperately in South Bend, and give her the good news that Howard was on his way home.

Woolverton's statement had read, "Through fear of being followed and wanting to communicate with my family in South Bend immediately, decided to phone a close friend of our family in Chicago to in turn telephone my family and ask that she relay the message by telephone to my family in South Bend."

Normally, when a man's kidnapping is covered nationwide, when it earns a dozen mentions on the first and second pages of his hometown newspapers, when it galvanizes military-level law enforcement deployments in three states, when some $10,000 (worth almost $200,000 in 2020) is raised in a single afternoon to catch the abductors, the phone call from a friend to the man's family revealing that the man is alive, safe, and headed home should create something of a stir.

We might imagine that Mrs. Woolverton, on learning from the Chicago woman that her husband was free and due by train within a few

128

hours, would notify the many authorities looking madly for him. She might not have been expected to contact every state officer, amateur sleuth, or ad hoc committee established in the past twenty-four hours to save her husband's life, but a quick courtesy call to, for example, South Bend Chief of Police John Kuespert might have made sense.

We might also expect her to have let the people in the household and the many police officers gathered indoors and out know that Howard should be showing up soon. Mrs. Woolverton was a talker. She said what was on her mind. She told the police everything she knew, despite the explicit threat of what would happen to Howard if she did so. Had she gotten that call herself, we must imagine she would have announced the news to the nearest ears before she'd finished setting the phone back on its cradle.

Or, at the very least, the wife of the man torn from her in the dead of night by two murderous thugs might be expected to wait up for her husband's return, even if she kept his imminent arrival to herself.

Did anything like that happen?

No.

By most accounts, Howard Woolverton's arrival was a complete surprise.

We might speculate about what happened: After Howard Woolverton called that mysterious female friend in Chicago—let's call her Ms. X—and asked her to alert his family, Ms. X got distracted by something. Ms. X might have been one of the Woolvertons' closest friends, and she might have been quite worried about her dear Howard, assuming she read the *Chicago Tribune* that day and its blazing, top-of-the-page headline: "RICH MAN HELD FOR $50,000."

But after Howard Woolverton—the day's most famous citizen, grabbed in the dark of night by thugs and publicly threatened with an ignominious death—placed that call to her to ask the small favor of notifying Mrs. Woolverton that her husband wasn't lying dead in a ditch somewhere, Ms. X discovered something more pressing to attend to. Her child or one of her pets distracted her, perhaps. Another friend called, needing some other favor. She was late for a social engagement.

It also may be that the woman tried every means possible to place that call to the Woolverton household but couldn't get through. Maybe the line was constantly busy with friends, family, well-wishers, and the merely curious. Maybe there was no service. Telephones were still a relatively new technology in that era, and they'd already failed once that day in South Bend, the lines jammed for a time to city hall and the police department.

Or maybe the whole thing was a lie, made up by Howard Woolverton and immortalized in his federal statement because calling his family directly, or calling his friend and asking her to call his family, was what he should have done and what he wished he'd done, but it was not what he actually did.

Instead, Woolverton most likely placed his first postliberation call to G. A. Farabaugh, his attorney, and the two worked on a scheme together that involved clumsy lies and, ultimately, a very effective, ninety-year cover-up.

While Farabaugh would later deny that any calls had been made, multiple publications suggested otherwise, courtesy of Farabaugh himself.

"Earlier in the night," reported the *Indianapolis Star*, Farabaugh "had said there 'might be' a development about midnight."

According to the *Chicago Tribune* of January 28, 1932, "Earlier in the evening Attorney G. A. Farabaugh, former city judge and friend of the family, stated that he expected to hear from the extortionists shortly and intimated that Mr. Woolverton would be released before midnight."

The *South Bend News-Times* of January 28 declared, "During his contacts with newspapermen[1] early Wednesday evening, Mr. Farabaugh had indicated that he might have some development in the Woolverton kidnaping case by midnight."

In the next paragraph of that same *News-Times* article, however, Farabaugh "declared that the family had received no communication from Mr. Woolverton or his captors." But that statement might be considered factually correct if Howard Woolverton had called only Farabaugh on his release.

One more piece of evidence, an eyewitness account no less, hints at a secret call and suggests Farabaugh discreetly brought Mrs. Woolverton the news, but with the expectation she would say nothing.

Mary Jay, formerly Mary Frances Bowers—who was mentioned earlier in this book as one of Betty's closest friends—was interviewed over the phone and via email (the latter through her daughter, Sue Hunter) several times in 2019 and 2020, and says she was in the Woolverton home on the night Mr. Woolverton returned.

Jay had no recollection of a phone call, from a Chicago woman or otherwise, announcing Woolverton's liberation and imminent arrival home. But somehow, the hopeful news had been imparted.

"Betty told me that he was coming home but she did not know how he got away," Jay said.

If Betty knew, so did her mother. For most people, however, including the many authorities still looking for the man, Woolverton's arrival was a complete surprise.

Mary Jay recalled that she and Betty Woolverton were still awake, near midnight on January 27, 1932, when Howard Woolverton stepped into the home.

"When the police who stood guard at the door said that he had arrived, we went to the hall," Jay reminisced in an email written by her daughter. "At first it seemed that no one said anything as his appearance was so different. He was very haggard and looked very tired and when he took off his hat, his hair had greyed a lot making it look white in the light. He was more serious and upset than jubilant looking. There was hugging and talking, but mostly more reserve than lots of merry making."

How does Jay recall his first words?

"He was certainly glad to be home and that his family was all right, and I think he asked for a drink."

In the first stories of Woolverton's arrival, several newspapers yielded to sentiment, presenting Howard Woolverton as appearing weary but unharmed and rushing upstairs to give the good news in person to his distraught, bedridden better half.

The *South Bend News-Times*, not above sensationalizing the kidnapping as the work of a band of seven career criminals whose repertory included torture, said Woolverton was "haggard but unharmed" when he arrived home, and his first words there were notably mundane: "Well, here I am. Where's Florence?"

According to the *Belvidere Daily Republican*, Woolverton was told on arriving home "that his wife was upstairs, suffering from tortured nerves resulting from the tension of waiting for word about her missing husband. Woolverton dashed upstairs to his wife's bedside" where he "discovered his wife in a state of nervous collapse and under care of physicians who were administering opiates to relieve the painful strain. Bearing up bravely for many hours after her husband was torn away from her, Mrs. Woolverton finally crumbled to the floor yesterday when it appeared the kidnapers might murder their victim unless their demand were met at the appointed time, eight o'clock last night."

Jay's account offers another take on why Mrs. Woolverton, if she knew her husband was coming home soon, didn't rise from bed to wait for him downstairs. Until she saw her husband in the flesh, Jay recalls, "Mrs. Woolverton was still very worried about what might have happened to him while he was being held."

Further, Jay added ominously, Betty told her the family was "very worried about what the kidnappers or their friends might do next."

No doubt Mrs. Woolverton was well aware of the story published earlier that day by the *South Bend News-Times* announcing that Woolverton had been taken by an experienced band of criminals who bound their victims hand and foot and used "torture and terrorism" to get their cash.

Yes, my husband seems to be on his way home, Mrs. Woolverton might have been thinking as the opiates worked their magic. But in what condition?

The *Chicago Tribune* offered one of the most detailed accounts of Mrs. Woolverton's state as the kidnapping ended: "Dr. Stanley A. Clark, a neighbor of the Woolvertons, remained at the home most of the night. He was called Wednesday afternoon to administer relief to Mrs. Woolverton who was reported to have collapsed under the strain. Nurses were also on duty at home when Mr. Woolverton returned. Mrs. Woolverton, however, appeared completely recovered on her husband's return."

Mrs. Woolverton, the paper added, "laughed and cried intermittently" after Howard came home.

Howard Woolverton, on the other hand, appeared in many press accounts to be less burdened by emotion and more focused on secrecy and cover-up, his intentions obvious from literally the moment he arrived on his property.

"Woolverton's appearance before his house last night amazed a heavy detail of state troopers and city police who were guarding the building," said the *Belvidere Daily Republican*. "But, before they could ask any questions the 52-year-old secretary-treasurer of the Malleable Steel Range company literally leaped up the stairs of the front porch and dashed into the house."

The *Indianapolis Star* detailed what happened after Woolverton arrived home with these words, building the twin themes that Woolverton's homecoming was anticipated by select others, and that he had no interest in speaking to the authorities: "On arriving home he went into conference with his wife, other members of his family and attorneys."

Quite a welcoming party for a man whose whereabouts, whose very existence, was questionable until the moment he stepped through his front door. What were lawyers doing there?

The clearest evidence of cover-up, however, came from the *South Bend Tribune*, which included several otherwise unexplainable passages: "Chief of Police Kuespert, who worked on the Woolverton case for 22 hours after the report of the abduction, was not informed of the manufacturer's safe return until after state troopers had placed Mr. Woolverton behind guarded doors to prevent anyone from questioning him."

The paper quoted Kuespert directly on when he learned that Woolverton was alive and home safe: "The first I knew of it was when a police car came to my home about midnight and informed me that Mr. Woolverton had returned."

If a cover-up was indeed afoot, the first order of business would be assembling a team. Stonewalling on this magnitude isn't a one-man job, after all.

The *South Bend News-Times* succinctly summed up Woolverton's cover-up crew in its January 28 edition:

> Before and after the return of Mr. Woolverton the situation within the house was being handled by Mr. Farabaugh, Secretary of State Frank Mayr, jr., and John and Hugh Woolverton, brothers of the victim. Captain Risher was there in command of a detail of state police.
>
> Secretary of State Mayr, a neighbor and close friend of Mr. Woolverton had hurried here from the state house at Indianapolis, Wednesday, accompanied by the executives and expert investigators of the bureau of criminal identification.

In short, from the first moments of Woolverton's arrival home, everything about the case was under the direction of Woolverton, his brothers, his lawyer, and his good friend and neighbor, who happened to be Indiana's secretary of state.

As we shall see in the coming pages, everyone else, from the cops to the vigilantes, was shut out, blocked, stonewalled.

The press—the eyes and ears of a terrified people—wouldn't have it.

13

The Man Who Came Home

HOWARD WOOLVERTON'S ABDUCTION TRIGGERED police mobilizations in three states, wire stories across America, and the dawn of a new understanding of the crime's implications: they're coming for us all.

Given the crime's importance, total silence that night wasn't going to wash where the newspapers were concerned. In fact, there were times in the evening when the press was literally wrestling for information. According to the *South Bend Tribune*, "Lieutenants Guy Sears and Ray Fisher of the Indiana state police were stationed at the front door of the Woolverton home most of Wednesday evening using their weight to keep newspapermen from making contact with persons inside the house."

Looked at with ninety years' hindsight, the Woolvertons' front door represented far more than a barrier between curious reporters and state police. The entrance to the stately home became the first demarcation of a historic conflict—one between a man who had thrown in with the kidnappers, promising them money and his silence, and the press, duty-bound to uncover the nature of this new threat to the American Dream.

The fight would continue for weeks, combatants including a lawyer whose name still graces an annual Notre Dame scholarship, and a

The Woolverton home, in a photo taken in winter 2022. On the evening of January 27, 1932, after Howard Woolverton dashed through the front door following his kidnapping, local journalists staged a near-riot on the porch, demanding answers. Some of those answers would lay buried for almost a century. *Photograph by Travis Childs.*

scrappy reporter who a few years later would be sentenced to death in Spain.

The press, armed with nothing but the power to ask questions and publish the answers, won the war, mostly, exposing lies, forcing retractions, and infuriating the Woolvertons in the process. Without their presence on the Woolverton front porch on that cold night in January, we would know far less about the kidnapping, for it was their persistence that forced G. A. Farabaugh to step outside and offer a statement.

The narrative was woefully incomplete, however, and one must wonder if it had been hastily crafted by Woolverton and his lawyer with the intention not of informing the public or helping the police but only to telegraph to the kidnappers that Woolverton would be saying nothing important.

In a story published in the evening edition the day after Woolverton's liberation, on January 28, 1932, the *South Bend Tribune* attempted to create the impression that it had received Woolverton's kidnapping statement in person, writing that although "Mr. Woolverton talked a bit incoherently after his arrival, due perhaps to the excitement of his return home," the man pulled himself together quickly that night, and "twenty or more relatives, friends and police officers were grouped about him while he told his story."

Chances are, however, the journalists of the *South Bend Tribune* saw no more of Howard Woolverton than any other reporter that night, and they cobbled together a first-person account of Woolverton's storytelling based on others' recollections and their own imaginings.

Where and how was Woolverton's story actually told to the press? Outside, after midnight, tersely, and by someone other than Howard Woolverton, according to the *South Bend News-Times*: "In a conference with the newspapermen on the porch of the Woolverton home early Thursday morning, Mr. Farabaugh and Rex Risher, captain of state police offered brief and sketchy accounts of Mr. Woolverton's 24 hour adventure with the abductors."

Most likely, the *South Bend Tribune* had to settle, like everyone else, for the statement Farabaugh delivered.

Given everything else we know, it seems probable that Woolverton and Farabaugh carefully crafted the story told that night—complete with several fabrications—in the twin hopes of satisfying the kidnappers' demands for secrecy and stilling the press's clamor for a more complete accounting of the abduction.

Farabaugh's statement as presented in the *Tribune* began with an explanation of how he had money for the papers and trains, and included the lie that he was dropped off not in Chicago but in Michigan City, Indiana: "When the kidnapers released their victim on the outskirts of Michigan City they took from him a billfold containing $96. They handed back a $10 bill, however, explaining that it was for carfare. When he was first kidnapped, Mr. Woolverton related, he succeeded in secreting $25 in bills in the watch pocket of his trousers."

In the next paragraph of the *Tribune*'s account, as delivered by Farabaugh, the Michigan City lie continued to grow.

"Mr. Woolverton told his wife that he sat in the South Shore waiting room in Michigan City for a half hour waiting for the train and purchased two evening newspapers there.

"'It certainly was an unusual experience to open them and find your own picture staring at you and big head lines to the effect that you were missing,' he said."

Farabaugh insisted that Woolverton had placed no calls to anyone.

"During his half hour wait, he said, he made no attempt to communicate with his family by telephone or otherwise and had no thought of notifying the police," Farabaugh claimed, quoting Woolverton thusly: "I wanted to get home—that was the important thing . . . I'm mighty glad to be home and I'm going to do just as they told me—I'm not going to talk. . . . It's all over, and I'm glad of it."

The next portion of the Farabaugh statement, as presented in the *South Bend Tribune*, corroborated the details of Woolverton's federal statement, in which he described riding with the kidnappers, being forced down when cars passed, and being blinded with goggles and a muffler. But the words were strange, referencing his "bandaged eyes."

The article continued, quoting G. A. Farabaugh: "Mr. Woolverton could not remember where he was taken by the kidnapers, did not know how many men had held him captive, did not know whether he was 'going straight ahead or in circles' and could give no descriptions of his captors, the attorney said."

The *Chicago Tribune* was one of several papers that reiterated the inability to identify the kidnappers and included a reference to a house that, two years later, would be an important detail in Woolverton's federal statement: "'I don't know where I was and I couldn't identify either of the two men who held me prisoner,' he said. 'I never saw them for I was blindfolded all the time. We drove around for what seemed a long time, and then stopped at a house. I don't know how long I was there. Then we drove around again. They treated me nicely.'"

Woolverton, speaking through Farabaugh, did acknowledge that he believed the kidnappers were going to kill him, but he didn't elaborate on why, didn't mention that they were furious that his wife had talked.

The January 28, 1932, *Palladium-Item* newspaper of Richmond, Indiana, provided a stark summary of Woolverton's feelings on that score:

> Woolverton said he was really frightened only once, and that was at the beginning of the ride last night which ended with his release.
>
> "We are going to take you for a ride," he said one of the men told him.
>
> Accepting the slang interpretation of the expression—a death ride— Woolverton said he thought the desperados were about to carry out their threats to kill him if $50,000 was not turned over to them at 8 o'clock last night.

Another version of the moment was provided by the *South Bend Tribune*: "Then they told me they were going to take me for a ride and I thought that the jig was up. They rode me around—I don't know where—and I felt certain they were going to kill me."

The end of the ride with his kidnappers, and Woolverton's first moments of freedom, were given several column inches in the *South Bend Tribune*. Other than the Michigan City lie, and a lie about the time he was released necessitated by that first lie, this portion of the article matches Woolverton's federal statement but adds some important detail, more drama, and a little humor:

> He said that he had no idea of his whereabouts when the kidnapers stopped their car, a sedan, and ordered him out about 10 o'clock Wednesday night.
>
> "We are going to take the blindfold from your eyes but don't look around or try to watch us when we leave—just keep going straight ahead," he quoted one of the pair as saying.
>
> "If you don't do as we tell you we'll kill you on the spot," the other man is reported to have said.
>
> Mr. Woolverton said he stood in the street as the car started and disappeared quickly. He then looked about him and saw a small business structure with the street number 2600 on the window. He walked another block and found a number in the 2500 block so he continued in the same direction, still not knowing what city he was in.
>
> A few blocks farther on he encountered two women in an automobile and asked them in what city he was.
>
> "They told me Michigan City," he related, "and looked at me as if I were drunk. Then they told me how to get to the interurban station and I walked on down town."
>
> Mr. Woolverton said the kidnapers warned him against using a telephone when he was set free, instructing him to go home unannounced.

Farabaugh, speaking for Woolverton, insisted that no ransom had been paid. The *South Bend Tribune*, one of many papers to repeat that assertion, put the claim in these words: "The attorney to-day maintained his denial that any ransom had been paid for the manufacturer's return."

Perhaps the most frustrating thing Farabaugh said on that cold front porch was captured in this line from the *Tribune*: Woolverton, Farabaugh said, "gave no account of any conversations he might have had with his captors."

Woolverton had spent almost twenty-four hours with the abductors, driving around with them, staying at a home with them, never sleeping. Surely they'd spoken. Surely the kidnappers had said something, anything, that might give clues as to who they were, how they operated, what they might do next. Did they speak with regional accents? Did they lisp, drawl, growl? Did the words they used indicate education or the lack thereof? But no, Woolverton claimed he'd been blinded throughout his ordeal, and now he was asserting that he'd been as good as deaf as well, turning the kidnappers into that most terrifying of enemies, soundless and invisible, swooping in, grabbing people, eventually letting them go at a time and place of their choosing, departing in the darkness, leaving not even a coherent memory.

How could anyone protect themselves from that?

And how could any reporter be satisfied with that?

So the morning after Woolverton's return, the reporters started digging. One fertile area of inquiry was how exactly had Woolverton arrived at his front door? Who had brought him from the South Bend train station?

Two years later, Woolverton told the feds some other unnamed Chicago friend, a man, commuted one hundred miles for the privilege of conveying Woolverton one mile more, from the train station to his doorstep. It just doesn't add up, and a raft of evidence points to something else entirely.

The evidence as detailed in multiple newspaper reports suggests strongly that Howard Woolverton, immediately after being freed by the kidnappers, made his first and probably only call to his lawyer, the man known in South Bend as Judge Farabaugh.

Allegations of a phone call were denied by everyone after Woolverton's arrival home, and his federal statement referenced only a highly dubious call to some unnamed Chicago woman, a call just as questionable as that ride home from the mysterious Chicago man.

Press accounts from the time suggest strongly that Woolverton lied about how he got home from the station, and we might speculate today that he was lying to conceal his lie about whom he did and didn't call from Chicago.

Several newspapers, one claiming to quote an official source, said Woolverton's ride home was not in the automobile of a friend, but in a taxi.

Quoting Farabaugh, the *Indianapolis Star* described the man's return this way:

> Arriving at South Bend, Woolverton took a taxicab to his home. Two state policemen, Lieut. Guy Sears and Ray Fisher, who had been detailed to watch the front door of the Woolverton home, were discussing the kidnaping with Woolverton's nephew, Roy Flannery of Chicago, when the taxicab stopped in front of the home.
>
> When Woolverton stepped from the vehicle, the nephew exclaimed: "My God, it's Uncle Howard," and ran to him. Together they went into the house to greet Mrs. Woolverton.

The *Palladium-Item* also mentioned a taxi: "Alighting from the train in the uptown district here, he hailed a taxicab while newsboys attempted to sell him papers telling of his continued absence. He proceeded home immediately, his cheery greeting choking off suddenly when he learned that his wife, Florence, had collapsed."

So, was Woolverton alone in that cab? The consistent answers gathered by newspaper reporters serve as exhibit A in this book's allegation that Woolverton did not call one or more unnamed Chicago friends after his release but only G. A. Farabaugh, to set in motion a cover-up that would keep Woolverton and his immediate family safe and produce historic, unintended consequences.

While much of the Woolverton kidnapping news went out on the wire, meaning the same words appeared in paper after paper, it's important to note that the stories of how Woolverton made it home from the South Bend Interurban station used different words and phrasing and presented different details or, in some cases it seems, different fabrications.

Each story, we may therefore conclude, represented independent reporting by journalists on the scene, lurking outside the Woolverton home or buttonholing officials wherever they could find them, each receiving corroboration of a central element of the Woolverton kidnapping story, which was subsequently denied.

Who picked up Howard Woolverton and brought him home? It wasn't a Chicago friend or a random cab driver, most likely.

It was a state cop, there under orders from no less than Frank Mayr Jr., Indiana Secretary of State.

"It was learned today from an authoritative source that the family of Howard A. Woolverton," announced the *South Bend Tribune* on January

28, "had advance knowledge of his release and that a state police officer awaited him at the South Shore interurban station."

"Late in the evening," reported the *Chicago Tribune*, "Capt. Rex Risher of the state police said he was going to make a search of some cottages near Wanatah, Ind., thirty miles from South Bend. Instead he was back in time to meet Mr. Woolverton on the train, according to an admission yesterday by his chief, Grover Garrot [*sic*], at Indianapolis."

The *South Bend Tribune* presented Risher's mission this way: "Grover Garrott, chief of the state police, and one of the leaders in the activity to bring about the safe return of Mr. Woolverton, said that Capt. Rex Risher, of the state police, was waiting in a taxicab at the South Bend station at 11:20 o'clock when Mr. Woolverton stepped from a car which had brought him from Michigan City, Ind."

Mary Jay, best friend of Betty Woolverton and the only surviving eyewitness to Woolverton's return home, certainly doesn't recall a mysterious friend from Chicago delivering Mr. Woolverton to his doorstep. Instead, she said in a 2019 telephone interview, "I thought that a policeman brought him home."

The story of how Woolverton reached his door was not without its humor. The *South Bend Tribune* added an amusing footnote to the scene at the station:

> Although his photograph has been emblazoned across the front pages of newspapers throughout the country during the last 24 hours and newsboys were hawking their "extras" all around him Mr. Woolverton walked from the South Shore station here to a waiting taxi cab and rode to his home without being recognized.
>
> One of the newsboys outside the South Shore station stepped up to him as he entered the cab and tried to sell him a newspaper, it was said.

Said by whom? The *Tribune* does not identify the source of this tidbit, but attributed the next paragraph to Woolverton or someone speaking for Woolverton: "As he left the interurban station here, he said, he encountered Will G. Crabill, local attorney, but was not recognized."

Other papers picked up on the significance of a report of an officer in waiting, building on it and hinting that someone was lying: "Another angle that remained to be cleared up," stated the *Palladium-Item*'s January 29 edition, "was the statement of State Police Chief Grover Garrott that one of his men met Woolverton at the interurban station. This was denied by members of the Woolverton family, who said they had no advance information of the manufacturer's return."

The *Indianapolis News* matched the central elements of this narrative, but then took it a good bit further, alleging that Farabaugh actively negotiated with the kidnappers. The *Indianapolis News* reported that Wolverton

> alighted from a South Shore interurban car at the South Bend station late last night and was hurried to his home by Rex Risher, captain of the Indiana state motor police, who had been awaiting his arrival. Although all concerned maintain a silence about Woolverton's whereabouts after he was abducted Tuesday night in the presence of his wife, G. A. Farabaugh . . . says he was in communication late yesterday either with the actual kidnappers or their representatives. It was he who sent Captain Risher to the station to meet Woolverton while South Bend police, under direction of John B. Kuespert, chief, were insisting no word had been heard from the missing man.
>
> A strict guard was maintained on the home by Captain Risher and Guy Sears and Ray Fisher, lieutenants of the state police force, while telephone negotiations were conducted by Farabaugh for Woolverton's release.

Because the account of Farabaugh's telephone negotiations appears to be unique to the *Indianapolis News*, is essentially unsourced, and doesn't match Woolverton's narrative or any other paper's reports, it may be fairly speculated that those details were, to be charitable, an educated guess on the part of that paper's reporter.

In the absence of hard fact, of course, newspapers do what individual people do: fill in the gaps with whatever information seems handiest, most logical, most interesting, most salacious. The consistency in reporting on certain details following Woolverton's return home suggests that the media of the day stuck mostly to things that had actually been said, although one must read as many papers as one can find to build a more complete picture of what was going on. For example, the January 29 *Star Press* of Muncie, Indiana, in its account of Woolverton's ride home, added an important new name: "A statement by Grover Garrott, chief of state police, that Rex Risher, a state policeman, met Woolverton at the electric railroad station here upon his arrival last night added interest to the situation. This assertion was substantiated by Frank Mayr Jr., of South Bend, secretary of state and close friend of the Woolvertons."

It was Mayr, recall, who raced home to South Bend on learning of his friend's abduction, ordering at least ten state motorcycle officers to the city as well. Secretary of state, an elected position, is Indiana's third-highest office and entails responsibilities over various aspects of Hoosier life, including elections, securities trading, and the registration of vehicle dealerships.

Powerful as the role might be, it seems Mayr needed to check with Farabaugh before he went making pronouncements. The declaration about how Woolverton got from station to home, shared by both Mayr and Garrott, "was in direct conflict with the one made by G. A. Farabaugh, attorney and spokesman for the Woolverton family," the *Star Press* of Muncie, Indiana, reported.

What was Farabaugh's declaration? At some point, after multiple newspapers had been told by multiple sources that Woolverton had been met by Rex Risher at the station and brought home in a cab, Woolverton's cover-up crew realized that part of the story didn't fit the rest of the narrative and needed to be denied from that point on.

According to the *Star Press*, Farabaugh "said Woolverton had been released by his abductors in Michigan City, caught an electric train and came to South Bend without the knowledge of his family or friends."

With that statement, Farabaugh had committed himself to that blatant falsehood about a drop-off in Michigan City instead of Chicago, and a highly questionable one, about whom Woolverton did and did not contact on his release.

Within a few days, the Michigan City claim would be battered down by several skeptical reporters and would have to be walked back altogether.

The second assertion of phone calls made or not made was handled with remarkable clumsiness when the *South Bend Tribune* raised the question.

Farabaugh, however, never relented on that assertion. His response to the account of an officer waiting at the station came in two phases, which might be labeled (1) Cover-up fail and (2) Cover-up mulligan.

Farabaugh, the *Tribune* reported, had claimed during the preceding evening, January 27, "that the manufacturer's return was unheralded and that it was not known that he had been released until he walked into his home, haggard and exhausted."

However, when confronted with Garrott's and Mayr's claims that Risher was waiting for Woolverton at the station, the *South Bend Tribune* reported that Farabaugh "said that the incident of Risher's appearance at the interurban station was an 'insignificant' one."

Farabaugh, a lawyer and former judge, must have known even as that five-syllable word left his mouth that he had spilled the beans, that dismissing as "insignificant" a central piece of evidence in the mystery of whether or not Howard Woolverton called anyone, and whom, was, to use a four-syllable word, incompetent.

No semi-intelligent murderer would describe their possession of the smoking gun as "insignificant," essentially a confirmation of its existence. No embezzler would use that word to brush away the mysterious arrival of a million dollars into their bank account.

So Farabaugh did what anyone armed with sufficient chutzpah, not to mention the full faith and credit of the Indiana state government, might do following such a disastrous admission: he changed his testimony.

"After first referring to the incident as an insignificant one Mr. Farabaugh flatly denied that Mr. Woolverton had been met at the station by Capt. Risher," the *Tribune* reported.

Was he flailing? Was G. A. Farabaugh simply throwing words out at random in the vain hope of protecting his client's story and his own professional reputation?

No, apparently not.

In the very next sentence of the *Tribune*'s article, we get the first hint that something bigger was going on, that G. A. Farabaugh might have used a careless word earlier in the day, but now the pieces were falling into place for the systematic and effective burying of information.

The article continued: "Both Chief Garrott and Risher had left the city to-day, ostensibly for Indianapolis."

The meaning of the sentence is clear: the two central actors in the pickup of Howard Woolverton from the South Bend train station were gone, unavailable, incommunicado.

They could be called in Indianapolis, of course, but telephones, then as now, were effective barriers to getting at the truth. Both men could simply never be available when it was a reporter on the line and never return the messages they left. And should someone make the drive to Indiana's capital city in the hopes of a direct confrontation, the same brushoff could be accomplished through secretaries and closed doors, or a terse "no comment." And eventually, the questions would cease, the press moving on to some other matter, the cover-up a success.

Just a little later in the story, we are treated to this defining paragraph of how things would be going forward: "The only information on the kidnaping and the return of Mr. Woolverton was to be obtained from Mr. Farabaugh, who is serving as spokesman for all members of the family. He declined to allow newspapermen to see Mr. Woolverton to-day and other members of the family referred all inquiries to the attorney."

Although he bumbled, behaved inscrutably, and attempted to deceive in his role as disseminator of the official abduction story, G. A. Farabaugh was no slouch. Today, ninety years after the kidnapping and sixty years after his death in 1961 at age seventy-seven, his eponymous Farabaugh Prize is still awarded to a top student at the Notre Dame Law School, where Farabaugh maintained his class's highest grade point average for all four years there.

According to his obituary in the *South Bend Tribune*, Gallitzin Aloysius Farabaugh, who received his ungainly first name as tribute to a Russian prince who served in the Alleghenies as a Catholic priest, was born on a Pennsylvanian farm, moved to South Bend to go to Notre Dame in the first years of the twentieth century, and stayed in the city the rest of his life. At twenty-seven, he was the youngest attorney elected up to that time to serve as judge on city court. He founded a law firm and a country club in South Bend and fathered a daughter and three sons.[1]

And in 1932, he played a key role in a historic cover-up.

The *South Bend News-Times* portrayed the complete news clampdown this way (a description, incidentally, that disproves the *Tribune*'s earlier suggestion that one of its reporters was physically present to hear Woolverton tell his postabduction story): "After the return of Mr. Woolverton Wednesday night, he refused to even show himself to newspapermen, and denied admittance to all interviewers. Attorney G. A. Farabaugh was nominated as spokesman for the family, and gave out a story to the effect that Mr. Woolverton knew little about his experiences; that no ransom had been paid, and that he would talk to no one."

The article doesn't state it explicitly, but we must imagine that, by this point, Secretary of State Frank Mayr, Indiana State Police Chief Grover Garrott, and anyone else who didn't have a Notre Dame scholarship named after them had gotten the memo: don't speak to the press about the Woolverton case.

At all.

G. A. Farabaugh will take it from here.

Even the decision on what vehicle to bring Woolverton home in smacked of deception. Recall that accounts of the drive from the station with state police captain Rex Risher consistently mentioned a taxi, not a police vehicle.

Why? Surely Capt. Risher had access to a car, indeed many cars, given the concentration of state law enforcement officials in South Bend and northern Indiana that day. The only reason to use a taxi, and incur the attendant fares, was anonymity. Cabs probably idled outside the station every time a train stopped there, none getting a second look. A state police vehicle, on the other hand, would have attracted inconvenient attention, not just among civilian passersby but from the South Bend police. And keeping the South Bend Police Department in the dark, as shall be made abundantly clear a little later in this book, was a central objective of the cover-up.

In fact, the presence of a taxi instead of a state car indicates that the cover-up Woolverton and Farabaugh orchestrated won the cooperation of remarkably senior state officials with remarkable speed.

But before we get into the porous nature of that information clampdown—for the press could not simply be batted away—we must ask: What was the drive home like for Howard Woolverton?

The South Shore Interurban terminates today at South Bend International Airport, but in Woolverton's time, the station stood at the corner of LaSalle Avenue and Dr. Martin Luther King Jr. Boulevard.[2]

The drive from the station to the Woolverton home on Jefferson Boulevard was a little over a mile, with a drive time estimated today at about four minutes.

Did they chat? Did Woolverton and Rex Risher discuss the weather? The state of the world? The day's headlines?

With the cab driver listening, we can imagine the men had little to say, Woolverton staring pensively out the window at a city he thought he knew, a city that would never feel quite the same.

From the moment he stepped off the train in his hometown, Woolverton was forced to retrace the steps of the previous evening. Recall from Woolverton's statement that the man in the back seat the previous night, waving a gun and threatening death, ordered Mr. Woolverton to cross the river via LaSalle, where Woolverton could see "the South Shore station to the right." Earlier in the evening, he'd also parked near the station to go to the movies.

Almost a century after Woolverton's abduction, we can only guess at the man's feelings on that drive home. His plans, on the other hand, his calculations regarding dealing with the practical questions of what had just happened to him, are easier to sum up, given the wealth of evidence at our disposal.

Howard Woolverton had been told in no uncertain terms what the kidnappers expected of him: pay $8,000 in accordance with a letter we'll be sending your brother in a few days.

And DO NOT TALK.

Your wife spilled the beans, the kidnappers probably said, and we could have killed you for that. But we're giving you a second chance. We'll let you live, we'll leave your wife alone, and we'll let your daughter grow up. But you've gotta pay up and clam up.

If you talk to the cops, they'll talk to the papers.

And we read the papers.

The kidnappers swore him to secrecy, but with the headlines blaring, that was going to be tough, he must have realized as soon as he'd picked up those newspapers in Chicago. So, as a wealth of evidence suggests, he immediately called his lawyer to hatch a plan to keep the kidnappers happy.

He succeeded.

14

Kidnapping? What Kidnapping?

LET'S IMAGINE THE FAITHFUL subscribers of the *South Bend Tribune*, readers who'd been on the edges of their seats all day Wednesday, January 27, 1932, worrying over the fate of Howard Woolverton.

His abduction was considered such a terrifying event that the police of three states—Indiana, Illinois to the west, and Michigan to the north—had been mobilized to military-grade vigilance as they both looked for the man and defended the citizenry from what felt like the invasion of a kidnapping army.

Now, let us imagine their befuddlement the next day when they picked up the *Tribune*.

"Family Reluctant," announced South Bend's largest newspaper in a front-page headline on January 28. "State Police Also Lose Interest."

The kidnappers were still at large and presumably no less worthy of a military-grade mobilization than they were while in possession of Howard Woolverton the day before. And yet, the *Tribune* reported, "A squad of a dozen or more state police officers, brought to South Bend by Secretary of State Frank Mayr, jr., close friend of the Woolverton family, had scattered to-day."

And so it went. Regardless of which newspaper one read or when one read it in the days following the kidnapping, the story was the same.

The Great State of Indiana had other things to worry about now.

Kidnapping?

What kidnapping?

A week later, on February 4, the *Chicago Tribune* confirmed that Woolverton still wasn't talking, and that was good enough for those whose job was to care about such things.

"VICTIM WON'T HELP SO OFFICIALS DROP HUNT FOR KIDNAPERS," read the all-caps headline, over a story that declared, "The kidnaping last week of Howard A. Woolverton, wealthy manufacturer, is regarded as a closed incident because of inability to get cooperation from the Woolverton family, authorities said today."

Even Indiana's governor appears to have been persuaded to stop worrying about some minor abduction somewhere in northern Indiana.

From the January 29 *Chicago Tribune*: "Gov. Harry Leslie, who on Wednesday expressed himself strongly on the subject of prosecution of the kidnapers, could not be reached yesterday to find out if he intended to ascertain just what the state authorities know and which the county authorities do not know about the release of Woolverton."

Woolverton wasn't talking, and that was that. Without his cooperation, officials were powerless to do anything.

Speculation over Woolverton's reticence followed a similar theme: fear.

"Captain Rex Risher of the state police declared Woolverton refused to converse with authorities or give details of the abduction," the *South Bend Tribune* noted. "Risher said he believed the kidnapers had threatened him with death if he gave any aid to police."

Rex Risher, recall, was the Indiana state police officer who, according to multiple papers, met Woolverton at the South Bend train station and came home with him in a taxi. Perhaps Risher drew his conclusions from something Woolverton said on that short ride home?

Comparable speculation appeared in the *South Bend News-Times*, but without the reference to Risher: "In kidnaping cases of this type where the plot is executed by clever 'mobs,' the victim is threatened with death unless he complies with their demands after his release and furnishes no information which might lead to their capture."

"The family is taking no part in any effort to find the kidnapers," the *Chicago Tribune* reported, adding this grim detail: "Woolverton and his wife are still fearful that their lives are in danger, and do not leave their home except when accompanied by several other persons, it was said."

Understandably, interest in the Woolverton kidnapping extended well beyond South Bend and even beyond Indiana state lines, given the habit of kidnappers to ply their trade wherever opportunities arose.

According to a front-page story in the *South Bend Tribune* on January 29, bylined in Chicago, Patrick Roche, chief investigator for the Illinois state attorney's office "told The Tribune there are some 'mighty peculiar angles' to the account of the kidnaping and Mr. Woolverton's return home 24 hours later."

Roche, however, was sent packing.

"I was in communication with the Woolverton home, Mr. Farabaugh and the state police throughout Wednesday while Mr. Woolverton was missing," Roche told the paper, "and they were anxious enough to have us help find him. But now that he's back I have heard nothing from them."

Had Woolverton wanted the kidnappers caught, Patrick Roche would have been a powerful ally.

Roche, who died in 1955 at age sixty of a cerebral hemorrhage, enjoyed a career in law enforcement both stellar and colorful.

Among his achievements with the state attorney's office was, according to his obituary in the *Chicago Tribune*, "his seizure of the records of Jack Zuta, former Chicago vice lord, after Zuta was shot down in a Wisconsin roadhouse. Roche beat the killers to the records, which paved the way for extensive criminal prosecutions."

"In 1924," the *Tribune* continued, "he gathered evidence which sent Hymie Weiss and Dapper Dan McCarthy, hoodlums, to jail for hijacking."

His investigative work once sent fifteen Prohibition agents to jail for taking bribes, noted the *Tribune*, another of many high points in a career that showed promise from the start, when he was a twenty-five-year-old rookie: "In 1920," the *Tribune* reported, "as a member of the Chicago police department, Roche made 469 arrests, an average of better than one and a half a day. He obtained 205 convictions, and scored 884 points in the police efficiency tables, more than any other member of the department."

Most relevant to the Woolverton case, on January 2, 1932—twenty-four days before Woolverton was kidnapped—Roche announced the roundup of "the worst gang of extortionists ever organized."

The story, featured on the front page of the January 3, 1932, *South Bend Tribune*, alleged that the group, based in and around Chicago, was responsible for "wholesale kidnapings that netted thousands of dollars."

Victims who wouldn't agree to pay up quickly were tortured. A Chicago druggist named Leo Gans had his feet "burned with red hot irons" before he agreed to produce $5,000, according to the article.

Eight members of the gang were arrested by Roche, with several more still on the lam and being sought, the article said.

According to the article, Roche identified a recent kidnapping trend pointed out by many other observers at the time, claiming that "he was drawn into the inquiry when the extortionists extended their activities, which previously had been confined to bootleggers, gamblers and others engaged in shady enterprises, to include reputable citizens."

Despite his expertise and his welcome to the case the day before, Roche was greeted with silence after Woolverton's return home, a development that seemed to leave him disappointed.

"This is an Indiana case and they don't seem to want our cooperation," he told the *Tribune*.

Roche's professional frustration is understandable. Less than a month before, he'd broken up a vicious gang of kidnappers. Now another had sprung up, hydralike, in its place. If he thought his work was done, Howard Woolverton's abduction proved the opposite. This isn't going to be a one-punch fight, he may have told himself. Anyone determined to stamp out kidnapping is in it for the long haul, and they'll need to look well beyond their own jurisdictions.

Roche reportedly saw no choice but to move on from the Woolverton case, however: "Insofar as he is concerned," the *South Bend Tribune* reported, "the investigation is at an end."

Woolverton's lack of cooperation with Roche, we might speculate, came from the same place as his claim that he'd been dropped off in Michigan City, Indiana, instead of Chicago. Admit to a Chicago drop-off, and it becomes a Chicago case and the focus of people there who know how to put kidnappers behind bars. Perhaps Woolverton, well aware of Roche's recent success in the city, decided on his own to say nothing about the Chicago angle. More likely, the thugs demanded he say nothing about Chicago and told him to hold Chicago authorities at arm's length.

The Secret Six, that band of Chicago vigilantes discussed earlier, also seemed to get the cold shoulder, according to multiple outlets.

"The Secret Six . . . offered their aid to South Bend authorities while Woolverton was a prisoner," claimed the *Chicago Tribune* on January 29, "but reported they were told their help was not needed."

The *Star Press*, in an AP wire story on the same day, detailed Woolverton's stonewalling of the irregulars this way:

> Officials of the "Secret Six," crime investigating group which recently announced it had discovered a national kidnaping ring, recalled its detectives from South Bend, Ind., today after "fruitless" questioning of Howard Woolverton, a victim of extortionists.
>
> Alexander Jamie, chief investigator, said Sergeant Roy Steffens and Detective Charles Touzinski reported that Woolverton did not give them a single clew to the identity of his abductors, and "did not appear to be concerned about their capture."

The Secret Six were particularly interested in the case, the *South Bend Tribune* indicated, because of recent developments in Chicago: "Col. Robert Isham Randolph, organizer of the Secret Six, said threats have been received by five intended victims in Chicago and that the threats came from another wing of the same gang which abducted Mr. Woolverton. He would not name the men selected for seizure by the kidnapers but said they will be given adequate protection."

The abduction of Howard Woolverton, the article implied, suggested that these threats weren't idle, but with the state of Indiana firmly in the cover-up camp, Howard Woolverton and his team had no trouble chasing away Illinois authorities and the vigilantes as well.

The South Bend police and the local prosecutor's office were another matter, however.

Just before midnight on January 26, 1932, South Bend Police Chief John B. Kuespert was roused from his home, and perhaps his bed, to meet with a very distraught Florence Flannery Woolverton at police headquarters.

He may not have gotten any sleep that night, nor the next day as he worked with the woman, other officials, and the press to protect the family and bring Howard home alive.

As soon as Woolverton walked through his front door, however, Kuespert got the cold shoulder.

"The determination of Chief Kuespert to run down the extortionists," declared the *South Bend Tribune* on January 28, "who are believed to be members of a large middle western syndicate, apparently found no support from the members of the Woolverton family and their attorney, nor did state police express any further interest in the case."

Unlike Illinois authorities or the Secret Six, however, Chief Kuespert couldn't simply walk. He had a city full of people to protect, a portion of whom were wealthy enough that they might be the next to fall victim to this new, at-large horde of people-snatchers.

"Chief of Police John B. Kuespert," announced the *Indianapolis Star* on January 29, "planned to continue investigation despite requests from the family that they wished the matter dropped. The chief scored the Woolvertons for what he termed lack of co-operation, and said that he was not informed of the man's return until after state troopers were guarding the residence."

A virtually identical theme was struck by many papers in stories published within a day of Woolverton's release, including this passage from the *South Bend Tribune*:

> Chief of Police Kuespert, who worked on the Woolverton case for 22 hours after the report of the abduction, was not informed of the manufacturer's safe return until after state troopers had placed Mr. Woolverton behind guarded doors to prevent anyone from questioning him.
>
> Nor did the family or Mr. Farabaugh communicate with Chief Kuespert this morning relative to any further investigation of the case in an attempt to bring about the capture of the criminals.
>
> Chief Kuespert said that although he conferred with Mr. Farabaugh and the family throughout the greater part of Wednesday afternoon he had no knowledge that the kidnapers were to set Mr. Woolverton Free.
>
> "The first I knew of it was when a police car came to my home about midnight and informed me that Mr. Woolverton had returned," he said.

One senses not just personal hurt in the sudden brushoff of Kuespert but perhaps some professional wounding as well. And Kuespert was no Keystone Cop, no common gumshoe. He served in the Indiana legislature from 1930 to 1931, according to the obituary published in the *South Bend Tribune* on March 15, 1967.[1] He'd been a vice president for the International Association of Chiefs of Police. He'd managed the city's airport for a time.

"Police Chief Kuespert said the Woolverton family had made no effort to assist him in running down the kidnapers," reported the *Star Press* of Muncie, adding, "He was disturbed that members of the state police department, instead, were given the confidence of Woolverton's family."

As the *Star Press* put it:

> Police Chief John B. Kuespert, smarting over what he termed the lack
> of co-operation of the Woolverton family with his department, said
> the fact that the man had returned home late last night unharmed and
> reporting that he had not paid any of the $50,000 ransom demanded
> would not halt his investigation.
>
> "Regardless of Mr. Woolverton's apparent desire to drop this case and
> whether some part of the $50,000 ransom was paid or not, I still con-
> sider this case a felony and will pursue it until we succeed in capturing
> the men or the trails fade out," Kuespert said.

"Chief Displeased," read the headline in the *Palladium-Item* of
Richmond, Indiana, over an article in which Kuespert promised that
"his forces would continue an investigation until all clews had been
exhausted."

While Kuespert never got to talk directly to Howard Woolverton,
Farabaugh apparently granted him an inconclusive interview the day
after Woolverton came home.

The question of ransom came up while the men talked, and Farabaugh seems to have swatted it away, forcing Kuespert to ruminate,
as reported in the *South Bend Tribune*: "Chief Kuespert declared that it
appeared certain that either ransom money had been paid to the kidnapers or a promise had been exacted from Mr. Woolverton to pay after
his release."

If there was to be a payment, the paper reported, "Chief Kuespert
made it clear that although the family was free to take whatever course
and pay whatever amount of money it saw fit, the police could not participate in any negotiations with the kidnapers. 'We cannot encourage
this growing criminal racket by entering into the payment of ransom
money,' he explained. 'To us this was and is simply an incident of major
crime.'"

Some sympathy did emerge through Kuespert's professional frustration, however, when he admitted to the *Indianapolis Star* that "Woolverton's apparent reticence to talk was probably engendered by fear of
gang reprisals."

That same sympathy broke through in an interview Kuespert gave the
South Bend Tribune: "'It is only natural that he would heed the warnings
of the kidnapers and keep still,' Chief Kuespert said. 'You or I no doubt
would have done the same thing.'"

Chief Kuespert was not the only local official worrying about the case and its implications.

St. Joseph County Prosecutor Samuel P. Schwartz's concerns, summed up in a front-page story in the *Chicago Tribune* on January 29, 1932, focused less on sympathy and more on responsibility.

Sixteen months after Woolverton's abduction, in May 1933, Schwartz would die of a cerebral hemorrhage.[2] One of South Bend's most prominent Jews, he was tragically young, at forty-one, and left behind a wife and daughter.

But in late January 1932, he was very much alive, his mind was very much focused on the essential questions of the crime, and he left us with a defining moral summary of the kidnap dilemma, as reported by the *Chicago Tribune*: "Feeling was high in South Bend, business and political leaders there holding that the latest kidnaping indicated that the field of underworld victims is exhausted and that every reputable business man is now subject to abduction. If the kidnapers of Woolverton received money and are to escape punishment, declared County Prosecutor Samuel P. Schwartz, their success will encourage outlawry everywhere."

Schwartz, the article continued, "admitted that the natural thing would be for Woolverton to wish to forget all about it and avoid any prosecution for the sake of his own safety and that of his family.

"'But such action is not in accord with public welfare,' Mr. Schwartz said. 'People who have an experience such as Mr. Woolverton had should think of the future safety of their fellow men and give every aid to bringing about proper punishment for the kidnapers.'"

Society had been looking the other way when crooks kidnapped crooks. But now that the bad guys were coming after upstanding folk, profiting and getting away, no one was safe, anywhere in America.

With the kidnapping of Howard Woolverton, and Woolverton's refusal to talk, Schwartz implied, success in America was under attack; doing well would bring down—on oneself, one's family, one's fortune—an unstoppable, unprosecutable visitation by the dark angels of the nation's underbelly.

The American Dream was dead.

Driven by what might be called an existential concern, then, Schwartz summoned the full weight of his office, threatening Woolverton with no less than a grand jury subpoena.

On January 29, the *Journal and Courier* of Lafayette, Indiana, alluded to this unique power of Woolverton's peers to get him talking:

The county grand jury will be asked to force Howard A. Woolverton, wealthy manufacturer, to divulge information regarding his abduction by kidnapers who demanded $50,000 for his release.

This was the announcement today of Prosecutor Samuel Schwartz who complained that Woolverton's refusal to discuss the kidnaping has balked all efforts to capture the gang.

The gambit worked, suggested the *South Bend Tribune*:

Prosecutor Samuel P. Schwartz, who entered the Howard A. Woolverton kidnaping investigation Thursday afternoon by announcing that he would question the manufacturer, has been promised an interview by the Woolverton family and is deferring his interrogation until the physical conditions of the victim and his wife permit.

"There are many confusing details of the kidnaping and the return of Mr. Woolverton," Prosecutor Schwartz said Thursday afternoon.

"If I am unable to obtain satisfactory explanations for all angles of the crime from this procedure," the prosecutor said, "I most certainly will place the matter before the grand jurors."

That shook Woolverton loose.

Sort of.

But first, Mr. Woolverton needed to recover. How was the man doing?

"A physician examined Mr. Woolverton and declared he had suffered no physical harm, only fatigue," reported the *South Bend Tribune* on Thursday, January 28.

The *South Bend News-Times* declared on the same date that "Mr. Woolverton arose late Thursday, refreshed after several hours of sleep induced by medical ministrations. He shaved and breakfasted, but remained in the seclusion of his home, denying himself to all interviews."

A day later, on Friday, January 29, the *Star Press* of Muncie reported further improvement: "Woolverton was reported today to have enjoyed a splendid sleep last night and to be feeling well. He planned to stay around his home and rest for several days before resuming his duties as secretary-treasurer of the Malleable Steel Range Company here."

By Sunday, the Woolvertons were ready to speak to Prosecutor Schwartz, and the results of the interview were summed up on Monday, February 1.

Bottom line: nada, zip, and zilch.

On Monday, February 1, 1932, the *South Bend Tribune* reported:

Unable to procure any new information which might provide clews to the identity of the kidnapers, Prosecuting Attorney Samuel P. Schwartz said to-day that the Woolverton kidnaping case will not be placed before the county grand jury which was convened this afternoon for its quarterly session.

The prosecutor conferred for two hours Sunday afternoon with Howard A. Woolverton, the 52-year-old manufacturer . . . and with the manufacturer's wife. The conference took place in the Woolverton home at 1246 East Jefferson boulevard.

"I learned nothing which I might use as a basis for a grand jury action," Mr. Schwartz said. "Mr. Woolverton gave me a detailed account of what happened from the time he and Mrs. Woolverton were abducted late Tuesday night until he was released by the kidnapers nearly 24 hours later. But he was blindfolded all of the time and did not once have an opportunity to see the faces of the kidnapers. Nor does he know the location of the place to which he was taken."

The prosecutor said he was convinced that the manufacturer had concealed nothing from him.

Did Woolverton admit that he'd promised the kidnappers $8,000? There was nothing in the paper about it from Schwartz, so presumably not. Did Woolverton talk about the farmhouse where he was kept or any of the other details he gave the feds two years later? One must assume not. In a passage of the statement to be discussed in the coming pages, Woolverton revealed several critical details about one of the kidnappers, but did Schwartz get the scoop? No. In fact, one might speculate that the Woolvertons spent all their time in that meeting with Schwartz making clear to him that nothing mattered as much as Betty's wellbeing. Maybe, they might have told him, the next South Bend kidnapping would involve someone who didn't have a twelve-year-old daughter. Subpoena them.

For whatever reason, Schwartz backed off. But that wasn't the end of Woolverton's cover-up to-do list. There was still one force to contend with: the press.

15

The Press Starts Digging

NOW THAT HOWARD WOOLVERTON was home safe, we may update the essential elements of his case.

Who: Howard Arthur Woolverton, fifty-two, wealthy Indiana industrialist; and at least two hoodlums still at large, with whom Woolverton spent almost twenty-four hours but never saw, never heard, and didn't wish to talk about

What: A kidnapping

When: Beginning a little after 11:00 p.m. on January 26, 1932, and concluding a little before midnight the next day, when Woolverton got dropped off, allegedly in Michigan City; once freed, he caught the train to the South Bend train station and from there was mysteriously transported home

Where: South Bend, Indiana, unknown wilderness west of the city, and possibly Michigan City, although that needs to be checked out

Why: Originally, for a $50,000 cash ransom, but now Woolverton and G. A. Farabaugh were claiming, dubiously, that no money had changed hands before Woolverton was let go, and that none had been promised

How: Guns, cars, a ransom note, a lot of driving around, and maybe a brief stop at a house, but something seems to be missing here

The Woolverton kidnapping story—a gripping, easily digestible tale the day before, with an innocent life in the balance, a distraught wife, an imperiled daughter, and a built-in cliffhanger—had in twenty-four hours devolved to something decidedly less satisfying to the average news editor: a chief source incommunicado and a morass of questionable claims and suspect assertions.

Half the story—the who, the why, and the how—was distressingly incomplete, and the when and the where weren't doing that well either.

Only the what—a kidnapping—seemed certain.

One must sympathize with Howard Arthur Woolverton, however. Menaced with his wife by a gun-wielding thug after a pleasant evening out; intermittently blindfolded and forced to endure almost twenty-four hours of cold, sleepless fear, concluding with a car ride that he believed was going to be his last; and beholden to the tune of $8,000 to the worst sort of people, the esteemed industrialist probably expected that fate might cut him a break, that karma might step in, that the beleaguered Howard Woolverton should get the two small things he most wanted: to conclude his dealings with the kidnappers with a minimum of fuss and attention and to see his version of the tale, as disseminated by his friend and spokesman G. A. Farabaugh, published without further inquiry by the media.

But it was not to be.

South Bend was in an uproar in the wake of Woolverton's abduction, and if Woolverton believed going silent would make everyone forget the whole thing, he was in for a rude awakening.

The midnight clamor of reporters at his front door was the first indication that the press wasn't going to take this one lying down.

As the *South Bend News-Times* described the scene: "A dozen newspaper reporters besieged the Woolverton home for two hours waiting for the story of the kidnaping from the victim. All requests for an interview with the victim brought the response that 'Judge Farabaugh was in conference with Mr. Woolverton and his wife and would soon have a statement ready.'"

Eventually, Farabaugh did come out and give that statement—although it was a decidedly incomplete narrative.

Perhaps the thronging journalists, leaving the Woolverton home late on that cold January night with notebooks full of the vague memories packaged up by Woolverton and his lawyer, allowed themselves a few moments to rejoice privately over the survival of the man and his return to his wife and daughter.

The sentiment didn't last long, however. After all, these were Depression-era newspaper reporters.

Do your job, get the scoop, beat the competition, and sell papers.

Or go stand in a bread line.

The statement Woolverton and Farabaugh had pieced together didn't add up, and the reporters, pounding out their stories on manual typewriters the next morning while the lead warmed up in the Linotypes, wouldn't have it.

Newspaper editors, faced with the daily task of edifying, informing, and titillating, must have despaired over a story that wasn't going to do any of the above for their paying customers.

When a well-to-do and respected man is picked up with his wife, threatened with death, and driven around by thugs who want $50,000, people need answers. Most importantly, they want to know it won't happen to them next.

With the bad guys still on the loose and Woolverton professing ignorance, answers were in short supply.

So the newspapers had their work cut out for them, and they collectively spread out their tentacles, looking for whatever additional tidbits they could turn up, whatever cracks appeared in the narrative's facade.

The American media, it must be said, can be both the easiest and the most difficult force to wrangle. Journalists don't carry guns, don't wear badges, can't demand admittance to a home, and don't issue subpoenas.

But if they don't get an answer to an awkward question, they can say so in print; they can pursue leads government investigators might not bother with; they can publish rumors and speculation more authoritative institutions can't.

They can also put the disturbing uncertainty of things front and center: "After having been in the hands of kidnappers for twenty-four hours," observed the *Indianapolis News*, "Howard A. Woolverton, South Bend manufacturer, was back in his home today, his silence adding to the mystery that marked his disappearance."

The *Dekalb Daily Chronicle* offered an even more ominous take: "Woolverton was not seen by any reporters when he arrived at the house and this gave rise to an unsubstantiated belief he might have been tortured or injured by the abductors in their effort to force payment of a ransom."

The press, as is obvious from the coverage of the day, was getting suspicious. Something wasn't adding up.

There appears to have been enough skepticism on the part of the Fourth Estate in South Bend that it left the kidnapping's official spokesman exasperated. The *South Bend Tribune* reported to that effect on January 28, the day after Woolverton arrived home and put his lawyer in charge of all communications:

> "Did that story I told you last night sound fictitious?" G. A Farabaugh, attorney for the Woolverton family, asked newspapermen to-day at the outset of an interview in his office.
>
> Mr. Farabaugh referred to the reluctance of the press representatives to accept the story that Mr. Woolverton was set free 23 hours after his abduction without the payment of any ransom or any communication between the family and the kidnapers.

The article did not include a response from any of the reporters present, but if it had, most likely the answer would have come out something like "Yes, that story you told us last night did indeed sound fictitious."

But how do you uncover lies and inconsistencies when all official organizations have gone silent or been rebuffed, and a private attorney has been named arbiter of all facts, large and small?

We might imagine the editors and reporters meeting in the (presumably) ink-stained and smoke-filled offices of the *South Bend Tribune*, tossing ideas back and forth, looking for holes in the story, determined to give their terrified readers what they were paying for: truth and reassurance.

The Woolverton kidnapping was major news—a front-page story in Chicago, carried nationwide on the wires, described in the *South Bend News-Times* as a crime that triggered "one of the keenest manhunts staged in the Middle West during the past few years"—and it happened in the *Tribune*'s front yard. Professional pride, if nothing else, demanded that they get to the bottom of whatever could be gotten to the bottom of.

As they brainstormed, we might guess, someone proposed talking to the conductor of the South Shore Interurban to ask if he remembered anything about a rumpled businessman getting on the train in Michigan City.

The idea, whatever its genesis, must have been considered a sound one and not that difficult to execute. Train conductors were easy to identify and find, back then as today, since their location at any given time while working tended to be widely published.

The *Tribune* found its man, got the interview, and presented its scoop on the front page of the January 28 issue:

> The story of the release of Mr. Woolverton on the outskirts of Michigan City, as related by Mr. Farabaugh and Capt. Risher, appeared to be growing fragile this afternoon when a representative of The Tribune talked with the conductor of the interurban on which the manufacturer is supposed to have ridden from Michigan City to South Bend.
>
> Otto Bartels, of Michigan City, conductor of the car which arrived here at 11:20 o'clock, said that he did not remember any person corresponding to the photographs of Mr. Woolverton entering the car at Michigan City.

A few days later, on January 30, the *Michigan City News* backed up the *Tribune*'s reporting:

> Harry F. Hanley of 121 West Barker avenue, a dispatcher for the South Shore railway, reported that he rode on the same train Wednesday night from the 11th street station to the offices in Eastport, and that three other persons got on, but that all were local residents and Woolverton was not among the group.
>
> He declared that the train, due here at 10:26 o'clock was slightly late in arriving, and did not leave the station until 10:38 o'clock. Of the three getting on the train with Hanley, one man was an employe [sic] of the South Shore, a woman who was employed at the counter in the station, while the third person was a Michigan City Resident.

The press had done its job here, digging up what could be unearthed in stories that suggested Woolverton and his attorney were lying about the drop-off point.

On this score, Farabaugh eventually relented. But, true to form, his capitulation to the evidence was a piecemeal, halfhearted affair that spawned more laughable misinformation.

According to the *Chicago Tribune*'s January 28 edition, "Stories conflicted as to where Woolverton was released. Attorney Farabaugh declared the manufacturer did not know."

Farabaugh asked his audience to imagine, then, that a man able to read about himself in newspapers and to buy a train ticket to South Bend was incapable of gathering his faculties beyond that, his postabduction position on earth a complete mystery to him.

In a story published by the *Indianapolis Star* on the same date, Farabaugh seemed to be hedging a bit in the statement, hinting that a "slightly dazed" Woolverton might have gotten on the train farther up the line, but "the first Woolverton remembered, according to the statement, was when he regained his senses on the train at Michigan City, Ind., en route to South Bend."

The claim of a Michigan City drop-off was not officially abandoned until a week later, on February 4, when "unimpeachable sources" (most likely G. A. Farabaugh; more on that shortly) informed the *South Bend News-Times* that "Mr. Woolverton was released in Chicago and not in Michigan City."

Now, what of payment? What did Woolverton have to do to get free?

In the minds of the citizenry, the ransom question would be a central matter. Anyone with any means in South Bend must have wondered: If I'm kidnapped, what's the going rate for freedom, an end to the torture, and the safety of my family?

Woolverton himself provided, through Captain Rex Risher of the Indiana State Police, a claim that $0 was the going rate.

As the *Chicago Tribune* reported, "Concerning ransom Woolverton refused to talk on orders of the abductors, the captain said. Beyond stating he had paid no ransom and had promised none, Woolverton declined to talk further."

G. A. Farabaugh was similarly adamant, quoted in the *South Bend Tribune* as insisting that "there was no communication between myself and members of the family and the kidnapers and absolutely no ransom has been paid."

Indiana Secretary of State Frank Mayr offered insights as to how Howard Woolverton could have gotten away for nothing.

"His opinion was," the *Chicago Tribune* reported on January 29, "that the kidnapers released Woolverton because of the great amount of publicity given by the newspapers to the kidnaping."

Farabaugh offered his own theory to the *South Bend Tribune*: "The attorney said that he felt certain that the kidnapers realized that they had abducted a man who was unable to meet their demand for $50,000 ransom and that, rather than take a chance on being trapped, set him free."

The absence of hard information on many aspects of the kidnapping meant that there were lingering questions. Predictably, the answers came thick and fast from less-official parties, evolving by the hour as sources, anonymous or otherwise, crawled out of the shadows to whisper their assertions.

Multiple papers repeated variations of Farabaugh's declaration of no payment, but these were usually accompanied by counterclaims from other sources in the next sentence.

One example appeared on the front page of the *Dekalb Daily Chronicle*, which reported that "Attorney G. A. Farabaugh, representing the victim's family, denied flatly any ransom was paid. Other sources intimated that a sum not to exceed $20,000 had been agreed upon for Woolverton's release."

Similarly, the *Belvidere Daily Republican* reported without attribution: "Yesterday Woolverton's relatives offered to pay $15,000 for his release and it was believed possible that this amount had been delivered. Relatives, however, denied the payment of any price for the manufacturer's freedom."

Two years after the kidnapping, Howard Woolverton would claim in his federal statement that he had promised $8,000 in cash to the thugs. Somehow, that information got out and began circulating within a day of Woolverton's liberation.

The *South Bend News-Times* was one of several papers to claim on January 28: "Although it was announced that the Woolverton family paid no part of the $50,000 ransom demanded by the kidnapers, The News-Times learned from a source that was considered authoritative that Mr. Woolverton placed himself under heavy obligation to his captors to gain his release."

The *South Bend Tribune* reported similarly on the same date: "From one source close to the Woolverton family came the intimation that Mr. Woolverton might have been released after promising to pay for his liberty to-day or at some future time."

The next day, however—Friday, January 29, 1932—the *South Bend Tribune* abandoned mere speculation and piecemeal rumor, declaring that their sources knew, once and for all, how Howard Woolverton had gotten himself free.

After two days of rumors and scuttlebutt about what ransom, if any, had been paid to free Howard Woolverton, an entirely new version of things emerged.

On Friday, January 29, 1932, the front page of the *South Bend Tribune* presented a version of the ransom story divergent from all other newspaper coverage, Woolverton's federal statement, and a second ransom note handed down through the family that is now in the keeping of grandson Dave Hendry.

"CHICAGO GROUP TELLS OF DEAL IN OFFICE HERE," shouted the headline.

The story began: "The Secret Six, Chicago's mysteriously guided crime fighting organization, directed the payment of ransom for the return of Howard A. Woolverton, kidnaped South Bend Manufacturer."

The article claimed to be quoting "unimpeachable official sources," asserting that "at the headquarters of the Secret Six here to-day it was frankly admitted that ransom was paid for the release of Mr. Woolverton although the officials of the organization declined to divulge the amount." The article continued:

> Alexander Jamie, director of the Secret Six activities, and Sergt. Roy Steffens, one of the operatives, admitted their group participated in the deal for the prominent manufacturer's release and that ransom money was paid several hours before he returned home aboard a South Shore train at 11:20 o'clock Wednesday night.
>
> Sergt. Steffens went to South Bend Wednesday afternoon and sat in conference in the office of a business man not a member or a close friend of the Woolverton family, when the ransom payment was agreed upon.
>
> So definite is the information procured by the Secret Six It [*sic*] is learned, that its investigators have located the house where Woolverton was held prisoner. The house is about 60 or 75 miles from South Bend and is not headquarters of gang extortionists but was used by them specifically for the Woolverton kidnaping.

The story runs perplexingly contrary to most other information available about the case, both published and confidential. And it is quite likely all wrong.

Why would the Secret Six make such a boast? Featured in a 1931 movie, credited with anticrime efforts of heroic proportions, including building the case that sent Al Capone to prison for income tax evasion, the vigilante crime-fighting group was a year from dissolution when Woolverton was kidnapped and was already struggling. Propelled by the hubris of its own successes, perhaps, it had moved from plodding investigation work to the planting of bombs and the flinging of wild accusations, and at the time of the Woolverton kidnapping, it was the principal defendant in a $100,000 defamation lawsuit (which it would lose in December 1932), brought by a young man who'd been arrested on the group's flimsy say-so for extortion.

Taking false credit for freeing Woolverton might have represented a bid for restored relevance, a last-gasp reach for the glory days, an act of strategic marketing.

The next paragraph of the story suggests something along those lines: "It also has been revealed that part of the ransom money was provided by relatives and friends of the Woolvertons here and in Wheaton, Ill., and that they were instrumental in bringing the Secret Six into the case."

Have you had a kidnapping? the passage fairly exclaims. Has someone from your household gone missing after last being seen in the company of murderous thugs? Has a loved one vanished, leaving nothing behind but a threatening ransom note written in big, blocky letters? Never fear! Call the Secret Six, like the Woolverton family did, and this discreet group ("secret" is part of their name, after all) will negotiate on your behalf, gather the funds, deliver them to the designated place, and get your favorite abductee back home safe and sound!

If the story was more marketing than truth, the story's author probably can't be blamed. Bylines were rare in those days, but Everett R. Holles earned one for his thorough coverage of all things Woolverton, including that front-page *South Bend Tribune* story about the Secret Six and the ransom.

If anyone was going to break startling new Woolverton revelations, it would be Holles.

16

The Woolvertons Get Even

WHAT DO RESPECTABLE PEOPLE do when the newspaper coverage of their personal affairs—say, a messy divorce, a financial problem, or a widely publicized kidnapping—leaves them deeply wounded?

They might seek a financial remedy; for example, withholding advertising dollars or filing a lawsuit.

They might complain to the editor.

Or they might hit the offending publication where it really hurts: right in the scoop.

The scandalized Howard and Florence Woolverton, with the aid of G. A. Farabaugh, their maligned lawyer, chose the latter option.

We can only imagine their sense of affront on January 29, 1932, when they gazed on the front page of the *South Bend Tribune*, spotted that story by Everett Holles, and saw an account of Mr. Woolverton's liberation that had nothing to do with their version of reality.

This was the proverbial insult atop injury: a man who'd been taken from his wife by armed thugs, forced to cool off in a basement prison, and promised death, and who had successfully talked his way out of peril was now being subjected to a band of Windy City Sherlocks taking credit for it all, and South Bend's number one paper (which the Woolvertons paid to receive daily at home) swallowing the story whole, splaying it out front-page-style on January 29.

The article, along with calling Howard Woolverton a liar, also took aim at his attorney, it should be noted.

G. A. Farabaugh, his name often preceded in print by the honorific "Judge" long after he ceased to be one, was not granted that dignity of station in Holles's article.

Under a second all-caps headline, "DISPUTES FARABAUGH STORY," Holles wrote that the Secret Six's claim of arranging a ransom payment "completely shatters the account of Mr. Woolverton's release as given by G. A. Farabaugh, South Bend attorney and spokesman for the Woolverton family."

Under a section of the article headlined "Story Reported Changed," the piece took a second swipe at Farabaugh as the source of errata: "Although Mr. Woolverton's spokesman gave detailed accounts of the victim's release on the western outskirts of Michigan City about 10 o'clock Wednesday night and his walking 26 blocks to the South Shore station where he waited 30 minutes for an interurban train, information has been given The Tribune that he did not board the train at Michigan City but nearer the hideaway of the gang."

Judge Farabaugh wasn't just a casual liar, the article implied, not merely the fabricator of a convenient mistruth now and then. When called to it, the man could spin yarn by the spool. For an attorney who had, presumably, to appear regularly in local courtrooms presided over by judges who both cared about the truth and read newspapers, this paragraph must have cut particularly deep.

Neither Farabaugh nor the Woolvertons could be expected to take this one lying down, and the aggrieved three struck back, serving their vengeance lukewarm.

A week after the Holles outrage, on Friday, February 5, *Tribune* archrival the *South Bend News-Times* published a front-page story chock-full of the sorts of details everyone had been clamoring for.

The story closely matched Woolverton's federal statement, confirmed several rampant rumors, and corrected earlier official pronouncements.

And it was exclusive to the *South Bend News-Times*.

"News-Times Gets Detailed Story of Seizure," the headline crowed.

The article continued:

The price of freedom for Howard A. Woolverton, wealthy South Bend manufacturer, who was kidnaped last week and held for $50,000 ransom, was $8,000, The News-Times learns today from unimpeachable sources. The price was arranged between Mr. Woolverton and his abductors a week ago Wednesday night shortly before he was set free in the outskirts of Chicago after being held captive for 24 hours.

Whether the $8,000 has been paid or is yet to be paid could not be learned.

The abductors, who are thought to be members of a notorious kidnap gang operating in and around Chicago, were to mail Mr. Woolverton directions this week for sending the money to them, it was learned.

The letter containing the directions was to be sent to Mr. Woolverton in care of his brother, John Woolverton, 307 S. Lafayette boulevard, The News-Times informants said. Delivery of the money was to be made by a nephew of Howard Woolverton.

Because of the refusal to discuss the kidnaping by members of the Woolverton family, it could not be learned whether the letter has been received here.

To the delight of the Woolvertons and Mr. Farabaugh, no doubt, the *News-Times* story took aim at several assertions made in the article Holles had written for the *Tribune*.

Where the *Tribune* had claimed that the ransom was "believed to be $15,000 or $20,000," the *News-Times* declared, "The disclosure of the $8,000 agreement between Mr. Woolverton and his abductors discredits the reports that Mr. Woolverton paid his captors $15,000 or $20,000 for his freedom the night he was released."

As for Holles's revelation that the Secret Six had found the location of Woolverton's prison, "about 60 or 75 miles from South Bend," the *News-Times* offered this very specific rebuttal, courtesy of their unnamed source: "Disclosure of the fact that he was released from the gang's custody in Chicago also discredits earlier reports that he had been held in a house 50 or 60 miles from South Bend. Officers also deny that the location of the house in which he was held captive was discovered."

The story settled finally where Woolverton was dropped off by the kidnappers, noting that the disclosure by their unnamed source "established that Mr. Woolverton was released in Chicago and not in Michigan City where it was declared he was set free after he had arrived home at midnight a day after he was abducted."

In his statement to the *News-Times*, Farabaugh withheld some information about the ransom payment, but the paper had no problem filling in those gaps, thanks to the local rumor mill:

> It is believed the kidnap gang set its date for receiving the ransom almost two weeks after the actual kidnaping hoping that police activity for capturing the gang members then would have died out.
>
> Police here admitted this week that because of a lack of clues and the refusal of the Woolverton family to discuss the affair, they had given up hope for capturing the gang.

The article included a peculiar euphemism for cold-blooded murder, stating that the kidnappers "threatened to put Mr. Woolverton 'on the spot' but after compelling him to agree to their demands for money to be delivered to them after the receipt of their letter, freed him."

We must now put ourselves back in that hypothetical, smoky, ink-stained conference room of the *South Bend Tribune*, where Everett Holles has joined with the newspaper's editors to leaf through that day's edition of their biggest competitor.

Holles, according to his *New York Times* obituary, was born in 1902 in Hastings, Michigan, went to school at Michigan State University, and enjoyed a long and widely respected career.

At the time of the Woolverton kidnapping, he was twenty-nine and a new husband and father. In June 1930, he had married Carolyn Jacks (a former features writer for his paper's bitterest rival, interestingly enough, the *South Bend News-Times*), and the couple brought his only son, David, into the world in 1931.

In September 1936, a few years after the Woolverton affair, Holles had a near-death experience of his own.

Now an international correspondent, he'd come to San Sebastian, Spain, a focal point of the Spanish Civil War, mired in danger and intrigue. He'd arrived by boat, beseeching a dozen ship captains to bring him into the city before he found someone foolhardy enough to do so. The beautiful coastal city, located on the Bay of Biscay less than ten miles from the French border, featured an abandoned fort that Holles made the mistake of wandering into soon after his arrival.

Later that day, according to a story he filed with the United Press, he was taken into custody by Spanish loyalists who charged him with being a spy and sentenced him without trial to death by firing squad. His crime: investigating military structures.

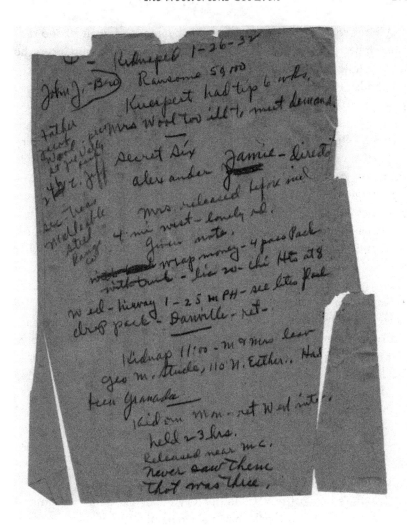

Notes taken by *South Bend Tribune* reporter Everett Holles on January 27, 1932, were preserved by the paper and now reside in the archives of David W. Hendry, Jr. *David W. Hendry, Jr.*

"'You'll probably be shot about 5 o'clock this afternoon,' the captain told me pleasantly," Holles wrote.

"My poor Spanish became voluble and its disorder seemed to persuade the captain that I was probably not an actual Spanish rebel," Holles reported. "Still, he said, he favored shooting me."

Where Woolverton got out of trouble by negotiating an $8,000 ransom, Holles got the French consul involved, and they convinced the Spanish militia to let him go.

Grandson Greg Holles, a family doctor living in Portland, Oregon, remembers the courageous journalist fondly.

"My grandfather was a lovely guy, very, very funny with a big bellowing laugh," Dr. Holles wrote in a 2019 email. "He was always very supportive of me in school and put a lot of emphasis on having a wide breadth of knowledge."

Intelligence, good humor, and a bright future notwithstanding, Everett Holles had some work do to on that first weekend in February 1932. His paper's biggest rival had just scooped him on the moment's biggest story, and an answer was due. As a young father at the time, Holles must have felt some disappointment, perhaps uttered a few obscenities (an exceedingly rare occurrence among 1930s journalists, of course, but it was known to happen) when he was called in by his editor to discuss the *News-Times*'s Woolverton story. Perhaps Mr. Holles had hoped to spend Saturday at home with his wife and toddler and may have said as much. And then, with the preambles over, they got down to the business of deciding what face-saving win could be wrested from this embarrassing act of revenge.

The *Tribune*'s answer arrived the next day, Saturday, February 6, and was given the minor treatment a secondhand story deserved, relegated to page four. Not surprisingly, it focused on the elements of the *News-Times* story that confirmed the *Tribune*'s coverage and mostly ignored everything else.

"Tribune's Disclosure Verified in Story Published Here," announced the headline, above an article that avoided naming either the competing paper or Farabaugh:

> A story, believed to have been provided by an attorney acting for the family of Howard A. Woolverton, was published in South Bend Friday afternoon confirming The Tribune's disclosures a week ago regarding the kidnaping and return of Mr. Woolverton.
>
> The published article confirms The Tribune's information that a "deal" was entered into between representatives of the kidnapers and the Woolverton family on Wednesday, Jan. 27, several hours before the business man's return home.
>
> The Tribune announced that it had learned from unimpeachable sources that ransom had been arranged for, although it was believed

that considerably less than the $50,000 demanded had been agreed upon. Friday's published article states that the kidnapers and the family compromised on $8,000.

The story published Friday also bore out The Tribune's statement that Mr. Woolverton was not placed aboard a South Shore interurban train in Michigan City by his kidnapers but boarded the train nearer Chicago. This fact was established by The Tribune the morning following Mr. Woolverton's return.

The article also got in one last lick against the veracity of Judge Farabaugh, who certainly didn't need to be named: "At the time all of these facts were emphatically denied by the Woolverton attorney."

With that final paragraph, the warring sides apparently settled on an uneasy truce, the answering of some of the most burning questions meaning it was time to move on to other news, albeit with several lingering mysteries: Was a second ransom note actually received? Was it truly for $8,000? Does it still exist? Was the ransom paid?

The answer to all four questions, after nine decades of silence and a cover-up that seems to have begun with a winter's eve call from a pay phone in Chicago, is yes.

Among the vast trove of clippings, relics, and artifacts assembled by David Hendry Jr. relating to his grandfather's kidnapping, the letter stands out.

Written in pencil in exceptionally neat cursive script, it maintains near-perfect evenness and line spacing on unlined stationery. It reads in its entirety:

Dear Sir. Give your nephew $8000^{00} securely wrapped in heavy paper, and have him take either your Pierce-Arrow, or Packard #20 and drive to St. Louis Missouri.

He must leave St Louis on Highway #40 so he can arrive in St. Charles Missouri at six P.M. Wednesday after noon Feb. 3rd. Leave St. Charles at five minutes past six oclock, on highway #40 going through Columbia to Kansas City. When he sees lights flash ten times stop car, and sit package on pavement and continue at least ten miles ahead. If he is not stopped, have him turn around at City limits of Kansas City and drive back to Columbia.

If this agreement is met, as we stated, your case is a closed issue with us. But if you fail you can rest assured, We will do every thing we told you.

The letter, showing creases where it was folded into thirds for mailing, was presumably sent to John Woolverton at his home at 307 S. Lafayette Boulevard.[1]

In fact, given a ransom drop deadline of Wednesday, February 3, the deal was presumably done, the money left on the pavement, the case a "closed issue" when Farabaugh went to the *South Bend News-Times* to give them that revenge-driven exclusive on Friday, February 5.

The Woolverton nephew tasked with delivering the cash wasn't named in the newspapers or the letter, but Dave Hendry is certain it was John Jacob Woolverton Jr., twenty-six-year-old son of Howard Woolverton's brother John.

John Jr. would go on to helm two of his grandfather's companies, chairing the boards of both the St. Joseph Bank & Trust Company and the Malleable Steel Range Manufacturing Company. He lived another fifty-five years after the kidnapping, marrying twice (his first wife died in 1971) and fathering two daughters. He was eighty-one when he died in 1987, and his death left us with a number of unsolved mysteries.

First of all, at what point was John Jr. appointed the delivery driver?

In his statement, Howard Woolverton said he was freed after promising to pay $8,000, which was to be delivered in accordance with whatever instructions were mailed to his brother John. Who specifically would make the drop wasn't revealed in his statement, however. Did Howard volunteer his nephew John's name while still in the kidnappers' clutches on the assumption the young man would be glad to get the job done? John Jr. had started working for the Malleable Steel Range Company in 1929 and was still unmarried and childless in 1932. He had time on his hands, therefore, and was probably already demonstrating the acumen that would earn him top positions at two family businesses.

Still, committing one's nephew to fulfilling the demands of a ransom letter without first consulting said nephew might be a bit presumptuous. So a second possibility remains, not recorded in Woolverton's statement or anywhere else, that there was some further communication between Woolverton or his representatives and the kidnappers or theirs, in which John Jr. was identified as having agreed to serve.

A second, bigger mystery: What happened on that long drive back and forth to Kansas City? This was a round trip of more than one thousand miles on modern roads, and surely both longer and more torturous in 1932. The question remains pertinent because the kidnappers, apparently, never got their cash.

Dear Sir

Give your Nephew $3000.00 securely wrapped in heavy paper, and have him take either your Pierce Arrow, or Packard $20 and drive to St Louis Missouri.

He must leave St Louis on Highway #40 so he can arrive in St Charles Missouri at six P.M. wednesday afternoon Feb. 3rd. Leave St Charles at five minutes past six oclock on highway #40 going through Columbia to Kansas City. When he sees lights flash ten times stop car, and, set package on pavement and continue at least ten miles ahead. If he is not stopped, have him turn around at city limits of Kansas City and drive back to Columbia.

If this agreement is met, as we stated, your case is a closed issue with us. But if you fail you can rest assured, we will do every thing we told you.

The second ransom note, in neat cursive and far more professional than the first, but still concluding with a threat. *David W. Hendry, Jr.*

The only record of the money drop and what came after seems to reside in the memory of David Hendry Jr. When he was old enough, his mother, Betty—the woman who as a girl of twelve required a police escort to go to school—told him all she knew.

"Everybody thought the ransom was delivered," Hendry said in a 2019 telephone interview. "Until the phone calls started coming in."

For a year at least after the kidnapping, or possibly closer to two, the sanctity of the Woolverton household was violated repeatedly by a mysterious woman who called to insist the cash hadn't been received.

Betty never answered the phone for any of these calls, Hendry said, but she later learned of them.

"The threats were graphic and nasty," Hendry said he was told, and many were directed against Betty.

The threats were reported in a front-page story in the *South Bend Tribune* on March 2, 1932. And the Woolvertons weren't the only ones receiving such messages.

> It was also disclosed to-day that a guard had been maintained at the home of G. A. Farabaugh at 1019 East Colfax avenue, and that Mr. Farabaugh, who is attorney for Howard Woolverton and served as spokesman for the family at the time of Mr. Woolverton's disappearance, recently received a series of telephone threats.
>
> The threats came from a woman who tersely informed him:
>
> "You're next, Mr. Farabaugh."

We might imagine that the kidnappers, deprived of their cash, knew from media reports that Judge Farabaugh had been the family's go-to in all kidnapping matters and might be coerced into putting together a second money drop.

The article went on to hint at the fear that would become a postkidnapping theme of life in South Bend.

"A week ago," the article read, "Mr. Farabaugh sought some means of obtaining firearms permits and special deputy badges for guards at the homes of the Woolverton Family."

In the story, Farabaugh confirmed the telephone threats coming into the Woolverton household, as well as the arrival of more letters: "At that time he admitted to a friend that Mrs. Howard Woolverton had received intimidating letters and telephone calls."

While none of the threats were carried out, and the calls eventually ceased, they would soon upend Betty's life.

These badges, issued by (*from left*) the State of Indiana, St. Joseph County, and the South Bend Police Department, are believed to have been worn by Howard Woolverton when he was acting as a deputized law enforcement officer after his kidnapping. He and other family members also obtained gun permits in answer to ongoing threats. *David W. Hendry, Jr.*

Did the girl know her well-being was routinely menaced in messages to her parents? Apparently not. Her son Dave Hendry and her best friend Mary Jay are both certain the parents suffered in silence, never speaking to their daughter of the messages or their graphic detail.

What happened to the money? No one knows.

"Maybe John Jr. decided 'Well, I'm just going to drop it here,'" Hendry speculated. "There's just so many things that can go wrong with that kind of a money drop."

Hendry also wonders if word got out.

"Did someone else know about the ransom note?" Hendry speculated. "How tough would it be where somebody else sets the stage, where someone else knows about it?"

The arrival on February 1 of the second note at his great-uncle John's house, Hendry observes, would have been communicated immediately to at least four South Bend households: those of Jacob Woolverton and the patriarch's three surviving sons.

And each of those homes employed multiple servants—cooks, nannies, laundresses, chauffeurs, gardeners. Even if they were sworn to secrecy, how could the domestic staff be expected not to talk about what was surely the most exciting news any of them had encountered on the job, ever?

There was a fatal flaw in the kidnappers' methodology, Hendry added. The well-publicized first ransom note instructed the driver to drop the money on seeing headlights from behind flash ten times. The second ransom note included the same instructions.

An opportunistic household staff member, or someone who'd caught wind of things thanks to someone else's loose lips, wouldn't need to know much to intercept the package. If they'd been told no more than that John Woolverton Jr. was leaving Wednesday to drop the cash off somewhere, they could follow discreetly, flash their lights at some strategic moment, and earn several years' income with a single night of work.

Hendry said:

> I have to believe that there was somebody in one of the households that knew about this that wasn't a family member, that followed him. How hard would it be to follow him to where he was supposed to be?
>
> At some time, someone gets behind him and starts flashing the lights 10 times, and he drops the money, and they pick up the package, and they're on their way.

A doublecross is certainly another plausible theory. The last chapter of many kidnappings in the era when they were rampant was a final reckoning among the abduction team because money didn't always get distributed fairly or handed out at all. Many resulting revenge slayings were dutifully covered by the press of the day. So whoever had been assigned the chore of blinking those lights and grabbing that cash might have neglected the final step of equal compensation, stashing it someplace safe and then claiming they'd all been stiffed.

Whatever happened, Hendry is certain that the well-wrapped package of cash didn't just end up moldering by the side of the road: "Somebody got 8,000 bucks."

Strangely, Howard Woolverton's federal statement in 1934, two years after the kidnapping, includes no mention of the money drop or the threatening phone calls.

The next few sentences of his statement do add some other interesting details to what we know, however. What was presented in the press as a broad-brush stonewalling of all investigations into the abduction wasn't quite so monolithic.

Recall that in his statement, Woolverton said he phoned that mysterious Chicago woman, was picked up at the South Bend station by that mysterious Chicago man (neither of whom existed, most likely), and arrived home to find his dwelling "surrounded by many cars and police motorcycles who were in and out of the house."

The next passage suggests that Woolverton was more cooperative with the Secret Six than news stories indicated at the time. Although Secret Six officials were quoted in a widely-distributed Associated Press story as saying Woolverton "did not give them a single clew to the identity of his abductors, and did not appear to be concerned about their capture," several Secret Six officials were invited to a lengthy, wee-hours conversation with Woolverton at his home, or so says the statement:

> Alexander Jamie of the Secret Six and one of his operators, Mr. Steffin as well as one other whose name I cannot recall were present at my home when I arrived. Among them was the captain of the Indiana State Highway Police namely Rex Risher[2] with several of his men. They questioned me about the details of my kidnapping and I sat conversing with them until about three A.M. the following morning January 28, 1934 [*sic*: 1932], at which time I went to bed. Also interested in the investigation of this case were the following named men: Frank Mayr, Jr., Sec. State of Indiana; Chas. Bolte, formerly associated with the above named man and now conducting a privately owned detective agency in Indianapolis, Mr. Bolte was at that time employed as an operator in the Bureau of Criminal Identification of the State of Indiana under the new Secretary of State, Frank Mayr, Jr.

Notably absent from that early-morning meeting: anyone with the South Bend Police Department or the St. Joseph county prosecutor's office.

In the next passage of his statement, Woolverton confirms receipt of the second ransom note, as well as two more threatening missives, probably the letters G. A. Farabaugh mentioned as being sent to Mrs. Woolverton in that March 2 *South Bend Tribune* article. Those letters have apparently been lost to history, but they weren't simply tossed out. In fact, what Woolverton claims was done with them offers another hint that he provided more assistance to the Secret Six than press accounts of the time suggested:

> The letter mentioned in the first part of this report which was to contain the instructions for the payment of the ransom money was received by my brother, John, at his residence 307 S. Lafayette Street on February 1st. The photostatic copy of this letter you have turned over to J. T. Martin of the Division of Investigation, U.S. Department of Justice. I also turned over to Mr. Martin an original ransom note received

by me together with another photostatic copy of another ransom note. The originals of the above mentioned photostatic copies are in the custody of Mr. Jamie of the Secret Six, Chicago Illinois, with which organization Colonel Robert Randolph was identified. The letter which was given to my wife at the time I was kidnapped was turned over by her to the Chief of the South Bend police, John Kuespert, and is (now) in his possession.

Perhaps Woolverton, exhausted as he must have been on the night of his release, wracked his brains for every scrap of evidence he could share, made clear that he would do everything in his power to bring these evil-doers to justice, recounted the kidnapping from start to finish before the gathered investigators and officials, and promised further documents to the Secret Six and other organizations as soon as they arrived.

None of that mattered, however. The people of the Kidnapping Crescent, and the great nation beyond, were told only that law enforcement could not act because Woolverton was incapable of assisting them, that the practitioners of the ancient art of kidnapping were now coming for upstanding men who, on being freed, were so terrified by their ordeals they knew nothing, remembered nothing, said nothing.

Two years later, in that statement to the feds, Howard Woolverton seemed to know a great deal more than any newspaper was able to uncover in the first few days after the kidnapping, or any law enforcement official was able to share publicly.

Because of his powerful state connections and his single-minded focus on shutting down any investigation, however, Woolverton's kidnapping stands out in the annals of American abductions for its ominous, terrifying silence.

So, in winter 1932, with the people up in arms over the terrible things that could happen for the crime of being successful, there was nothing to go on but rumors, nothing to read about but what the newspapers could allege or invent.

In the coming days and months, fear in South Bend would metastasize.

There would be breathless coverage of the criminals and their new, terrifying methods, a near-fatal shoot-out between police and private detectives, the deputization of armed citizens' patrols, and extraordinary efforts at keeping self and family safe. The Woolvertons would be victimized, over and over, by the kidnappers, forced by ongoing threats to make a painful decision about their daughter.

And none of it would ease anyone's fears—in South Bend or the rest of America—about a new storm brewing, an unprecedented cultural whirlwind that threatened, like none other in American history, to wrench the life out of those most quintessential elements of the American spirit: creativity, innovation, ambition, progress.

Hope.

However, faced with an invisible, noiseless enemy who proved with the Woolverton case that it could swoop in, threaten, take, and vanish—depositing its speechless, amnesiac victims on desolate curbs in distant cities—the people of the Kidnapping Crescent, and in the great nation beyond, did something else quintessentially American.

They fought back.

17

Tales of Terror and Torture

HOWARD WOOLVERTON WAS NOT a child, a gambler, a gangster, a celebrity, or a tycoon. He was a regular guy, doing well by playing it straight. He was what most people were—or hoped someday to be. In the third year of the Great Depression, many Americans were waiting for their ship to come in. The kidnapping of Howard Woolverton raised the question: Is this the price I'll pay when it arrives?

Compounding the fear, Woolverton succeeded in a singular way with strangling the investigation in its crib. His friendship with Indiana Secretary of State Frank Mayr Jr., his recruitment of bulldog attorney G. A. Farabaugh, and his general standing in South Bend and Indiana meant that when it came to that most important question of the crime—whodunit?—he could plead utter ignorance and demand a halt to the probe, and that's how it would be.

Perhaps Woolverton believed that satisfying the kidnappers' demands that he say nothing would make people forget and return to their regular lives.

Ironically, Woolverton's unique ability to sweep the abduction under the rug was one factor that gave the crime its singular power.

When people are deprived of information about something that frightens them, they typically make up things that are far worse than reality, and the media of Woolverton's day, with its habit of citing un-named sources and publishing wild speculation, led the charge. They had no choice, of course. Any newspaper that considered itself the eyes and ears of the people, the informational best friend of the citizenry, the beacon of truth that would warn its subscribers of danger and how to avoid it, had to cover the Woolverton kidnapping with all the facts they could dig up, make up, or get someone to allege.

The Woolverton kidnapping wasn't just another topic for the press's standard speculation machine, it must be noted. Several accidents of timing elevated the crime to its unique standing in the annals of abduc-tion history.

In mid-1931, half a year before Woolverton was taken, the Secret Six turned their investigative powers to the new kidnapping craze, and they eventually dug up a raft of alarming intelligence they considered worthy of sharing.

So, on Sunday evening, January 24, 1932—forty-eight hours before Howard Woolverton was kidnapped—the Secret Six announced their findings, in a story distributed widely by the Associated Press.

Under headlines like "'SECRET SIX' UNCOVERING HUGE KIDNAP-ING RING," the story ran in dozens of papers across the country over the next two days. The news of the Secret Six's work was published ex-tensively in the Midwest, of course, but also in papers as far away as California, New York, and Florida, often on the front page.

The content of the story varied from paper to paper, but many ver-sions mentioned the push for a federal law imposing the death penalty for kidnapping (supported by the Secret Six) and mentioned the use of torture among the kidnappers' repertoire.

The story, datelined Chicago, cited Alexander Jamie, chief investiga-tor for the Secret Six, who claimed to have "developed important evi-dence against the leaders of a huge kidnaping syndicate."

The version of the story published in the *Nebraska State Journal*, typi-cal of many such articles, continued, "Jamie declined to reveal specific kidnapings of which the syndicate is suspected. He said, however, there have been five kidnapings in the Chicago area within a year in which the victims were tortured or terrorized into paying a total of about $375,000 ransom (worth $6.6 million in 2020 dollars). The syndicate operates, Jamie said, like a well organized business concern. Certain members of the gang, he said, specialize in searching out wealthy persons as victims, others carry out the actual abduction, and a third group is assigned to collect ransom from relatives and friends."

Most of the papers went with the Associated Press version, but the *Times* of Streator, Illinois, seems to have had its own reporter taking notes on the Secret Six announcement, as its story included details about the investigation and its victims not part of the Associated Press copy. "Col. Randolph,"[1] the *Times* reported, quoting another Secret Six official, "said material was at hand which had been collected during eight months' undercover work. It concerns at least fifteen cases where women have been abducted, he said."

It was a compelling story, and its genesis in Chicago makes who didn't cover it strange: the *Chicago Tribune*.

Also ignoring the story: the United Press and all of its subscribing newspapers.

Perhaps the Secret Six chose to release their story only to the Associated Press, or perhaps the *Chicago Tribune* and the United Press were offered the announcement and took a pass. Either way, once the story of a major ring of torturing kidnappers went out through one channel, the decision-makers at competing channels seemed to have viewed the item with professional disdain, turning up their collective noses at the sordid claims of these Chicago amateurs.

"So what if the Secret Six has uncovered a huge gang of kidnappers?" the United Press might have sniffed. "We don't believe our subscribing newspapers, or their readers, will care that a corporate-level and growing band of toughs is taking respectable people en masse, torturing them, threatening them with death, and generating revenues in the six figures."

It's all about saving face, of course, then as now. When one publication or wire service gets a scoop, the competing outlets are confronted with that eternal journalist's dilemma: repeat the story, admitting that it came from a hated rival, or ignore it and pretend it just wasn't that important anyway.

The United Press chose the latter course.

And that might have been it. The Americans who read the papers that subscribed to the Associated Press received a tale of growing terror. The other Americans, who read only United Press newspapers, received no such story and never would.

And then, Howard Woolverton got himself kidnapped.

Woolverton's abduction gave the United Press and its member papers the chance for a do-over, the opportunity to tell their readers that same compelling story of a vast syndicate of kidnapping and torture, but to tell it better than the Associated Press, more urgently, and with a fresh victim to hitch it to.

All they needed was a little help from the Secret Six.

And the Secret Six was, apparently, glad to oblige.

We might imagine that the United Press reporter, tasked with presenting Woolverton's case within the larger context, asked their Secret Six source for something new, something that hadn't already been run in the Associated Press story two days before. Name some of the other victims, they might have pleaded to the vigilantes. Give us some new dirt.

And perhaps it was Alexander Jamie himself who obliged, who agreed to share the organization's less official findings as long as neither he nor the Secret Six were specifically identified.

And so arrived that United Press story, mentioned earlier, which was distributed while Woolverton was still missing and which attributed the crime to a "band of seven super-criminals."

Dozens of United Press papers that ignored the first kidnapping story ran this new article, among them the *South Bend News-Times*, along with papers in the Midwest and the East, and as far away as California and Oregon.

Many papers edited the story to fit, added details, and wrote their own terrifying headlines.

The *South Bend News-Times* went with two headlines: "South Bend Man Believed Held by Huge Abduction Band" and beneath it, "Operations of Kidnap Gang Have Cost Victims $600,000 in This Area, Survey Shows."

The *Indianapolis News* headline summed things up with fewer but more terrifying words: "South Bend Kidnapping Linked With Noted Gang of Torturers."

The content of the stories varied from paper to paper, but the version published in the *South Bend News-Times* described Woolverton's kidnappers as a "band of hardened criminals in the prime of life, each with a long and notorious individual record in crime, operating in vicious boldness as a result of a year of kidnapings throughout the Middle West which have netted them more than $600,000."

Some newspapers, including the *Indianapolis News*, included this passage: "The Woolverton abduction was described as a typical 'seven' crime. Its finesse illustrated the degree of perfection in the crime specialty of the close-knit organization."

The article as published in many papers claimed that the gang had conducted similar kidnappings in Michigan, Missouri, Wisconsin, Iowa, Indiana, and Illinois.

Reported the *South Bend News-Times*, "Only once during the two years of terrorism by the 'seven gang' has it failed to extort money from bankers, business men, gamblers and their wives. Fear forced them to kill Mrs. Clyde Garrison in Peoria, Ill., after she and her husband almost escaped in October, 1931."

The version of the wire story published in the *Indianapolis News* put the ages of the seven at "over 35 and under 40" and claimed that each member "made a name for himself in the underworld as a bank robber or a holdup killer. Two years ago they decided they could make more collecting ransom money than robbing banks. They pulled a kidnaping. It was crude compared to the way they work now, but it worked."

The gang members are doing well, the article claimed. They "live in the best hotels, dress like millionaires and have expensive luggage and costly jewelry."

Once they decide to conduct another kidnapping, the article alleged, they "send one of their number into a city to look around for a prospect. Before anyone gets suspicious, the advance agent is called in and another takes his place."

And then, when the preliminary work is done, the terror for the victim begins in earnest, as detailed by the *South Bend News-Times*:

> the gang swoops down upon the victim. They work fast, but with care. They are too wise to wear masks, but the man who approaches the victim holds his hands over his face. All the victim sees is a pair of eyes under a hat brim. A sedan door is opened. The victim is thrown inside. Arms seize him and clap a pad made of billiard cloth and fitted with adhesive tape over his eyes. The prisoner is taken to a hideaway, bound hand and foot and tortured, particularly if any publicity is given the case. He is transferred to perhaps half a dozen places and all the time he is told that he will be burned alive or his wife and children killed. In most cases the money they demand is delivered at the spot they specify.

As the story of the seven super-criminals made the rounds, it picked up steam. The *Ames Daily Tribune* (Ames, Iowa), in its version of the story on February 1, 1932, reported additional, more horrifying details. Along with being threatened with getting burned alive, "The captive then is told he will be . . . cut to pieces, or his wife and children tortured unless the amount demanded is forthcoming."

Given that the Woolverton kidnapping happened in its state, the *Indianapolis News* included passages other papers left out:

> In most cases, the money is delivered at the spot the extortionists specify. They always get it in $5, $10 and $20 bills. They are easy to spend and hard to trace.
>
> Usually the "seven" pass as traveling salesmen. In their large brief cases they carry machine guns. In smaller brief cases are pistols. These cases are known to the gang members as "violin cases." "Bring your violin case," means there is likely to be a need for a machine gun.

The United Press story never hinted at the identities of any of the seven super-criminals, odd in a day when suspected perpetrators were routinely named in the papers before arrests and before any charges had been filed. Perhaps the Secret Six was trying to avoid another lawsuit from someone who could prove their innocence?

Right, wrong, or indifferent, the wire stories, the latter inspired by Woolverton's kidnapping, represented an early attempt to take the full measure of the nation's new kidnapping menace, and the Secret Six was the most prominent but not the only source of such data. As noted earlier in this book, the findings of a 1931 kidnapping survey sent to police departments nationwide by St. Louis Chief of Police Joseph Gerk also received prominent play, often running as a sidebar to the main story of Woolverton's abduction.

In the weeks to follow, more stories would be written, building on each other, adding to the terror, all owing their inspiration, it seems, to Howard Woolverton.

Like the stories to come, the United Press story offered what became a national consensus about how the American kidnapping industry had gotten cranked up—kidnappers started out by preying on wealthy criminals and other men living on the edges of legitimacy, but they were running out of such victims, forcing them to pursue respectable people like Howard Woolverton. The story as published in many papers, including the *Indianapolis News*, also provided details on ransom revenue and expenses:

> Dozens of gamblers, race bookmakers and other nightlife figures paid from $7,500 to $200,000 each. The minimum demand was $7,500. In one

case, the same man was kidnapped twice. The first time he paid $7,500. The second time the cost of freedom was $50,000.

Despite the enormous sums they have extorted, the "seven" are now low in funds. Since turning to bankers and business men after reaping the cream of the gambler ransoms, their "jobs" have been less frequent. Besides, they have spent money like water. Parties costing $1,000 to $2,000 for two nights are a regular occurrence.

Like Howard Woolverton, the article continued, "Most of those who paid ransom for their release, however, kept silent through fear."

The difference with Woolverton, of course, is that his abduction was front-page news, while many victims were taken discreetly: "Police constantly are getting unofficial reports of men who were kidnaped months ago, who paid, and who are afraid even to admit to their friends the reason for unexplained absences."

The United Press story, a gripping read with the strong local tie-in of Howard Woolverton, ran in only one South Bend paper, the *South Bend News-Times*. Because it was not a United Press subscriber, the *South Bend Tribune* got shut out of that story. And it was a good one. But the editors of the *Tribune* had Everett Holles, and Mr. Holles had ambition, so he wasn't about to let his city's junior paper beat him at the Woolverton kidnapping story.

In the last days of January 1932, Everett Holles, intrepid reporter for the *South Bend Tribune*, headed to Chicago to meet with the Secret Six and write the last word on kidnapping, Woolverton or otherwise.

He had already worked with the Secret Six to break one dubious story, published on January 29, 1932, about the work the group claims it did to negotiate, collect, and pay the ransom that got Howard Woolverton freed. Now Holles needed another story, this time not just about Woolverton's kidnapping but also about the big picture, the trends and practices of abduction, and who was behind this new threat to the American way of life. Perhaps Holles was told not to come back to South Bend without something that would keep his readers up at night.

The Secret Six, it turns out, must have liked his January 29 story, because it was glad to cooperate again.

And here we have another accident of timing.

Why were the Secret Six, whose name implied discretion, anonymity, and a preference for working in the shadows, suddenly so eager to go public?

As discussed earlier, because they knew they were dying.

Yes, in early 1932, the Secret Six were still riding high, getting called into big cases, testifying before Congress on occasion, making pronouncements the press picked up eagerly. But they were also getting sued at that time for what was surely the worst thing they could be accused of: shoddy detective work. Almost as bad, they were being rendered irrelevant by legitimate law enforcement. Although they had spent most of 1931 investigating a huge midwestern kidnapping ring, it was Patrick Roche of the Illinois state attorney's office who rounded up a gang of torturing abduction specialists in early January 1932, filing charges against a half dozen of them. Nothing in the published reports of the time indicated Roche received any help from the publicity-starved Secret Six.

Facing obsolescence and an embarrassing hit to their professionalism, the Secret Six weren't going down without a fight. Indeed, at the dawn of 1932, the Chicago group seemed ready to franchise their crime-fighting model nationwide.

Secret Six leader Colonel Robert Isham Randolph, in a February 2, 1932, address before the Pittsburgh, Pennsylvania, Chamber of Commerce, insisted that "organization of a 'Secret Six' in Pittsburgh or any other large metropolis where crime is a major problem would sound the death knell of the gangster."

Randolph, as quoted in that day's *Pittsburgh Press*, declared with admirable boldness that "virtually all large cities face the same problem we are solving in Chicago."

The ideal solution, in Pittsburgh or elsewhere, according to Randolph, was not better law enforcement but "a secret committee of businessmen."

Woolverton's kidnapping, then, couldn't have come at a better time for the vigilantes. Before he was taken, most kidnapping coverage focused on the individual crime, story after story proceeding formulaically: who was taken, when, where and how, when were they freed (or found, lifeless), what ransom was demanded, what was paid, who did it or was suspected.

Beginning at the time of Woolverton's abduction, and for several critical months afterward, the approach to kidnapping stories shifted significantly, from the simple who-what-where of the single crime to the bigger picture, to an attempt to capture the broad scope, the complete range of nefarious methods, and the terrifying and growing reach of America's new kidnapping industry.

While the press was compelled by the Woolverton kidnapping to take the full measure of this new threat, the Secret Six, with the freshest and the best (or at least the most frightening) information on hand, were glad for their own reasons to toss secrecy out the window and become the official dispensary of kidnapping knowledge.

So, when Everett Holles showed up in Chicago, seeking something darker and more compelling than the sordid United Press details the *South Bend News-Times* had just published, the Secret Six were glad to oblige.

Holles thought perhaps he was being done a favor. Most likely, the benefits were mutual.

On February 1, 1932, the partnership bore fruit.

In that day's *South Bend Tribune*, Holles declared, "It was nearly two years ago that a group of fearless gangsters—killers when necessary—began spreading the terror of kidnaping for ransom on a syndicated basis and during those two brief years their operations have netted nearly $1,000,000."

Holles had spent two days in Chicago with the Secret Six, as well as with Patrick Roche, he reported, to compile "an amazing picture of the operations of this syndicate."

The kidnappers, Holles said he was told, believe "they have the safest racket of all in these crime-ridden times because the intimidation methods which form the basis of every job rarely fail to freeze the victim with fear. The victim's safe return to his home and family and his escape from death or hideous torture are, of course, more important to him than tracking down his abductors."

According to Holles, Roche told him that kidnapping is "the boldest, most vicious form of crime we have to-day." Continued Holles, "The six men and one woman Roche arrested in early January form a branch of the big syndicate, it is believed, and worked a 'territory' assigned them by the leaders."

Holles wrote of three "common kidnaping methods" used by the syndicate. In the first, the victim is treated well and released when the money is paid. The second method is held at the ready, however: "When the ransom demand is unproductive immediately the victim may be forced to suffer while burning brands are touched to his bare feet, water may be dripped for several hours on his head until it seems that he will go mad, or he may be horse-whipped. When the victim is about to collapse a pencil and paper is thrust before him and he is ordered to write a note to his family pleading with them to submit to the kidnapers' demands immediately."

The third method, the rarest according to the article, was used with Woolverton: the victim is allowed to go free on the promise of payment. This method is used, Holles wrote, "only when the kidnapers are certain that they have so thoroughly intimidated him that he dares not go back on his promise to pay for fear of his life."

There is a contradiction here, of course. In Holles's January 29 story, mentioned a few chapters back, the Secret Six took credit for paying Woolverton's ransom before he was released. Three days later, the group seems to have abandoned that claim, acknowledging that Woolverton fit into the category of those who promise to pay after they're let go. Perhaps the Woolvertons or Farabaugh had privately corrected the record on that point. A more public correction, of course, would arrive with that exclusive published by the *South Bend News-Times* on February 5.

Holles's February 1 article implied that Woolverton would be too fearful not to pay his ransom, but it went on to counter the image of Woolverton as a quivering lump of upper-middle-class jelly. No less than Alexander Jamie himself, chief investigator for the Secret Six, weighed in on Woolverton's courage in Holles's *South Bend Tribune* story: "Mr. Jamie described Mr. Woolverton as having 'plenty of nerve' in dealing with the kidnapers."

Holles wasn't the only journalist thinking about kidnapping trends in the context of the Woolverton abduction. On the same date Holles's article was published, the *Ithaca (New York) Journal* presented a concise summary of the new narrative: Howard Woolverton's abduction confirmed that kidnappers are now going after upstanding folk, the enterprise was growing, people were getting tortured, and the crimes couldn't be investigated because no one was talking.

"Kidnaping, as the newest and most readily lucrative form of criminal activity," wrote the author, Owen L. Scott, in a story datelined Chicago, "has gained further impetus after the successful abduction, presumed ransom and release of Howard A. Woolverton, wealthy South Bend, Ind., business man and civic leader."

The article noted that Woolverton "said that he could not recognize his kidnapers and did not know where he had been held prisoner while negotiations were going on. This left little for detectives to work on."

The article made the obligatory reference to "fiendish torture for the victims" and noted that although "much of the activity has centered in Illinois, Missouri, around St. Louis, and in Michigan," kidnapping more recently "has spread to other districts as far West as Denver."

Anyone who had succeeded was at risk, the article implied. "The kidnap gangs now are bolder and are prepared to direct their activities against wealthy and prominent members of communities."

A month after Holles's and Scott's stories, two major new kidnapping compendia would be birthed, one by the *Daily News* of New York City, the other by the Newspaper Enterprise Association, a service with subscribers around North America. Both efforts—arguably prompted by the Woolverton case—would be published widely, thanks to another accident of timing: the stealing of Charles Augustus Lindbergh Jr. from his crib, a kidnapping that took place five weeks after Woolverton's and is still considered one of the defining crimes of the twentieth century. (The importance of the Woolverton case to the Lindbergh abduction— and vice versa—will be explored a little later in this book.)

The *Daily News* of New York City published a veritable book of kidnapping trends, statistics, and terrifying anecdotes. The series of sixteen "chapters," published between March 3 (two days after Lindbergh was snatched) and March 19 and authored by Fred Pasley, presented individual kidnapping stories interspersed with data, trends, and expert opinion.

But the primary takeaway for the average reader was a stark warning, summed up in the headline on the first day's article: "No one is safe."

The point was driven home throughout the series: "You may be next," Pasley wrote on March 4. "No man, woman or child . . . is safe from the kidnaping racket."

Pasley wrote that kidnapping had

in the last five years . . . preyed almost entirely upon legitimate society, hand-picking its victims for their wealth, prominence and high standing.

I shall show [Pasley promised] how kidnaping as directed against organized society has assumed its present national proportions in the gradual breakdown of law and order in the past decade through out the length and breadth of the United States.

While the crime threatened the nation at large, Pasley noted that much of it was focused in the Midwest:

> I stood in the office of Walter B. Weisenberger, president of the St. Louis Chamber of Commerce looking at a map chart of the United States. It was dotted with circles, representing the number of kidnappings of record. The St. Louis Police Department sent questionnaires to 548 cities, asking for reports over a three-year period. To date, 502 replies have been received.
>
> Boston had seventeen cases and New York but ten. It is in the Middle West that the racket thrives. The chart shows forty-nine for Illinois, thirty-four for Ohio, twenty-six for Michigan, twenty for Indiana, and eleven for Missouri.

The article, which estimated that there had been four thousand kidnappings nationwide in the previous ten years and two thousand in the last two traced the roots of the problem to Prohibition and the Volstead Act, the 1919 law that forbade alcohol consumption. Americans, being American, still wanted to drink, so for the next decade, criminals filled the void, growing rich off a cash cow so lucrative they would fight to the death to control their turf.

One method for the elimination of enemies gave rise to the next phase in kidnapping's development. Pasley wrote:

> Earl (Hymie) Weiss, deadliest of the prohibition Big Shots, found that the best way to evade an annoying inquest in eliminating a rival was to put him in a car, shoot him, then dump the body outside the city limits. It was remarked that the victims generally became abject with terror when informed of the purpose of the ride. A member of Dion O'Bannon's crew spoke up one night after a foe had been left in a ditch northwest of the city:
>
> "That punk said he'd kick in with a hundred grand if we'd let him loose."
>
> "That's an idea," Dion had said.
>
> The idea was soon thereafter put into execution when the gang's funds got low. Gamblers, speakeasy proprietors and enemy gangsters had at first been the victims. Then the gang had widened the scope of its activities to shady stock brokers. These always kicked in, and never reported to the police. Kidnaping them developed into almost an everyday business both in Chicago and New York.
>
> The transition was perhaps logical from the brokers to other business and professional banking men. Anyway, it occurred, and now the kidnaping industry is on a sound footing as the greatest easy money phase of organized crime.

The series presented details of more than a dozen kidnappings, many of them tragic, horrifying, or salacious. Abducted children sometimes came home and sometimes didn't. The lifeless body of fourteen-month-old Lloyd Keet, snatched from his Springfield, Missouri, crib in 1917, was found in a well. A Chicago gambler named John "Jack" Lynch had his ribs broken. Chicago insurance broker Theodore Kopelman, Pasley wrote in that *Daily News* series, paid up after being "threatened with blinding by hot poker." Chicago doctor Max Gecht and his wife, Georgia, who was described as young, blonde, and attractive in stories of the day, were kidnapped in December 1931 and chained to beds in two separate rooms at a home in South Chicago. The kidnappers freed Dr. Gecht to round up the $2,000 ransom, leaving Mrs. Gecht with her abductors for another two days. The clever woman got close enough to one of the kidnappers to make a date with him after she was freed.

She didn't show up for the dinner, but the cops did. (It was a lucky break. The man they arrested led them to that gang of torturing kidnappers Patrick Roche rounded up in early January 1932.)

"In thirteen incidents," Pasley noted, "the kidnapers made good their threat to murder their victims."

Murder, torture, tragedy. Pasley's series offered it all. But even for him, the abduction of Howard Woolverton, five weeks before the first article of his series was published, seemed to stand out and very well might have been his project's impetus.

"An amazed world read in January, of this year," Pasley wrote in chapter 11 of the *Daily News* series, on March 14, 1932, "of the spectacular kidnaping in South Bend, Ind. of Mr. and Mrs. A. Woolverton, and the holding of him for $50,000 ransom."

The Woolverton case represented to Pasley something new from the kidnapping industry. A turning point, perhaps. A culmination.

"Indiana was stunned by the Woolverton kidnapping, which for brazen audacity has no parallel," Pasley wrote. "It climaxed a series of such crimes in the Middle West, the victims of which were wealthy business men."

As with other observers of the day, Pasley found a deeper meaning in the Woolverton abduction. It wasn't just another assault on one man, one household, one wealthy citizen in one Midwestern city. Kidnappings of people like Howard Woolverton, he wrote, "represent a challenge to organized society."

Organized society. Civilization. The American Way. In 1776, the Declaration of Independence declared the pursuit of happiness to be an inalienable right, an essential principle, indeed a foundational premise for the most important experiment in self-governance the world had yet seen.

The Prohibition Era–kidnapping of the upper-middle class, like perhaps no other factor in the nation's great history, put the lie to that promise of a century and a half before.

Yes, go ahead and pursue happiness. Reach for it. Grasp. Hold. But once it is yours, always look behind you, because they are coming. They'll take you, your child, your wife. They'll torture, maim, and kill. If they want to, they'll take you twice. They are legion, organized, and growing rich. And the oath of silence you will swear when they're done with you ensures they will never be pursued, caught, or convicted.

And yes, they are concentrated in the Midwest now, but as long as there are cars, an expanding network of good highways, and growing profits, they will radiate like a disease, franchising outward, perfecting their methods as they swallow new territories until all of America and all of the people in it who have accomplished something are theirs, waiting to be harvested.

If the American media were asked, in winter 1932, to select a poster child for this terrifying new assault on America's most treasured values, Howard Woolverton would very likely have been chosen.

"Woolverton is one of the most prominent of the recent kidnaping victims in the mid-West," insisted the *Indianapolis Star* the day after Woolverton arrived home.

Why, then, has the once-famous man from South Bend been forgotten?

Because of the very silence that made the case so important in its time.

The lack of information may give a particular crime an immediate, terrifying boost, and that's what happened with Woolverton. Imagine if Lee Harvey Oswald, the alleged killer of President John F. Kennedy, was never found or if the perpetrators of the attacks of September 11, 2001, remained anonymous, officials declaring that, since no witnesses to the crime would say what they knew, the investigation was over.

Terrifying as they were, the facts of the Howard Woolverton kidnapping were also sketchy, and history requires fact, not emotion.

As Pasley noted, Woolverton "returned to his home and declined to give the police any aid or say whether he had paid the ransom. It is believed he did."

Even for Pasley, writing about a case a little over a month old, the truth of the Woolverton kidnapping was already becoming elusive, malleable, and error-ridden.

Several mistakes made their way into his account of the South Bend incident. For example, he repeated that widely circulated non sequitur about the goggles, claiming they were put on as soon as the kidnapper entered the car, Woolverton driving blind through South Bend and into the hinterlands west of town. Pasley wrote of three men, while Mr. and Mrs. Woolverton's published and private accounts and most other reports mentioned only two. And he wrote that Woolverton was held for three days, clearly wrong.

The Associated Press condensed the first story of Pasley's series and distributed it nationwide, where it was picked up by newspapers in at least two dozen states.

"2,000 in U.S. Abducted for Ransom in 2 Years," shouted the headline in the March 3, 1932, *Fort Worth Star-Telegram*.

The *Los Angeles Times* put the story on page three and gave it several urgent headlines. "Gigantic Scale of Growing Racket Disclosed," said one, followed by "Millions Paid by Victims of Kidnaping Gangs."

And Pasley wasn't the only one working on a kidnapping series in the weeks after Woolverton got kidnapped.

Also winning broad distribution, including in a two-page spread in the *Vancouver Sun* of Vancouver, Canada, on March 26, 1932, was a three-article project by the Newspaper Enterprise Association.

The series, by Bruce Catton, started making the rounds in early March and ended up in dozens of papers in the United States before it reached the neighbor to the north.

Like the series by Pasley, it covered the standard list of abductions, and it gave Howard Woolverton special attention. But the picture of American kidnapping was evolving quickly at that time (thanks, arguably, in large part to Woolverton), and Catton presented some unique intelligence and, of course, some new tortures.

"In one city after another, little groups of half a dozen or more took to preying on the shadowy and wealthy big shots of gangland," Catton wrote. "From city to city the racket spread."

Catton, like Pasley, made clear that kidnapping was becoming a threat to everyone, particularly those who had done best: "Then began the development which ought to relieve the ordinary citizen forever of his comfortable belief that gang wars don't really matter because the gangsters only shoot each other. Emboldened by their success, the kidnapping rings started to reach out for law-abiding citizens—men of money and position and absolute integrity."

Catton pointed out the distinct significance of the Woolverton abduction in a section of the story that featured pictures of Mr. and Mrs. Woolverton. "The amazing way in which kidnapping has become a major underworld industry is nowhere better shown than in the events of the past few months in the middle-west," Catton wrote, adding a quote from Alexander Jamie of the Secret Six: "Gambler after gambler in Chicago and downstate has been victimized. Now, however, it seems that the ring has taken about every possible victim from the rackets and is branching out to seize reputable citizens. The seizure of Woolverton, the banker, is evidence of this."

Along with ignoring Woolverton's primary job in manufacturing (he did do some work for his father's bank, though), the article perhaps goes a little too far in letting the Secret Six self-aggrandize, permitting them to make the dubious—and immediately self-contradicted—claim that they had single-handedly discovered an organization running virtually all kidnappings in the Midwest.

"Existence of the kidnapping ring has been discovered by operatives working for Colonel Robert Isham Randolph, founder and head of the Chicago Association of Commerce's 'Secret Six,'" the article stated, adding that "kidnapping . . . has ceased to be the work of isolated criminals working on their own and has become the job of a highly organized syndicate of desperadoes with headquarters in Chicago, Detroit and St. Louis."

The statement of course raises the question: What "highly organized" business enterprise has three headquarters?

But that was a minor detail for the Secret Six, who even conjured up someone directing the whole operation, a supreme captain of kidnapping, if you will, a veritable snatch-racket CEO: "The man at the head of it," said Jamie in the article, "whose identity we haven't yet discovered, is evidently a highly capable business executive."

The article, true or not, was at least as terrifying as all the rest.

The kidnapping corporation even maintained its own prison system, Catton wrote, "for keeping its victims while the ransom money was being collected. One house they owned, for instance, contained an attic room especially fitted for the prisoners; in another house, a special cell was built in the basement."

An essential element to all such stories was some previously unmentioned torture.

Catton's article offered two.

When a Detroit gambler refused to pay, "they tied him up in a barn and fired a few rounds of machine-gun bullets at a spot a foot from his head."

For the price of a handful of machine gun shells, the kidnappers earned $20,000.

And then there was Freddie Strauss, who "made a fortune by speculation in Oklahoma oil lands. He was seized as he walked down a Kansas City street and taken to a house on the edge of town where the gangsters tortured him by tearing off bits of his flesh with pliers. When he was unable to stand this any longer, he consented to telephone and arrange for the payment of $50,000."

A few days after Pasley's and Catton's articles, on March 6, 1932, the *New York Times* published its own shocking compendium of kidnapping trends—another story that Woolverton's abduction may have triggered, directly or indirectly. But that paper avoided the pitfalls of the uncertain Woolverton case by ignoring Woolverton altogether.

The *New York Times* described kidnapping as "a species of felony that is centuries old, yet which has recently showed signs of being organized on an unprecedented scale and with unheard-of extremes of cruelty and audacity."

The article quoted Colonel Randolph of the Secret Six, who no doubt remembered sitting in the home of Howard Woolverton six weeks before, when he said, "Rings of kidnappers in Detroit, Chicago, St. Louis and probably other cities have turned their attention more and more from underworld characters to respectable business men and even women."

The *New York Times* article paid particularly stark homage to torture. Under the bolded subheadline "Some Victims Tortured," the article announced that "A Chicago 'torture chamber' used by one gang hinted at almost unbelievable horrors. There were indications, detectives said, that this chamber had been used frequently."

The article offered a fleeting assurance that "probably most of the victims [of the torture chamber] were underworld characters." The next passage took such reassurances away, however. Citing the knowledge of the Secret Six and other authorities, the article warned that "with the present evolution of kidnapping no one is safe."

You will not just be taken temporarily out of your comfortable life, the article implied in its own contribution to the growing chorus. You will not just be forced to endure a few days of fear and privation before you part with a fortune. If you succeed, if you arrive at the place that defines your American Dream, there will be waiting for you or your loved ones a room specifically built and equipped to cause you "fiendish" torment, to render irrelevant the creature comforts of a nice home, fine clothing, good food.

Thanks, at least in part, to the forgotten kidnapping of Howard Woolverton, this was the terror Americans took to bed with them at night in the winter and spring of 1932.

Woolverton's abduction might have been climactic, spectacular, and unparalleled for its "brazen audacity," as Pasley put it, and the Lindbergh kidnapping accident of timing meant that Woolverton's abduction seems to have served as the catalyst for a new wave of both comprehensive and highly personalized kidnapping stories (kidnapping is everywhere; it brings torture and death, and you might be next). But Woolverton's silence and his ability to quash the investigation meant a frustratingly incomplete account, an uncertain story, a tale lacking the clarity of many other kidnappings. Anyone summing up the nation's epidemic of kidnappings during the Prohibition Era would have plenty of less ambiguous cases to choose from.

In fact, there was no reference to Howard Woolverton on Wikipedia as of summer 2020, and he was ignored in David Stout's *The Kidnap Years: The Astonishing True History of the Forgotten Kidnapping Epidemic That Shook Depression-Era America*, released in April 2020.[2]

Howard Woolverton was a forgotten victim of a forgotten crime wave. He wasn't even a footnote.

Neither the man nor the crime wave that swept him up deserve a place in history's dustbin. Both played essential parts in making America what it is today.

But even at the time when kidnapping reigned, it didn't always receive the attention it deserved. As Pasley noted in his *Daily News* series, kidnapping got no mentions in the vast 1931–1932 Wickersham Commission reports, America's first comprehensive study of crime and law enforcement.

"Kidnaping is a feature crime today," Pasley stated, arguing that the nation should be paying closer attention. "Big business in the underworld has turned from bank robbery, train robbery, hijacking and the spectacular crimes of the past to specialize in it almost exclusively."

Within six weeks of Howard Woolverton's abduction, helped along by a perfect storm of terror and timing, kidnapping was considered important enough to have earned notice from papers outside the United States, as well as in the halls of Congress. Different as these two venues were, the focus was the same in both cases: an existential threat to the American soul, delivered by people who knew how to torment, terrify, and torture.

From the pages of newspapers in Canada to the halls of power in Washington, DC, the stories continued.

"TALES OF TORTURE TOLD HOUSE GROUP," announced an all-cap headline in the *Evening Sun* of Baltimore, Maryland, on February 25, 1932.

The US House of Representatives Post Office Committee, the paper reported, which was considering a law that banned the use of the US mail to send extortion notes, had invited speakers to testify in support of the law.

The Secret Six sent several witnesses to the February 24 hearings, including two men who, four weeks earlier, had been at the Woolverton home to discuss his kidnapping.

The *Evening Sun* related:

> Robert Isham Randolph of Chicago, executive secretary of the well-known "Secret Six" which is fighting master minds of the criminal world in that city, characterized blackmail as "the most profitable racket in the world."
>
> "Murder isn't to be compared with kidnapping, it is merciful by comparison," he declared, exhibiting to the committee a piece of rope, which he said had been sent in a large envelope to one woman with the warning that unless she came through her little daughter would be strangled.
>
> Lieut. Roy Steffins of the Chicago detective force, told of one victim submerged in a quarry filled with water sixty feet deep. The man was placed in a diving suit and tortured until he signed notes involving large sums of money, Steffins said.

Thanks, it may be argued, in large part to Howard Woolverton, the newspaper readers of America got their kidnapping terror delivered with both barrels—the Associated Press, then the United Press. Other outlets followed, doing their part, many of them armed with new data from the struggling, no-longer-so-secret Secret Six, all competing to see who could scare people the most.

The importance of this new trend in kidnapping journalism, from individual cases to big-picture presentations of national statistics and methods, might best be understood from the individual reader's perspective: these were no longer stories about what happened to other people; now, they're about what could happen to *me*.

There needed to be arrests, charges, trials, and long sentences, the average reader must have concluded. But how can that happen when victims won't talk, when the new class of abductees are so respectable that they can not only refuse to talk but also demand a halt to official probes as well?

Who are these kidnappers? readers must have wondered. Who kidnapped Howard Woolverton? Will we ever know? Is there any chance we'll ever identify and arrest them, or are all of us who achieve and succeed condemned to merely waiting until our turn comes to be snatched, blindfolded, threatened, tortured, made poor?

Despite its obscurity now, the Howard Woolverton kidnapping provoked the full range of responses, from those breathless press reports to a generalized terror to calls for public action.

Six months after his kidnapping, Woolverton's name was still coming up as far away as New York City. According to a United Press story published, among other places, in the *Logansport (Indiana) Pharos-Tribune* on July 21, 1932, Richard Mueller, who'd escaped from prison in Indiana in 1929, was tracked down to a New York hotel room.

"Mueller's capture was effected by detectives Wallace and McHale, who entered the fugitive's room with drawn guns," read the article. "Mueller was in bed. He reached for the revolver on the table but Wallace leaped forward, getting it first."

Mueller, who also went by the name Sam Reibman and gave his age as twenty-five, had been convicted of robbing and kidnapping Dick Johnson, a South Bend bank president, of some $13,000 in May of 1929. Johnson, performing his official duties apparently, had climbed into a taxi with the cash, worth about a quarter million in 2020 dollars. In a crime with strong similarities to the Woolverton case, Johnson's cab driver, Curtis Pruett, was forced to the curb by the robbers' car, according to the May 30, 1929, *Indianapolis Star*. Two gunmen leaped from their car and got into the cab, and Pruett was forced to drive to a vacant cottage outside South Bend, where both men were tied up. The men freed themselves within half an hour, but by then, the crooks and the cash were gone.

Mueller, aka Reibman, and the rest of the gang were captured soon thereafter and sentenced to long terms, but they escaped in September 1929. Mueller, the last to be recaptured, was on the loose at the time of Woolverton's kidnapping, and the New York detectives who collared him were apparently well enough versed in the details of the South Bend case to ask about it.

Back in custody, Mueller seemed proud of his exploits, according to the article.

> He boasted that he was a "big shot" and told detectives that he had escaped from the St. Joseph's [Indiana] county jail. Awaiting removal to west side court for arraignment, Mueller leaned back in a chair, put his feet on a desk and chatted amiably with detectives. When one of the officers suggested that he was bragging and did not really kidnap Johnson, he seemed offended.
>
> "I'll swear to God I did," detective Wallace said he said.
>
> "Do you know anyone by the name of Woolverton?" another detective asked him.
>
> "Never heard of him," he replied.

Who kidnapped Howard Woolverton? History has settled on three names, none of them Mueller, aka Reibman. But two new names have now emerged from the fog, courtesy of Woolverton's forgotten statement.

Before we get to that, however, we must reckon with the immediate and longer-term aftermath of the kidnapping, in South Bend and beyond. Forgotten today, the kidnapping produced waves of fear, outrage, and suspicion, provoked a near-fatal shoot-out in a quiet South Bend neighborhood, and changed the course of history.

"*Now you resine and dam quick or the way you go for a ride and a good one. . . . If you dont know call that gui in South Bend he will till you. I mean Woolferton.*"

—Anonymous, as quoted by the *South Bend Tribune*, February 16, 1932

PART III

The Unique Significance of the Woolverton Case

18

Fear and Loathing in South Bend

ON THURSDAY, DECEMBER 15, 1927, a man showed up at Mount Vernon Junior High School in Los Angeles with grim news: Perry Parker, a wealthy banker, had been hurt in an accident, and his twelve-year-old daughter Marion was needed at home. Marion's twin sister, Marjorie, was also a student at the school, but the man didn't ask that she be excused. Only Marion was sent off with the man.

It was all a lie. There had been no accident, and distress turned to panic for Marion's parents when she didn't come home that night.

They heard from the kidnapper the next day, and by 7:30 p.m. Saturday, the terms by which the Parkers could get their daughter back had been worked out: $1,500 in $20 gold certificates, to be delivered at a street corner in northwest Los Angeles.

The *South Bend Tribune*, like papers throughout the country, published the horrifying details of what happened next, drawing from an Associated Press story on December 18, 1927: As Mr. Parker waited to recover his daughter, a small roadster pulled up to the intersection. Parker could see Marion in the passenger seat of the car, but he was told she was asleep. He handed over the money, and then, "according to the agreement, the man after taking the money drove ahead of the father a little

207

way and, climbing out of the car, laid the body of the girl on the grass . . . Parker ran frantically to his daughter's side, clasped her in his arms and found she was dead."

She had been strangled and mutilated, her arms and legs cut off, her torso stuffed with rags.

A nineteen-year-old drifter named William Edward Hickman was quickly caught, convicted, sentenced to death, and hanged the next October. In the meantime, the *South Bend Tribune* covered the crime and its aftermath extensively, including the horrifying fact, published on December 31, 1927, that Hickman was "reported to have said in his confession that life was not completely extinct when he began dismembering her body."

A little over four years after the details of twelve-year-old Marion Parker's abduction and murder were seared into the brains of parents around the nation, Howard Woolverton was kidnapped and released after promising to pay $8,000.

Woolverton attempted to pay, but something went wrong, and when the money didn't turn up, the kidnappers began sending letters and making phone calls, threatening the family and the Woolvertons' own twelve-year-old daughter, Betty.

Any accounting of the impact of Howard Woolverton's kidnapping—citywide, statewide, nationwide—must first report what it did to the Woolverton family itself.

Woolverton's abduction, and the subsequent threats to himself, his wife, and their daughter, were sandwiched between two terrifying child abductions, the Parker and Lindbergh cases.

The Woolvertons, avid newspaper subscribers raising a girl at the height of America's kidnapping era, were surely well aware of both cases, and the painful decision they soon would make about Betty's schooling was probably informed as much by those crimes as by the kidnapping of the father.

In fact, on at least one occasion, the Woolverton and Lindbergh stories appeared literally side by side in a paper the Woolvertons likely read. On page nine of the *Indianapolis News* of March 3, 1932, a story about threats being made against the Woolvertons and their daughter appeared next to a picture of the missing baby Lindbergh, sitting in a chair and kicking a ball.

For the Woolverton family, the first order of business was securing the home.

According to David Hendry Jr., who played in the home as a child and visited the current owners there in 2019, the modifications to the area of the house that held Betty's second-floor bedroom are still visible.

"You come up around the stairs and that was where you'd want to block anyone from gaining access to the nanny and my mother," Hendry said in a 2019 telephone interview. Security there was added with a sliding pocket door. "It's heavy hardwood," he said. "It's got to be 3 inches thick, probably twice as thick as a typical pocket door."

The bolt to lock the door, he added, was "super heavy-duty. If you didn't know what was going on, you'd say wow this is really overkill."

The Woolvertons used that same thick wood to seal off all the windows, Hendry recalled.

The parents also narrowed Betty's social circle down significantly, telling her to choose one friend to play with. She chose Mary Jay, whose older sister was part of the deal, meaning Betty got two companions.

"Both my older sister Virginia Bowers and I were good friends with Betty and she could visit and play with both of us," Jay recalled, noting that the Woolvertons also employed a nanny, Martha, who "was always nearby." The family kept guards on hand as well for the first two years after the abduction, Jay recalled.

Jay said she and her sister "were chosen because Betty liked us best and Martha knew us and our family very well."

But even isolating Betty to a pair of sisters wasn't enough in a world where children could be pulled through second-floor windows and criminals who'd been caught and convicted could leave prison seemingly at will, their escapes duly noted by the press of the day.

So, sadly, a year and a half after the kidnapping, in the fall of 1934, the fear became too great, and fourteen-year-old Betty Woolverton was sent away to Miss Hall's School for Girls in Pittsfield, Massachusetts.

Archives maintained by the school suggest that she struggled there, academically as well as emotionally.

"We found her trying in every way to do her best," Headmistress Mira Hinsdale Hall observed in June of 1935, at the end of Betty's one year there. "She was always even tempered, sweet natured, unselfish and a most polite girl. From her record it will be seen that there was some difficulty scholastically. This we felt could partially have been solved by certain medical or psychological attention."

Letters from the school commented consistently on Betty's sweet disposition. "Her year with us was her first experience away from home," wrote Margaret Hinsdale Hall, Mira's successor as headmistress, "and in many ways it was difficult for her to adjust herself, since there were certain nervous tendencies in her temperament."[1]

In a summary of Betty's time there provided via email in 2019, school archivist Marieanne Clark wrote that Betty left the school in 1935 "in order to find a more appropriate academic match. After (Betty) left the school, her father wrote to Mira Hall of his daughter that "She has a deep feeling for your school and often speaks of it."

"Based on comments in our files, it appears that prior to attending Miss Hall's School," Clark wrote, Betty "had been somewhat isolated as a result of the kidnapping incident, which may have had some effect at the time on her mental well-being."

Jay's memories of Betty's year away are brighter, including a lot of letter writing and trips home for the holidays, and she does not recall the decision to go away to school as particularly difficult for her friend.

"Betty did not mind going off to Miss Hall's," Jay said in a 2019 telephone interview. "She could be happy anywhere as she made friends easily and loved going to new places."

The Miss Hall's school files include a neatly handwritten note from the girl to Miss Hall that seems to confirm Jay's memories.

Sent on Hotel Bermudiana stationery and dated March 29, 1935, the note reads, "You would find, I am sure, Bermuda a most enjoyable place. Even though I am having a lovely time, I will be glad to return to school the fourth of April on the New York Train. Hoping this finds you enjoying your vacation as we are ours."

Betty's year away, born of desperation, had plenty of dark moments, however. Perhaps the most poignant artifact from her time at Miss Hall's was the Western Union telegram sent November 5, 1934—the date of Betty's fifteenth birthday.

"Mary-Elizabeth Woolverton," the telegram began.

Not "Betty."

Why?

One must assume parents, daughter, and school had all agreed that the girl who'd been known by her nickname since a few weeks after her

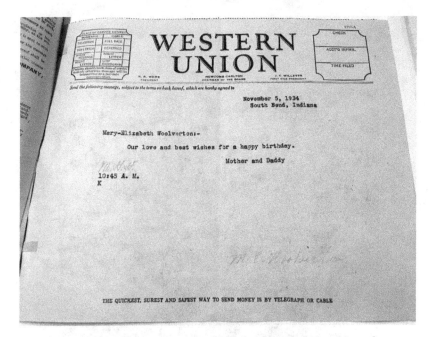

The telegram Betty Woolverton received from her parents on her fifteenth
birthday. She'd been sent to school in Massachusetts for safety.
Miss Hall's School for Girls.

birth must go by her given name now, to throw off any vengeful kidnappers sniffing around a girls' school in Massachusetts.

"Our love and best wishes for a happy birthday," continued the short
telegram, signed simply, "Mother and Daddy."

Mother and Daddy would not be seeing their daughter on that day,
would not be sharing birthday cake with her or giving her presents to
unwrap. Thanks to a kidnapping and the threats that followed, Betty
would celebrate her fifteenth birthday a thousand miles away from those
who loved her most.

According to a note sent by Howard Woolverton to Miss Hall in
June 1935, the parents decided to bring their daughter home for good
after that one year in Massachusetts, but her childhood travels were
not over. Betty's passports, still in Dave Hendry's possession, record
four cruises to Europe, each of which lasted a month or more. Hendry
recalls that his mother described the trips as treasured memories, as
educational as anything else she did in those days. But Hendry believes

Betty and her parents prepare to embark on a cruise in 1938.
Photographer unknown; David W. Hendry, Jr.

there was a second purpose to the journeys. Betty's first cruise was taken in 1932, just months after the kidnapping, and provided the Woolvertons a much-needed respite from the kidnappers' threats. Travel abroad was not without its own perils, of course. In 1939, they took a cruise that stopped in Poland, just weeks before Nazi Germany invaded that country and launched World War II. The antiques Mrs. Woolverton ordered in Poland were never delivered.

After returning from Miss Hall's, Betty may have attended a private school closer to South Bend, but Mary Jay does not believe her friend ever graduated from high school.

A page from Florence Woolverton's 1934 passport, granting fifteen-year-old Betty permission to travel to Great Britain. *Photographer unknown; David W. Hendry, Jr.*

"Betty liked to go out to socialize," Jay recalled in emails written by her daughter, "and was very interested in meeting boys." By the time she got back from Miss Hall's, Betty was almost sixteen and growing "quite independent of her parents," according to Jay. Jay's fondest memories of those days were from "several years after the kidnapping when they were dating and more into parties. Many of the best times were down in the finished basement of the Woolverton's home where they played games and there was a refrigerator that was kept filled with beer. They played charades, put on skits and sang. Betty hosted a lot of parties and loved to go to all the dances. Betty was a very good swing and ball room dancer."

Occasionally, Jay added, the Woolvertons' chauffeur would take them all to Colonel Carlisle's Castle.

Disruptive as Woolverton's abduction had been, the kidnappers never made good on their threats or even attempted to. Tales of the letters

From left, Florence and Howard Woolverton, Betty Woolverton, and best friend Mary Bower (later Mary Jay), in a picture taken around 1938. *Photographer unknown; David W. Hendry, Jr.*

and phone calls were handed down through the generations among the Woolverton descendants, but no harm came to Betty.

The same cannot be said of South Bend and the outlying regions. Fears ran rampant, the cops stepped up their game, and people died.

The kidnapping of Howard Arthur Woolverton, for the people of South Bend, was not just another crime story, another interesting but ultimately inconsequential tale about the latest machinations of society's less respectable elements.

No, the Woolverton kidnapping pervaded the psyche of South Bend and surrounding environs like few other events of the day.

Kidnappings happened. The newspapers reported them. And then everyone moved on.

But this one was different, for a variety of reasons: because Woolverton's kidnapping was reported while he was still captive and under threat of death, making it particularly sensational; because his wife and daughter were in peril as well; because he was respectable; because he insisted on saying nothing.

And most of all, because state authorities walked away, content to leave the crime uninvestigated, the perpetrators free to perpetrate again and again.

In one of the sharpest ironies of the tale, Indiana Secretary of State Frank Mayr. Jr.—the man who ensured nothing would be done on the state level to apprehend Woolverton's captors—lamented to the press about South Bend's postkidnapping angst and terror.

"The recent kidnaping of Howard Woolverton," wrote the *Muncie Evening Press* on February 10, 1932, "has cast fear of similar outrages over the entire city, Frank Mayr, Jr., secretary of state, said today."

The article noted that Mayr's home "is in South Bend near the Woolverton residence" and he is "a personal friend of Woolverton."

But Mayr indicated not a shred of culpability in the story when he claimed that "many wealthy South Bend persons have employed guards to protect their families" and declared that, in South Bend, "a peaceful community has been turned into an armed camp. Men of wealth are afraid both for their own safety and for their wives and children. Conditions are deplorable and pitiful."

And then of course came the kicker, the reminder that vital facts about the crime were secret and would remain so: "Mayr declined to comment on a report that Woolverton paid the kidnapers $8,000 for his release."

So, if you're the next to be kidnapped, the article said in not so many words, you're on your own. The great state of Indiana isn't even going to tell you what the going rate is to buy your freedom and preserve the safety of your wife and children. When your turn comes to be tossed into the back seat of a black sedan, tortured, and given a choice between death and dissolution, Indiana and its elected authorities are very sorry for you, and they wish you good luck.

In the face of such uncertainty, as Mayr noted, the people of South Bend and beyond responded as people do, by arming themselves.

Some of them nearly got killed in the process.

"Since the Woolverton kidnaping," announced the February 18, 1932, edition of the *South Bend Tribune*, "10 South Bend citizens have taken out gun permits, according to records in the office of County Clerk Frank N. Nevins, and several others are reported to have made applications."

Four members of the Woolverton clan applied, the story said: Howard's brothers John and Hugh; John's son John Jr. (he of the Missouri ransom drop, recall); and John's son-in-law, James F. Learmonth. The story's headline confirmed the reason for the requests: "Four of Family, Fearing Kidnapings, Get Permits."

Howard Woolverton was not listed among those requesting a permit in that article, but David Hendry says his grandfather did carry a gun following the kidnapping, as well as what was called at the time a "bullet-proof suit." After being donated to the South Bend Police Department, the suit may have ended up in a local museum, Hendry says, while the gun was handed down through the generations until it arrived in Hendry's possession. He donated the gun to the Piedmont, California, Police Department in 1998.

Guns were just a part of the response in South Bend to Woolverton's kidnapping; self-protection became something of a cottage industry there for a time.

"The homes of a dozen or more prominent South Bend residents [are] being guarded by police officers," announced the *South Bend Tribune* on March 2, 1932. "Special officers are watching the homes of . . . John Woolverton at 307 South Lafayette boulevard and Hugh L. Woolverton at 727 West Washington avenue and the father, Jacob Woolverton, prominent banker, at 313 South Lafayette boulevard."

The article wasn't just about wealthy adults, however, and for any reader with a heart, it was this paragraph, about little Betty Woolverton, that must have cut deepest. Before the family sent her away to safety at a school in Massachusetts, "the daughter of the kidnaped man has been staying at the home of relatives and friends of the family for short intervals since her father's abduction to block any kidnaping scheme."

The kidnapping of Howard Woolverton opened the floodgates of terror in South Bend, and what followed didn't help. Indeed, the apparent success of the crime seems to have marked it in the ensuing months as a place with ready cash for the ruthless.

"Wholesale kidnaping and extortion threats are being received by leading South Bend residents, it was learned today," announced the *Indianapolis Star* on May 11, 1932.

The story was prompted by an early-morning, near-fatal shoot-out at the home of John B. Mahoney, who had recently hired private guards for his home:

Mr. Mahoney, it was learned, has received numerous threats dating back to the kidnaping here of Howard A. Woolverton, wealthy manufacturer, last January. Mr. Mahoney is an engineer and high official at the Bendix plant.

It also was learned that other Bendix officials, including Vincent Bendix, have been receiving letters threatening them similarly.

For details of the shoot-out between South Bend patrolmen Steven Molnar and Joseph Hecklinski on one side and "private watchmen" John Doucherty and Joseph C. Mentel on the other, we must turn to the *South Bend Tribune*, which covered the 3:00 a.m. incident on the front page of its May 10, 1932, edition.

The story is given no attribution, and it needs none. This is undoubtedly the work of Everett Holles and, we might imagine, is one of the stories he added to his portfolio to show prospective employers, for it remains a marvel of clean, concise storytelling, twenty column inches that reduced a highly complex incident to an easily followed, gripping tale:

> Patrolmen Molna and Hecklinski were driving along Wayne street on their rounds. One of them thought he saw shadows of men against a garage.
>
> "That's that place we were told to watch. Let's see what is going on," Molnar told his partner. They stopped their car and started on foot up the driveway.
>
> "Here comes someone," Doucherty whispered to Mentel. Together they took cover behind an archway.
>
> After leaving their car, the city policemen had not been sure they had seen anything. Shadows are deceptive at night. One cannot be sure.
>
> But when they were only a few feet away from the archway, Doucherty, not recognizing them as officers, though they were in uniform, leveled his gun at them and cried, "Stick 'em up!"
>
> Almost immediately he began firing his gun at point blank range. As the bullets whizzed near their heads, Molnar and Hecklinski ducked back to their car for cover. Molnar fired one shot back at a shadow in the archway, missing his mark.
>
> "Kidnapers!" thought Doucherty and Mentel, hurrying into the house and barricading the windows.
>
> "Kidnapers!" thought Molnar and Hecklinski, as they prepared to lay siege to the place.
>
> Windows began to come up in nearby homes as householders stuck out their heads to see what was going on.
>
> "Hurry, there is a gun battle going on in the 1300 block, East Wayne street. Two policemen need help," someone told Desk Sergt. William Hudak over the telephone. Minutemen Benjamin Roberts and Fred DeLee hurried to the scene.

As they were arriving, Molnar got on a telephone.

"Send out everything. We have 'em cornered and they show fight. We're in for it," he told Hudak.

While tear gas bombs, armored vests, shotguns, flares, and extra men were being gathered, Roberts had an inspiration. He went to a telephone and called the Mahoney home. He succeeded in convincing those inside that only police officers were outside. By the time Night Capt. Edward Morris arrived in the riot car with extra men and the trappings of war, the situation had clarified itself. The contestants were out in the yard, conversing and comparing notes on how it feels to be shot at at very close range.

Protesting the near-tragic wave of weaponry and vigilantism was South Bend Police Chief John Kuespert, who urged his constituents to stand down in a March 30, 1932, address to the Lion's Club:

> "There is no need for the citizens of South Bend to be alarmed, as some have been since the kidnaping of Howard Woolverton," the chief declared. "Speaking of the number of permits to carry guns, I would say that they are better off without them, for if a professional crook goes after them and they make a move toward their gun, it is suicide, that's all."
>
> The chief said that crime is being steadily reduced in South Bend, the story noted, quoting Kuespert as asserting directly, "There is no crime wave in South Bend."

Kuespert could point to statistics, but the citizens of South Bend and the Kidnapping Crescent, and the media that gave shape to their fears, were experiencing something that would not yield to mere numbers.

"The kidnaping of Howard A. Woolverton, South Bend manufacturer, must compel attention and a determined community resentment everywhere," read an editorial in the January 29 *Lansing (Michigan) State Journal*: "The old practice of extortion through kidnaping was largely a practice of unsettled conditions. As civilization advanced the practice died out. But now it is back again, perhaps more threatening than ever before. Unless there is a determined stand, a definite public reaction in the matter, the practice is likely to increase ... scarcely anyone who has some reputation for being well-to-do will be safe from methods of extortion."

Discussed, dissected, described across the nation, the Woolverton case broke through to that highest level of awareness: it became a meme.

According to a front-page article in the *South Bend Tribune* published on February 16, 1932, the Woolverton incident was invoked by a crank angry over a vote by South Bend councilman Will H. Menaugh. The borderline illiteracy demonstrated by the writer suggested he or she didn't read much, newspaper or otherwise, and yet even they knew about Howard Woolverton.

"Now you resine and dam quick or the way you go for a ride and a good one," urged one of two letters sent anonymously to Menaugh's home.

"You will divide one way or another," the letter continued. "If you dont know call that gui in South Bend he will till you. I mean Woolferton. Now no monky business. This is final. We will wait for next concil meetin and then goodby."

Although Menaugh didn't resign from South Bend's City Council, he was not taken for a ride. Nor did he, it is probably safe to assume, call Howard Woolverton to learn more about being taken for a ride.

Perhaps the height of published outrage in the wake of the Woolverton kidnapping—and the government inaction Woolverton orchestrated through his friends in high places—appeared in a *Chicago Tribune* editorial on February 3, 1932. It had been eight days since Woolverton had been kidnapped, seven days since the police of three states had been mobilized to military levels of vigilance, six days since state officials had declared that, because Howard Woolverton saw nothing, heard nothing, and didn't want to talk regardless, the state of Indiana was done with it, no investigation needed.

"It is the public officials of Indiana who are on trial at this moment," the editorial asserted. "The kidnapers can be caught if a determined search is made for them with no sparing of expense, no weakening of the will to succeed, and no tiring in the pursuit. It may be safely assumed that at least four men were direct participants in the kidnaping and, no doubt, a dozen others know who is guilty. A dozen men and women cannot keep a secret. If Indiana officials want to find out who kidnaped Mr. Woolverton they can certainly do so."

The editorial noted that "indignation is running high in northern Indiana, as well it may. It is to be hoped that the justified anger of the community does not spend itself in futile curses addressed to the kidnapers, but takes the more intelligent form of insistence upon the capture of the criminals with no excuses for failure."

And then, the self-proclaimed "World's Greatest Newspaper" threw down the gauntlet, ending the editorial with a theory of Indiana law enforcement inactivity that had nothing to do with the machinations of Howard Woolverton and his high-powered friends, and everything to do with far more sinister motivations:

> The conclusion is inescapable that if the kidnapers are not caught and punished it will be because the political leaders of the state of Indiana are in partnership with the criminals. That is a conclusion which the voters of Indiana cannot afford to overlook or forget. If one of the most prominent business men of South Bend can be kidnaped and held for ransom under the threat of torture and death, the life and property of no man in Indiana are secure. And if the kidnapers remain unpunished it will be because the political powers of Indiana are sharing, directly or indirectly, in the plunder.

So there you go, Frank Mayr Jr., Indiana Secretary of State.

How do you like them apples, Governor Harry Leslie?

Maybe you were just trying to do a frightened constituent a favor, but that's not what it looks like to the rest of us. We think you turned your back on the whole affair because you're on the take.

The *South Bend Tribune* immediately ran most of the *Chicago Tribune*'s editorial, leaving off that scathingly accusatory final paragraph. Not that they needed to include it. Surely, more than one clipping of the *Chicago Tribune*'s full commentary was passed on to the indicted and to any other official in the Kidnapping Crescent, elected or otherwise, who might have been tempted to look the other way when kidnapping was afoot.

Consequentially, things were about to get a lot hotter for those who thought kidnapping was a solid business opportunity.

19

Law Enforcement Takes a Stand

IN THE WAKE OF the Woolverton kidnapping, Indiana law enforcement, from the governor on down, gave the impression they were content to walk away because Woolverton wouldn't talk. And without the support of the state, and lacking Woolverton's cooperation, the investigations of the South Bend police and other entities with an interest in the case fell by the wayside, the people left with a hopeless fear.

But ironically, the powerful impact of his case was compounded by Woolverton's silence, as can be observed in law enforcement actions soon after he came home. If they couldn't go after Woolverton's kidnappers specifically, they could go after the general problem, and that's what they did.

"A new offensive against the growing scourge of ransom kidnapings has been launched by Chicago's principle crime fighting forces—the crime commission, the secret six and the state's attorney's office," announced the Associated Press on January 29, in a story picked up by many subscribing papers, including the *Dispatch* of Moline, Illinois, which featured the story at the top of page one. "The spur was this week's kidnaping of Howard A. Woolverton. . . . South Bend is ninety miles away and local officialdom expressed belief a Chicago gang was responsible."

The organizations proposed a "standing reward" for the conviction of kidnappers, offered guidance for businesspeople who wished to protect themselves from being grabbed, and guessed at the usual suspects, including Sam Hunt, James "Red" Forsythe, Lee Turner, and Eddie La Rue (named Edward Doll at birth, and one of those FBI director J. Edgar Hoover would go on to blame for the Woolverton kidnapping).

The story also reported one of the first salvos in this reinvigorated war on kidnapping: the extradition of Louis Alterie to Chicago from Colorado to face trial for kidnapping Chicagoan Edward Dobkin.

Dobkin was a "bookmaker," the papers said, a gambler, in other words, and someone who helped others to gamble.

He wasn't respectable, but that didn't matter anymore; the authorities were no longer looking the other way when crooks kidnapped crooks.

In July of that year, a jury would acquit Alterie when Dobkin claimed he couldn't identify his captors, but several others went to prison for the crime.

And the fight was on.

In June of 1932, a Chicago gambler named Morris Schecter had been told to come up with $5,000 or face a kidnapping. Schecter made an appointment with the extortionists to hand over the money, but he also placed a call to Patrick Roche of the Illinois state's attorney's office.

Without the Woolverton coverage of a few months before, including the promise that unprecedented heat would be brought to bear against the new kidnapping industry, it seems unlikely Shechter would have called Roche. Shechter was just another small-time criminal, being asked for a little money from other rogues. But in the post-Woolverton phase of America's kidnapping era, things were changing quickly and dramatically.

Roche could have hung up the phone and told Shechter to fend for himself. Instead, according to an Associated Press story picked up by many papers around the nation, including the June 17, 1932, *Herald and Review* of Decatur, Illinois, after Schecter called Roche, Roche's team went to work: "A buzzer system was arranged between his office on the second floor at 208 North Wells street, just outside the loop, and an office across the hall, where a squad of detectives was hidden."

The three kidnappers—Harold Partner, Frank Rogers, and Sam Katz—entered Schecter's office shortly before four o'clock Thursday afternoon.

"Have you got the dough?" one of them asked.

"I can't raise $1,000," Shechter replied.

All three intruders drew pistols, police said, and the leader told Schecter: "Come on, then, you're going with us."

Schecter pressed a buzzer button and the police burst into the room. The trio pointed their weapons toward the police. One fired. The police returned the fire and all three men fell, two killed almost instantly and the third dying 10 minutes later.

The *Daily News* of New York, one of many papers that published the wire story, noted that the shoot-out "sent other tenants of the office building scattering."

A month later, the incident was credited with a significant dampening of the abduction enterprise.

"Several weeks ago," reported the *Jacksonville (Illinois) Daily Journal*, "Roche and his aids trapped three gangsters in the act of extorting $25,000[1] from a local gambler and shot the trio to death. Since then the kidnap business has slumped noticeably here."

It took a little longer to catch John "Handsome Jack" Klutas, leader of the College Kidnappers, but the tales of his exploits in the kidnapping trade and graphic accounts of his death made the wires nationwide.

The cabal of toughs led by Handsome Jack could indeed claim a passing acquaintance with higher education. Klutas graduated from Sterling Township High School in 1919 and enrolled at the University of Illinois in Urbana in September of that year.

For five semesters, through the spring of 1922, according to his university transcripts, Mr. Klutas demonstrated a fierce determination to show up. He got As in gymnasium, hygiene, and two military courses, drill and tactics, but marks for everything else fell a bit short. The second semester of his freshman year was particularly bad. In the spring of 1920, our future kidnapper earned E's (a failing grade) in principles of accounting, college algebra, and what was listed as an "Elementary Course."

And yet, Mr. Klutas kept at it, with slightly improved results: in the first semester of the 1921–1922 school year, he earned D's in accounting, trigonometry, and economics.

John Klutas gave it, literally, the college try until the first semester of the 1922–1923 school year, when he signed up for classes but received no grades for any of them. On January 10, 1923, the student identified in his transcripts as the son of a retired farmer officially left the University of Illinois to seek his fortunes elsewhere.

Postcollege, Klutas lived on the edge, and that's how he died.

Under the headline "Klutas, Gang Kidnaper, Slain," the January 7, 1934, *Des Moines (Iowa) Register* provided its readers—and any enterprising businesspeople thinking about going into the kidnapping field—a clear account of one way such a career might end.

Police, who suspected Klutas not just of kidnapping but of multiple murders over the previous few years, had learned that Klutas and his gang were hiding out in a small home in Bellwood, on the outskirts of Chicago.

The cops, led by Lieutenant Frank Johnson, forced their way into the home and arrested three suspects at about 2:00 p.m. on Saturday, January 7, 1934, the article said. It continued: "Two officers were posted inside the house with machine guns trained on the door. Other members of the squad deployed about the building. Shortly after 5 p.m. Klutas drove up with another man. They had packages in their arms and apparently were returning from a grocery store.

> "We're police officers," one of the officers shouted to Klutas, first to enter the house. . . . In reply, Klutas opened fire.
>
> "Give it to 'em," ordered one of the officers. The machine guns roared and Klutas fell dead. Nearly 50 shots were fired, most of them striking Klutas.

The bloody end of Handsome Jack was sent over the wire by the Associated Press, his death described by the *Kansas City Star* and some other fifty newspapers coast to coast this way: "Johnson's squad opened fire and Klutas fell with bullets splattered through his body."

Perhaps more than one dream of gaining riches through kidnapping died on that day. The field might have appeared exciting and lucrative to those pondering new careers, but Klutas's story was instructive. Even if you're good at abducting people, retirement comes early, and unpleasantly.

Now the cops were paying attention, and the guns were blazing. If you were kidnapping people in the Chicago area after the Woolverton kidnapping, you might want to get into a new line of work.

Would this prove to be America's rescue? Would the new eagerness of law enforcement in the Kidnapping Crescent stamp out, once and for all, the kidnapping menace?

Probably not. Like a cancer that spreads to new organs when it's eradicated in its first host tissue, kidnapping wasn't something that could be crushed with a few local measures. The crime, a simple idea, was metastasizing across America every time another successful caper was published in the papers.

A national problem needed a national answer. In response to a series of recent and high-profile kidnappings in Missouri, Senator Roscoe C. Patterson of that state announced his introduction of a national antikidnapping bill. If passed, according to the December 11, 1931, *Kansas City (Missouri) Times*, the bill would "make the transportation of a kidnaped person across a state line a federal offense with the maximum penalty of death."

The *Times* story, like others that ran the announcement that month, cited the 1930 kidnapping of Kansas City drugstore president Michael Katz, as well as abductions in St. Louis and "many others which do not get into the newspapers" as inspirations for the bill.

Senator Patterson claimed for the story that "this kind of racketeering is extending to include respectable citizens as victims, where formerly it was limited mostly to underworld characters."

The logic behind the bill, which received a simultaneous introduction in the House by Missouri congressman John J. Cochran, seems today unassailable, and graphic arguments for its passage were made within a few weeks of its introduction.

In an interview with the *St. Louis Star and Times* published December 31, 1931, local attorney and former police official Arthur J. Freund argued for the law by noting:

> It is a federal offense . . . to take a stolen automobile from one state into another. . . . Similarly, under the Mann act, if a couple drives across state boundaries and a woman is being taken for immoral purposes from one state to another, the man is subject to a penitentiary sentence, under federal law; yet if this same woman is seized, bound and gagged and thrown forcibly into an automobile in one state and driven into another state and there held for ransom, no federal offense has been committed. . . . It seems to me that the government should recognize that it is a greater crime to transport a stolen human being across state lines than it is a stolen automobile.

It was the automobile that had changed things, Freund noted. Before the adoption of the horseless carriage a few decades before, interstate kidnappings were virtually unheard of, "for the only feasible methods of conveyance were by a horse-drawn vehicle or by train," he observed. Having a gas-powered vehicle meant kidnappers could quickly and discreetly put many miles, and a state border or two, between themselves and the scene of the crime—a strategy that reduced the chances of being noticed and also hampered state and local police officers, who had to ask permission to investigate crimes outside their jurisdictions.

If the bill were passed, Freund insisted, "the federal government will be able to send its agents into any part of the United States to locate the kidnaped person and to arrest the kidnapers. Federal agents will not be bound by state lines or local police practices, and such a law will have the further great benefit of assuring society that a speedy trial will be had for the kidnapers, freed of technicalities and separate trials that accompany most cases of this sort in state courts."

There lay the rub, however—in that new raft of federal powers.

Since its founding, the United States has sought a more perfect balance between being united and being an amalgam of separate, independent states. Many citizens favored the latter, a political philosophy summed up as state's rights, or the right of each state to run things as it saw fit. In many minds, a federal kidnapping law represented another chipping away at the foundations of that philosophy by introducing a new means by which the federal government could meddle in matters states might wish to keep under their own authority.

While a number of papers issued editorials supporting the new law in the first months of 1932, including the *Detroit Free Press* on February 16, 1932, the paper acknowledged legitimate grounds for objection.

"It is true, too," the *Press* declared, "that the States ought to be jealous of any tendency on the part of Washington to encroach unnecessarily on their police powers or upon their authority to administer justice exclusively within the bounds of their natural jurisdictions. Federalization of criminal law enforcement could easily become a definitely vicious thing."

That concern and the age-old bugaboo of funding were mentioned in a syndicated editorial that ran in many papers in early March 1932, including the *La Crosse (Wisconsin) Tribune* on March 2: "There have been two barriers to enactment of a federal anti-kidnapping law, economy and states' rights. Attorney General Mitchell raised the first objection, holding adequate enforcement of it impossible on the present pinched budget. The second so far has been a cause of hesitation in congress."

Congressional opponents of the bill included Hatton Summers, chair of the House Judiciary Committee. He was a Texas Democrat and such a strong proponent of states' rights, that he fought against a federal antilynching law in the 1920s.

Lynching should fall under the purview of the local government, he argued, and when a lynching happened, all the blame rested on the officials in those jurisdictions. The frequent decision not to prosecute that kind of murder, or to allow the perpetrators to go free after sham trials, was no one else's business, Summers believed.

The same went for kidnapping, he declared. The *Courier-News* of Bridgewater, New Jersey, quoted him thusly on March 2, 1932: "[Kidnapping] is not possible among a self-governing people. It is a terrible penalty that local communities have to pay for their failure to control the elements in their midst."

And then there was the Secret Six, expressing support for the federal antikidnapping law in testimony before Congress but calling for someone other than the federal government to investigate the crimes and pursue the kidnappers.

As discussed earlier in this book, Secret Six leader Colonel Robert Isham Randolph told the Pittsburgh, Pennsylvania, Chamber of Commerce on February 2, 1932, that the best answer to kidnapping was "a secret committee of businessmen" set up in Pittsburgh and other cities.

Two days later, a message with a slight but significant difference was pushed by another Secret Six member, suggesting the group was working on a coordinated public relations strategy while their ambitions grew.

This message was issued from Chicago, home base of the Secret Six, and attributed to Frank J. Loesch, whose official title was president of the Chicago Crime Commission but who was most likely also a Secret Six member.

According to the statement, picked up by the February 4, 1932, *New York Times*, Loesch was not just proposing—as Colonel Randolph had two days before—that each city form its own version of the Secret Six. Instead, Loesch called for "the establishment of an interstate secret organization to combat kidnappers."

"No one outside the membership need know who are the members," Loesch declared. "The head should be an experienced man, publicly known. . . . This organization must be as secret as the criminal organization tries to be."

In two short days, then, the modest proposal of the Secret Six that each city start its own secret organization, presumably with guidance from the Chicago group, had evolved to something far grander: a national antikidnapping posse under the authority of a single, secretive group—the Secret Six writ large.

The Secret Six were, apparently, alone in their prescription for a private force against kidnapping, and the voices clamoring for a federal law with federal enforcement were far louder.

In fact, among the reasons given to support the law in the first few months after it was introduced—an argument forgotten today but vital then: Howard Woolverton's kidnapping.

"Woolverton Case Revives Kidnaping Bill in Congress" blared the headline at the top of the front page of the *South Bend Tribune* on January 28, 1932. It was but one of many stories about the kidnapping to run that day in the *Tribune*, but historically, it was surely the most significant.

"Spurred by the kidnaping this week of Howard A. Woolverton, South Bend Manufacturer," the story, datelined Washington, began, "passage of the Patterson bill making transportation of kidnaped persons from one state to another a federal offense appeared probable to-day as soon as the bill can be placed on the senate calendar. Passage by the house is also virtually assured.

"The Woolverton case aroused new interest in the bill, especially among western senators."

Two weeks later, Woolverton's name was still being invoked by the bill's supporters. In a story headlined "Indiana Police Directors Influenced by Woolverton Case," the *South Bend Tribune* of February 12, 1932, reported, "As a result of the recent kidnaping of Howard A. Woolverton, South Bend manufacturer, the directors of the Indiana Police association, have decided to support the federal bill which would make interstate kidnaping punishable by death."

The article added, "Chief of Police John B. Kuespert recently expressed himself as heartily in favor of the measure and Congressman Samuel B. Pettengill, of South Bend, has announced that it will have his full support."

Favorable commentary was also reported by the *Indianapolis News* on February 26, 1932: "The inclination of the congress to tackle the kidnapping problem has met with a wide public response, judging by

Woolverton Case Revives Kidnaping Bill in Congress

The Tribune's Special Service.

WASHINGTON, Jan. 28.—Spurred by the kidnaping this week of Howard A. Woolverton, South Bend manufacturer, passage of the Patterson bill making transportation of kidnaped persons from one state to another a federal offense appeared probable to-day as soon as the bill can be placed on the senate calendar. Passage by the house also is virtually assured.

The Woolverton case aroused new interest in the bill, especially among western senators.

Representative Samuel B. Pettengill of South Bend is strongly in favor of the measure, he informed Chief of Police John B. Kuespert of South Bend on Jan. 4.

The measure, sponsored by Senator Patterson, of Missouri, was instigated by Chief of Police Joseph A. Gerk, of St. Louis, who wrote Chief Kuespert about it. Senator Waterman, of Colorado, chairman of the sub-committee considering the bill, has been ill, delaying hearings and the measure is expected to be reported to the senate after action on President Hoover's financial program is completed.

Published in the *South Bend Tribune* on January 28, 1932, this story points to the importance of the Woolverton kidnapping to a vital federal law. *South Bend Tribune*, January 28, 1932.

communications coming to senators and representatives in support of proposed legislation to curb this form of crime. The mail of the Indiana senators and congressmen is loaded with endorsements."

In the flood of mail hitting Washington supporting both antikidnapping and a measure outlawing the use of the US Postal Service to send ransom notes, one letter in particular must have stood out: "Among the Hoosier indorsers of the legislation is H. A. Woolverton, South Bend manufacturer, who recently was a victim of kidnappers," the paper reported. "In a letter to Senator James E. Watson, he said: 'Being one of the most recent victims of acts covered by these bills, I cannot urge you too strongly to give favorable consideration. In my estimation from my personal experience these two measures are of extreme importance.'"

Not surprisingly, businesspeople were rallying around their own, the call for chambers of commerce to get involved generating strong support in Indiana.

"A. P. Ederlin, secretary-manager of the Evansville Chamber of Commerce," the *Indianapolis News* noted, "in a letter to Representative John W. Boehne, First Indiana district, recalled that 282 kidnappings had been reported in 1931.[2] 'This is the most heinous of all crimes,' he added. 'Pass these two bills. Make it a federal offense to steal human beings.'"

The law was proposed. It found detractors and supporters; the latter significantly bolstered by the taking of Howard Woolverton.

And then came the Crime of the Century. Thirty-three days after Howard Woolverton was left on a curb in downtown Chicago with his life and enough money to buy a train ticket home, twenty-month-old Charles Augustus Lindbergh Jr. was kidnapped from his crib on the evening of March 1, 1932.

A homemade ladder had been propped up against the side of the home. The kidnapper reached the baby's second-floor bedroom through a window.

A ransom of $50,000 was paid, but the badly decomposed, animal-gnawed remains of little Lindbergh, son of the famous aviator Charles Lindbergh, were found in the woods two months later. The child had died of a head injury, believed to have been suffered in the first moments of his abduction, when his kidnapper dropped him while climbing down the ladder.

Momentum for the kidnapping bill grew considerably after the Lindbergh abduction, moving successfully through both houses of Congress, but it was put on hold while Lindbergh was still missing but possibly alive. Lawmakers were concerned that if the law were passed before the child was returned to his family, the kidnappers would simply kill him and cut their losses to avoid federal prosecution. But when the child's skeletal remains were found on May 12, 1932, nothing stood in the way of federal penalties for the transport of kidnapped persons across state lines, and President Herbert Hoover signed the law into effect on June 22, 1932.[3]

The law is commonly known as the Lindbergh Law, so important was the child's abduction to the law's passage. His kidnapping was not, however, the inspiration for the law; kidnappings of adults in Missouri were. Nor did the Lindbergh kidnapping contribute to early support for the law. Woolverton's kidnapping did, and widely publicized congressional hearings on kidnapping were conducted in late February, after

Woolverton's kidnaping but a week before Lindbergh was snatched. Written endorsements for the law were also being sent to Congress that February, including that letter from Woolverton himself and from police chiefs across Indiana who were motivated specifically by the Woolverton case.

There was something else going on, however, beyond dry debates and the bloodless letters and petitions stacking up in the halls of Congress.

As mentioned earlier, Woolverton's abduction also seemed to be a leading force behind a new way of covering kidnapping—another accident of journalistic timing, one of several that gave the Woolverton case its historic punch.

Recall that on March 3, the *Daily News* of New York City published the first of its sixteen-part series focused on the national kidnapping menace, with its central theme that "no one is safe."

Around the same date, Bruce Catton's kidnapping piece, written for the Newspaper Enterprise Association, started making the rounds of newspapers from Oregon to Florida, Texas to New York.

Fred Pasley's and Catton's series both began with a reference to the March 1 kidnapping of Charles Lindbergh Jr., which was then but a day or two old. Given the timing, however, neither series could have been inspired by Lindbergh's abduction. Clearly, Pasley and Catton had researched their stories for weeks, with Pasley traveling a fair distance to visit the St. Louis Chamber of Commerce.

Both must have spent considerable time gathering anecdotes, statistics, and expert opinion. Before the internet, fax machines, photocopiers, or even a reliable phone system, the efforts must have been all-consuming, days of poring over old newspapers and working the phones. That their series were finished just as Lindbergh was snatched must have seemed like a blessing from the newspaper gods. The baby's abduction meant that their projects on this new crime spree were ready to go just as the taking of little Lindbergh was on everyone's mind. The child's snatching wasn't an isolated incident, readers across the nation were warned, but part and parcel of a terrifying new national trend.

So, why did Pasley and Catton embark on their projects?

Here we must speculate, but the kidnapping of Howard Woolverton featured prominently in both series and very well might have served as inspiration. For Catton, Woolverton's abduction was a prime indicator of the new trend of grabbing respectable citizens, and Pasley, in his *Daily News* report, labeled Woolverton's kidnapping a "spectacular" crime that "climaxed a series of such crimes in the Middle West" and "which for brazen audacity has no parallel."

So Pasley and Catton, we might theorize, were prodded by the Woolverton case to write their kidnapping stories, hooking them to the Lindbergh kidnapping at the last minute, and giving their many subscribers in New York and across the nation a full, terrifying picture of American kidnapping just as the citizens were most ready to receive it.

Howard Woolverton—kidnapping poster child for a time, forgotten kidnap victim today—deserves at least a share of the credit for the passage of the kidnapping law and perhaps the lion's share, for he was arguably not only the chief inspiration for media coverage of kidnapping trends at a critical time; his case also served as one of the chief struts of support during the law's deliberations.

Proposed in December 1931 and opposed immediately over states' rights and budgetary concerns, the law received key support from Woolverton during one of the first waves of promotion by the law's supporters in early 1932, helping to promulgate that critical new message: kidnapping wasn't just the tragic taking of the occasional child or something gangsters did to each other. It was a new American enterprise, growing, profitable, and professionally conducted, with hundreds of victims already and more every month, many of them respectable, many of them rendered too terrified to speak. This was a new business that threatened financial ruin, the loss of loved ones, and torture for every citizen who'd accomplished something.

The law might still have passed on the strength of Lindbergh's kidnapping alone, or it might have died under complaints of federal overreach. Baby Lindbergh wasn't transported over state lines, after all.[4] Without the Woolverton case, there might not have been those urgent stories, and cooler and less emotional heads might have prevailed. States' rights advocates might have convinced their peers in the House and Senate that the kidnapping of a single child in New Jersey, tragic as it might have been, didn't merit a new excuse for federal agents to go tromping from sea to shining sea.

How much support for the law in Congress was inspired by the taking of that child, and how much was provoked by the Woolverton case, by fears that the very fabric of American life was under attack, the American Dream being ripped apart, piece by piece, one kidnapping at a time?

We can only speculate, but if we give Woolverton any credit at all for its passage, if we imagine that at least a few of the votes in favor of the law were made with him in mind, or under the influence of the broad newspaper coverage of kidnapping arguably sparked by his case, then we must credit the forgotten man for doing far more than his share to build the America we know today.

But did the new kidnapping law really matter? Did it make a difference?

In a word, yes.

20

The Rules Have Changed

THE BOOK *PERSONS IN HIDING*, J. Edgar Hoover's 1938 paean to the FBI and its war on Depression-era crime, is not remembered as great literature. It gets things wrong, it ignores things that shouldn't have been ignored, and it reduces America's criminals to comic book caricatures, tough-talking cowards who broke the law primarily so the feds could lock them up. It could have used a better title.

But if one wishes to understand why kidnapping is no longer the scourge it once was, no longer the drumbeat of terror, the newspaper refrain, the nightmarish coda to the American Dream; if one wishes to find in a few words why Americans today can strive, build, achieve, and succeed, with never a thought to being snatched off the street or having to wait for a phone call or a ransom note while a loved one languishes in a basement prison or a torture chamber or a shallow grave, Hoover gave us the answer.

In the book's tenth chapter, titled "Bill Dainard Was Paroled," Hoover detailed the 1935 kidnapping in Tacoma, Washington, of George Weyerhaeuser, the young son of wealthy lumberman J. P. Weyerhaeuser.

And in that narrative, Hoover laid out in exacting detail what happened when there was an interstate kidnapping, now that Hoover's men had a federal law to back them up.

The kidnapping was a sensational one, covered widely in the press: on May 24, 1935, nine-year-old George Weyerhaeuser was grabbed on his walk home from school, driven into Idaho (triggering federal involvement, per the new law), chained, put in several shallow holes, handcuffed to a tree for a time, and driven around in the trunk of his captors' car. After a week of captivity, a $200,000 ransom was paid and he was released unharmed. He went on to help with the prosecution of the criminals and eventually to succeed his father at the helm of the Weyerhaeuser company, a firm that lives on, owning or managing eleven million acres of timberland in the US alone.[1]

The crime occurred three years after passage of the Federal Kidnapping Act, more than enough time for Hoover to have built up a sophisticated and aggressive national antikidnapping program.

"The Federal Bureau of Investigation," Hoover wrote, "had answered the kidnap call to Tacoma with a celerity made possible by highly geared procedure(s) devised for such cases. Once the red light National 7117, the 'kidnap number,' glows upon the switchboard in the Communications Room of headquarters in Washington, men leap to action throughout America."

The ransom notes received by the family were flown to FBI headquarters for examination, Hoover wrote, and a list of the serial numbers of every bill included in the $200,000 ransom was also sent to Washington, DC, by plane. There, "shifts worked night and day in our multigraphing plant" and "within thirty-six hours of the moment that list had reached Washington it was on the way out again in thousands upon thousands of bound copies, shooting forth by airplane to every newspaper, bank, department store, post office, and law enforcement agency throughout the West."

Alert bank clerks and merchants in Salt Lake City, Utah, began spotting the ransom bills immediately, Hoover wrote. Two of the kidnappers, Harmon Metz Waley and his wife, Margaret Waley, were caught in that city within a month of the kidnapping and were sentenced to forty-five and twenty years, respectively.[2]

The third kidnapper, Bill Dainard,[3] remained free a little longer, but he read the papers, and he knew that he'd been identified by the victim as one of the abductors. He also knew what had become of his partners in crime, and how they'd been caught.

No city or state police department had the resources to create, copy, and distribute nationwide a list of thousands of currency serial numbers, a strategy key to rendering the ultimate objective of kidnapping—money—worthless. Only the FBI had these capacities. And they worked.

His ill-gotten loot unspendable, Dainard, Hoover wrote, "again became a hobo, beating his way to California, on freight trains."

And only a national police force could accomplish what the FBI did next.

Hoover wrote that once Dainard was in California, he "found that, in ways mysterious to him, Special Agents had reached into his old haunts. Finally he learned that our kidnap squad, augmented by the activities of every necessary member of the thirty-seven strategically placed Field Offices throughout the United States, was compiling a slow, painstaking directory of his entire life. Already old friends had been told that if they harbored this man they would be prosecuted relentlessly. The underworld began to greet Dainard only with the snarling order: 'Get away from us! And stay away from us!'"

Dainard was still on the loose, toting a bag stuffed with the 2020 equivalent of more than a million dollars in cash, but his life on the lam could scarcely have been called free or pleasant.

He attempted to modify some of the ransom currency, buying paints to change the numbers, but the work wasn't perfect and served only to give cashiers something new to look out for.

He did get married, to a waitress he met in Los Angeles, but that was nothing more than a ruse, Hoover wrote, and man and wife had to move often, rousing her suspicions. "She insisted on asking questions: Where had he lived? Who were his mother, his father, his sisters and brothers? Why must they hurry constantly from town to town?"

On April 30, 1936, his criminal sixth sense telling him the feds were closing in, Dainard was forced to abandon his wife in Reno, Nevada, Hoover wrote. He told her he'd meet her in Denver, Colorado. She took the car, driving south. He caught a train headed north.

She didn't know it, but her marriage was over.

A week later, on May 6—almost a year after the kidnapping of nine-year-old George Weyerhaeuser—Bill Dainard was arrested in Los Angeles as he approached his car. The car contained a bag holding $29,000 in virtually worthless ransom money.

He got sixty years.

Bill Fliss, who helped Dainard launder some of the kidnap cash, got ten.

Kidnapping used to be fun.

And profitable.

But a law had changed all that, and the same federal resources brought to bear and described in detail by Hoover in the Weyerhaeuser case were already in place two years earlier, ready to be moved—for the first time under the new law—against the perpetrators of a sensational abduction in Oklahoma City.

Charles Urschel, Walter Jarrett, and their wives were playing bridge on the sunporch of the Urschels' Oklahoma City mansion about 11:30 p.m. on Saturday, July 22, 1933, when Berenice[4] Urschel observed, "This is the last rubber."

Moments later, according to stories published two days later on the front page of the *Oklahoma News*, "a large blue sedan rolled into the driveway and stopped. The motor was not stopped. Instantly, it seemed, two men burst into the sunporch. They were armed with machine guns.

"Everyone keep quiet," snapped the leader, a two-hundred-pound man neatly dressed and coatless.

Mrs. Jarrett said both men looked like Italians.

"Which one of you is Urschel?" one of the men demanded. "We want Urschel."

Urschel volunteered himself, according to the paper.[5] "Well, come on, you're going with us," he was told. Jarrett was also ordered to follow, and the four men left the porch, the abductors issuing a final threat to the women: "Keep away from that telephone and don't say a word or we'll blow your heads off."

"A few seconds later the powerful car roared away," reported the *Oklahoma News*. "The women sat frozen with terror for a moment."

Soon, however, Mrs. Urschel was on the phone. "'They've kidnapped Mr. Urschel and Mr. Jarrett,' she screamed into the telephone to the police."

Police immediately ordered a "general search of all cars." One vehicle escaped the dragnet, according to a witness: a "large blue sedan careened off 19th-st into Classen-blvd, a mile to the West, and sped northward. Some witnesses said a smaller car followed."

Jarrett was released about an hour later on the side of the highway, picked up by two youths who brought him back to the Urschel home. According to the *Oklahoma News*, after speaking to Mrs. Urschel, Jarrett went to the police station, "where he remained in conference with federal and local officers."

On July 24, her husband gone for two days, Mrs. Urschel twisted a napkin around her fingers over breakfast as she sought to communicate directly with the kidnappers.

"I am in no way interested in your capture or prosecution," began the message she shared with Noel Houston, a reporter for the *Oklahoma News*. "I care only for the safe return of my husband. To facilitate this, I have had police withdrawn from my house and there is no one here now except our family. We are sitting beside the telephone waiting for you to call."

Mrs. Urschel declared that Arthur Seeligson, Mr. Urschel's closest friend, would be in charge of negotiations and the arranging of payment.

Like Florence Woolverton eighteen months before, Mrs. Urschel was presented in the newspaper as a wife holding up under enormous strain: "Displaying a courage which is equalling that undoubtedly being shown by her wealthy husband, wherever he is held captive, she talked rationally and sensibly about the case."

Those in the home were waiting for the phone to ring and for that most important question to be answered: How much?

Mr. and Mrs. Urschel were relative newlyweds, each losing a spouse and finding each other, marrying quietly in October 1932. They were also, together, fabulously wealthy. Mr. Urschel was a successful oilman, and Mrs. Urschel brought an estimated $23 million to the union, a sum worth close to half a billion dollars in 2020.

They would have no trouble paying any reasonable ransom, Mrs. Urschel promised.

The kidnapping made national news as it dragged on, the family continuing to claim for more than a week that no word had been heard from the kidnappers, that no negotiations were underway.

But at about 9:45 p.m. on Monday, July 31—nine days after the kidnappers stormed that bridge game—a man showed up at the Classen Barbecue Stand just north of Norman, a town on the southern edge of

Oklahoma City. The man, in short sleeves and a straw hat, took a seat, asked for a cup of coffee, and grabbed a newspaper.

Eventually, according to the August 31, 1933, *Oklahoma News*, he asked someone there to call him a taxi. He paid five cents for the coffee and left in the rain.

The man was Charles Urschel, and he'd chosen to follow Howard Woolverton's peculiar postkidnapping playbook: saunter, read the paper, and enjoy your first moments of freedom privately.

But that's where the similarities ended. Because Urschel talked.

He talked to the cops. He talked to the newspapers. He and his wife posed for pictures.

Indeed, where Howard Woolverton ran onto his front porch, ducked into his South Bend home, and stayed behind a door guarded by state police officers, "the oil multimillionaire . . . greeted 14 newspaper men and photographers at 8 a.m. in the sun porch of his NW 18th-st mansion," reported the *Oklahoma News* on August 1.

Urschel smiled and joked the morning after his release, his elated wife by his side, while he told the reporters a terrifying story.

After he was taken and his friend Jarrett released, he said, he was forced to "lay on his back in the rear seat of the kidnapper's car and was given only a bottle of Coca Cola on the 14-hour drive."

Although his eyes had been taped shut (the evidence of that still visible to the reporters gathered there), he was aware of passing through "out-of-the-way country side roads, into a hilly, rolling region that might have been eastern or southeastern Oklahoma."

He was imprisoned in a shack, guarded by people other than the two men who kidnapped him, and "threatened with death, blindfolded and handcuffed for nine days."

According to the *Oklahoma News*, "he slept very little and had to get along with a brand of cigars other than his favorite kind. But he didn't complain, and remained on friendly terms with the snatchers."

He saw the light of day only twice, the paper reported, once so he could write a note begging for the payment of the ransom ($200,000, it was later revealed), once just before his release, to shave.

After the ransom was paid, Urschel was reportedly closer to death than anyone knew at the time. According to J. Edgar Hoover's account of the kidnapping featured in the *American Magazine* of February, 1937 (an important article we'll be revisiting in the next section) the sole woman on the kidnapping team, Kathryn Kelly, proposed that the millionaire oilman be disposed of.

The article's description of her input on the matter was colorful, if nothing else: "What I think," she snarled, "is that we're a bunch of saps if we turn this -- -- -- loose. Kill him! Then we won't have any more trouble with him."

She was alone in this opinion, Hoover wrote, and the other kidnappers had to work to change her mind: "It was a stormy session. The gangsters wanted to turn their victim loose as they had promised in the ransom letters. . . . At last the pleadings of the others won over [her] insistence that Urschel be murdered."

They let Urschel go on a highway south of Oklahoma City. After the coffee at the barbecue joint and the cab ride, he had one more challenge: getting into his own home.

"'At first, I'd planned to stop at a drug store and telephone, to make sure no officers were around and I wouldn't have any trouble,'" the *Oklahoma News* quoted him as saying. "'But I decided to come on home at once . . . I pulled up at the back and went to the back door. It was locked. When I tried to open it, I was met by a federal man and had to do some explaining before I could get in my own home,' he laughed again."

Available as he'd made himself that morning, however, Urschel withheld two critical details from the visiting reporters: the $200,000[6] ransom amount, which had been quietly negotiated in the preceding days and paid by E. E. Kirkpatrick on July 30, and his plan to do everything he could to bring his abductors to justice. He'd left his fingerprints all over the room where he was held. He'd listened, noting the twice-daily passing of a plane, as well as the day that rain forced it to take another route. When he could, he'd snuck a peek from behind his blindfold, noting his captors' faces.

Where Woolverton came home and clammed up, Urschel blabbed. In fact, his wife was talking to the FBI while he was still captive. According to some reports, when she called the federal kidnapping hotline, Hoover himself had answered.

Was the character of these two wealthy men that different, Woolverton cowering in his mansion while Urschel welcomed the press and the police into his?

No, probably not.

The differences in the kidnapping of Woolverton and Urschel spoke instead of the changing character of a nation.

Howard Woolverton had been kidnapped in one America.

Eighteen months later, Charles Urschel was kidnapped in another America—an America, it must be said, that Howard Woolverton helped create.

The change, in as few words as possible: the Federal Kidnapping Act.

Woolverton understood the conditions under which he'd been taken, and he behaved in accordance with those rules, logically and rationally.

But the rules of the game were entirely different by the time Urschel was taken, and he knew it. The kidnappers didn't.

In January 1932, Howard Woolverton's kidnapping was covered nationwide, and it prompted military-grade police mobilizations in three states.

But the feds never showed up, because no law authorized them to do so, and Howard Woolverton ducked through his front door and never came out, all his efforts focused on quashing any investigation and saving himself and his own.

Eighteen months later, Charles Urschel's kidnapping prompted another round of national coverage, and the mobilization of local and state police.

But someone new showed up this time: there was a national kidnapping law on the books, and the feds swarmed.

Recall that a "federal man" was in Urschel's home to greet him the moment he arrived.

There were certainly no federal men in the Woolverton home on that cold January night when he dashed up his front porch.

A small army was deployed while Woolverton was in the custody of his abductors, but it was an army of city and state police only, and it was dispersed as soon as Woolverton returned home and, with the aid of his friend Frank Mayr, quashed the investigations.

As shall be discussed in coming chapters, some of the same people who kidnapped Howard Woolverton were also reportedly in on the snatching of Charles Urschel. Two kidnappings, the crooks might have thought, one in winter, one in summer, one in Indiana, one in Oklahoma.

Same kind of job though, really.

Nope.

Different Americas.

Immediately after the safe return home of Charles Urschel, the FBI fanned out.

"A small army of 20 federal agents which has been held in check pending Urschel's release vanished along underworld trails," declared the August 1, 1933, *Oklahoma News*, "determined to bag the biggest game in recent kidnaping history."

Much of the federal investigation drew on the thorough recollections of the man himself. Using Urschel's memory of a regular flight that was diverted due to weather on one of the days of his captivity, federal investigators looked at airports, mail plane schedules, and weather reports, and brought their own aircraft to the effort, narrowing down the place where he'd been imprisoned to a farm near Paradise, Texas.

Only then could the FBI be confident that Urschel had been taken across state lines, of course. Until that discovery, the FBI's involvement had been highly speculative and perhaps a bit risky. If it was discovered that Urschel had been dragged to some other point in Oklahoma, the feds would have had no standing and been forced to slink back home and abandon the case into which they'd poured men and money. It was a risk Hoover was willing to take, a gamble with a payoff so great he couldn't hold back.

Hoover's calculus is easy to imagine. Catch Urschel's kidnappers and restore the Bureau's young, struggling legacy, already tattered by a massacre in Kansas City[7] and the failure to save Baby Lindbergh.

The cops raided that farm in Paradise on August 12, 1933. Among those arrested were the farm's owner, R. G. Shannon; his wife, Ora; their son, Armon; and his wife. Ora Shannon was Kathryn Kelly's mother, and mother-in-law to George "Machine Gun" Kelly.

Also nabbed was Harvey Bailey, who'd escaped from the state prison in Lansing, Kansas. (How did Bailey bust out? With the alleged aid of someone who quite possibly also kidnapped Howard Woolverton, but more on that in a bit.) Bailey was suspected at first to have been one of the Urschel abduction's masterminds, although many, including Hoover, said later that Kathryn Kelly planned it out. Bailey, called in some quarters "The Dean of American Bank Robbers," was found at the farm sleeping in an open garage when a dozen lawmen showed up.

"The federal officer woke Bailey by jamming a sub-machine gun in his face," reported the International News Service story about the raid.

When the officer promised to kill Bailey in the event of any resistance, Bailey reportedly replied, "Go ahead and shoot." But Bailey didn't resist, and he didn't die that day.[8]

They found some of the Urschel ransom cash at the farm, $700 of it in Bailey's pockets. The officers also discovered Urschel's strategically planted fingerprints in the room of a tenant building located on the property.

The indictments came down less than two weeks later, issued by a federal grand jury against fourteen people, seven in custody, the other seven still on the run, including Machine Gun and Kathryn Kelly.[9]

Urschel and his wife remained closely involved in the case. In fact, when Albert Bates, who with George Kelly grabbed Urschel from his porch, was flown into the Oklahoma City airport for trial, Mr. and Mrs. Urschel were there to welcome him.

Where Howard and Florence Woolverton were compelled to come to Chicago to look at an assemblage of crooks, and to speak to a grievously wounded suspect as he lay with his infected head and face in bandages (more on that soon), the Urschels had a better time of it, coming away with a positive identification the Woolvertons lacked.

The scene was described in wire stories picked up by many papers: "'Hello, Albert,' Urschel greeted the accused man as he stepped from the plane surrounded by federal agents armed with machine guns. Bates looked straight at Urschel and without a change of expression, replied, 'I do not know you.'"

The trials and convictions followed the arrests with remarkable speed by modern standards, conducted in September 1933 for those in custody.

But several suspected perpetrators were still at large, including Machine Gun Kelly and his wife, Kathryn, who were out there somewhere, dodging the cops, reading the papers, and growing murderously irate.

21

The Love Story of Kathryn and George "Machine Gun" Kelly

GEORGE AND KATHRYN KELLY possessed a flair for drama, beginning soon after they met. George's terrifying moniker itself was reportedly invented by his wife, who was a likely murderer and antisocial.

George Kelly Barnes was born in Tennessee, probably in 1900. In his twenties, he changed his name to George R. Kelly and embarked on the challenging career of illicit alcohol purveyance.

Kelly was not particularly good at the trade, if we are to judge his professional talents by his arrest record. According to the wanted poster the FBI published in August 1933, Kelly went to state prison in Santa Fe, New Mexico, in March 1927 for violating the National Prohibition Act. He was out four months later and lingering on the streets of Tulsa, Oklahoma, when he got hit with a vagrancy charge. Six months after that, in January 1928, he was charged with another violation of the National Prohibition Act, and that earned him a rap of three years in the US Penitentiary in Leavenworth, Kansas.

Good behavior got him out early, and he celebrated his freedom by getting married in 1930.

"When Kathryn Kelly met George Kelly in Oklahoma City not many years ago, he was a weak, loud-mouthed, overdressed bootlegger," wrote J. Edgar Hoover in *American Magazine*'s February 1937 edition.

244

Penned with the help of Courtney Ryley Cooper (a famous writer at the time whose life ended in a peculiar way, more on that in a bit), the story asserted that Mrs. Kelly, harboring fantasies of being married to a "super-villain" who would bring her wealth and fame (she was also interested in a film career), built Machine Gun Kelly from the ground up, buying him his Thompson submachine gun and talking up the small-time criminal who had already done time for bootlegging: "She embarked upon a popularity campaign in gangdom, where she was indisputably the best-looking and best-dressed gun moll of the lot. She rode in a sixteen-cylinder car, her silver fox furs floating from her shoulder. Apparently, whispered the underworld, Kelly must be a big shot—must be making good."

The article goes on to trace the wife-driven genesis of the legend of Machine Gun Kelly, stripping off all the chrome in the process.

"Not so very long ago," reads the article, "the name of George (Machine Gun) Kelly brought a shiver of fear into the homes of wealthy families in every city of the land. This trade-mark of crime—Machine Gun Kelly—was a symbol of kidnapping, of brutal power, ruthlessness, and cunning."

But behind the legend, Hoover asserted, the FBI found "a craven, blundering blowhard."

The Machine Gun Kelly brand, according to the article, "was the creation of his manager, press agent, and leading lady—Kathryn Kelly, his wife—one of the most attractive women ever to travel the crooked paths of the underworld—and one of the most vicious. She bought him a machine gun and kept score for him in practice until he was able to strip a fence-top of a row of walnuts. Upon at least one occasion, she collected the bullets and passed them out among her criminal friends like cigars, remarking, 'Here's a little souvenir for you—a bullet from George's machine gun—Machine Gun Kelly, you know.'"

Mrs. Kelly could make a good impression on anyone, according to Hoover's article, not just the denizens of the underworld.

"She played the piano with moderate ability. She used English that was far better than the average. She was attractive to look upon, of good carriage and pleasing manner."

Did she kill her third husband? The evidence points that way. She married bootlegger Charles Thorne in 1924, living well except when they were fighting, which was often. By 1927, she'd had enough of him, or so goes the story. Here's how Hoover's article put it:

One night, an automobile wheeled uncertainly into a Fort Worth fill-ing station. Kathryn leaned out and, brushing away black hair from her smooth forehead, thickly ordered gas and lots of it.

The attendant obeyed orders. Then he asked, "Where are you bound for, Kathryn?"

"Where am I bound for?" Fire glinted from her piercing eyes. "I'm bound for Coleman, Texas, to kill Charlie Thorne."

Gears meshed. The car whined away down the dark highway. The next day, Charlie Thorne was found dead, a revolver near by. There was a note—typewritten, even to the signature. It read: "I can't live with her or without her, hence I am departing this life."

The coroner's jury called it suicide.

Hoover's article doesn't mention one important detail, but other sources do: Charles Thorne was illiterate.

Other accounts of the incident offer a more colorful, less family-friendly version of what Kathryn Kelly said at the gas station: "I'm bound to Coleman, Texas, to kill that damned Charlie Thorne."[1]

This was a determined woman. When a wrong needed righting, she was there, doing what was necessary.

And arresting her mom and stepdad for the kidnapping of Charles Urschel, it seems, was a bridge too far for the would-be actress, and the letters started arriving even before the trials of their coconspirators were done.

One of the letters was presented in detail in an Associated Press piece that was picked up, among other outlets, by the September 21, 1933, *Fort Worth Star-Telegram*. It had been sent to Charles Urschel from Chicago via airmail.

Addressed to "Ignorant Charles," it began, "Just a few lines to let you know that I am getting my plans laid to destroy your so-called mansion, and you and your family immediately after this trial."

Kathryn Kelly, who bought her husband a machine gun, insisted he get good at using it, and gave him one of the gangster era's most famous monikers, was reportedly behind the intimidation campaign as well, dictating the letters while her husband printed and signed them.

Incensed that Urschel had agreed to testify against Kathryn's fam-ily, the Kellys wrote, "If the Shannons are convicted, look out, and God help you. . . . You don't seem to mind prosecuting the innocent, neither will I have any conscience qualms over brutally murdering your family."

Like the first Woolverton ransom note, the author of the Urschel letter used underlines and dashes and demonstrated a talent for good

English, irony, and dramatic prose: "In the event of my arrest I've already formed an outfit to take care of and destroy you and yours the same as if I was there. I am spending your money to have you and your family killed—nice—eh?"

And in a passage reminiscent of that genre of extortion notes boasting of impressive equipment and technologies (explosives, long-distant poison darts, etc.), the Kellys warned that Urschel's decision to testify meant he was "bucking people that have cash, planes, bombs and unlimited connections both here and abroad."

The letter, a screed mostly of insults and threats, offered matrimonial advice toward the end, albeit with its own ethereal bent: "Now, sap—it is up to you, if the Shannons are convicted, you can get you another rich wife in hell, because that will be the only place you can use one."

The letter's closing was equally unpleasant: "Adios, smart one," it read, that line followed by "Your worst enemy."

The letter was signed "Geo. R. Kelly," and, should anyone doubt its authenticity, it included a postscript: "I will put my prints below so you can't say some crank wrote this."

Police analysis of the area beneath those words confirmed the helpful presence of Machine Gun Kelly's actual fingerprints.

We must imagine husband and wife reading through the letter after it had been written, nodding with satisfaction over some of its more colorful passages, perhaps agreeing that this was why they'd gotten married—to savor such moments.

But they might have decided the letter was still lacking something, and they decided to add a second postscript, referencing Joseph B. Keenan, who headed up the Urschel kidnapping investigation as special assistant US attorney general: "Give Keenan my regards and tell him maybe he would like to meet the owner of the above. See you in hell!"

Inspired as it might have been, the Kellys' reign of mail-borne terror, as well as Mrs. Kelly's dreams of movie stardom and both their careers as hoodlums, came to an ignominious end two months after the Urschel kidnapping, on Tuesday, September 26, 1933.

More plodding detective work brought them down.

As part of their disguise, the Kellys would sometimes travel with a twelve-year-old girl named Geraldine Arnold, the daughter of acquaintances, and a girl who lent the desperadoes an air of domestic respectability. When they sent her back home to Oklahoma after a crosscountry ramble, the feds met up with her, and she talked.

A coded telegram George Kelly sent to J. R. Tichnor in Memphis, presumably to let him know the couple were on the way and needed a place to hide, also helped in the capture.

Thus tipped off that the Kellys had taken refuge at either a bungalow or rooming house (press accounts varied) in Memphis, US Department of Justice agents flew in from Birmingham and met up with Memphis police officers to make the bust.

"A cordon of police surrounded the dwelling and a detail of heavily armed detectives and patrolmen made their way to the entrance," stated the Associated Press story that ran on the date of the arrest in many papers.

The *Daily Oklahoman* edition of September 27, 1933, described what happened next:

> Detective Sergeant Bill Raney of the Memphis force rapped on the door. Kelly flung it open. He had a gun in his hand.
> Raney snapped his shotgun over the bad man's heart and drawled: "Drop that gun, Kelly."
> The weapon clattered to the floor and the desperado jerked his hands skyward.

Also arrested at the home were Kathryn Kelly; Tichnor, thirty; and S. E. Travis, twenty-six; the latter two charged with harboring fugitives.

In custody, Machine Gun Kelly remained defiant.

"Tell the world I'll be out of this jail before long," the *Daily Oklahoman* quoted him as saying. "He only smiled when asked why he came to Memphis, and refused to say anything when questioned as to the whereabouts of more than $175,000 of the Urschel ransom money which has not been recovered. Kelly had less than $10, his wife less than $7 when they were captured."

Where Mr. Kelly promised escape, his wife played the innocent victim.

Although she, like her husband, had gone to some trouble to conceal her identity ("She wore a red wig," reported the *Oklahoman*. "Kelly had bleached his black hair yellow."), now that she was in custody, it was time to do the acting for the cops and the public that she'd never get to do on the silver screen, time to play the part of a wife terrorized into hiding from the law by her ruthless husband, a woman but hours away from risking it all to see that justice was done. As reported in the *Daily Oklahoman*:

Mrs. Kelly said she wanted to return to Oklahoma to save her parents.

"I was going back tomorrow and give myself up. Kelly told me he would kill me if I did, but I was going anyway.

"I've got nothing to say about that guy," she said when asked about Kelly. "I don't want to have anything more to do with him. He got me into this terrible mess. It's my fault my parents are in this because I married him in the first place. I'm glad for one thing—that we're both arrested. For I'm not guilty and I can prove it, and afterward, I'll be rid of him and that bunch. Day before yesterday was my third wedding anniversary and what a swell anniversary."

The arrest of the Kellys was not without its legends and disputes. Mr. Kelly claimed he'd been unarmed when confronted with the shotgun-wielding lawman. Accounts of his simply dropping his weapon seemed to be particularly galling for a man who got his gangland nom de guerre from a firearm.

And most likely, Machine Gun Kelly didn't shout, "Don't shoot, G-Men!" when confronted by the feds. That detail was reportedly inserted into the historic narrative later by a creative journalist, but the line nevertheless was so famous it became the name by which FBI officers were known thenceforward.

That Mr. Kelly remained defiant in the days after his arrest isn't in question. In fact, a movie about the Urschel kidnapping the FBI created—complete with a reenacted car chase and a dramatic reading of the ransom note—included footage of the Kellys and their fellow kidnappers in court, and showed Mr. Kelly with a lump on his left temple. The injury was explained this way:

Even in the face of almost certain conviction, Kelly maintained his air of braggadocio and nonchalance. This was considerably disturbed, however, by a severe pistol whipping which he received at the hands of one of the federal guards after starting something he couldn't finish. He was warned that at any further show of violence, he would be shot. This warning evidently had the desired effect, because George was very respectful of the federal officers for the balance of the trial. Look at the knot on his head. He has another one on the back, and his yellow-dyed hair was streaked with his own blood as he appeared in court, a wiser and more subdued man.

In the end, the threats and the guns and the wads of cash came to naught, and George and Kathryn Kelly were sentenced to life in federal

A one-couple crime wave whose exploits included bank robberies, kidnappings, and a murder or two, ended in a courtroom in October 1933, when Kathryn and George "Machine Gun" Kelly were sentenced to life in federal prison. *Photographer unknown; public domain image.*

prison. So were her mother and stepfather. In all, about a dozen people went to jail for their roles in the kidnapping of Urschel or for helping cover up the crime.

The Urschel kidnapping was reportedly launched by the Kellys as a do-over for the financially unsuccessful Woolverton kidnapping, but it was a failure for another reason: it was the first abduction prosecuted under the Federal Kidnapping Act. The case, further, proved to be a spectacular win for J. Edgar Hoover and his fledgling FBI, and it served as the beginning of the end of the crime of stealing people for money.

22

The End of an Era

WHERE THE NEWSPAPERS USED to be full of encouraging stories about kidnapping as a means to quick riches, the Urschel tale offered a different narrative. The new law meant the feds would get involved, they'd distribute lists of the ransom cash serial numbers, and they'd go after everyone, everywhere, not just those directly involved in the snatching.

Kidnap someone, and the money is useless, the G-men are hot on your trail wherever you go, and the people you thought were your friends don't want anything to do with you, no matter where they live when you come knocking.

By the mid-1930s, the great American kidnapping era was all but finished. The Kidnapping Crescent could turn its attention to better things, and Americans could dream again, striving, succeeding, achieving.

No longer did the respectable and the well-to-do have to look over their shoulders, wondering if this would be the day they got blindfolded and shoved to the floor of a black sedan, or woke up to an empty crib, or waited at home for a child who would never return.

Official kidnapping statistics can be hard to come by. The taking of one's own children in a domestic dispute can constitute kidnapping, as does holding an ex-spouse or lover for emotional reasons. Some kid-nappings are done to make a political statement or for revenge. Even in kidnapping for profit, there are several kinds—forcing a stranger to drive to an ATM, for example, versus the variety of kidnapping focused on in this book: the premeditated abduction of a wealthy victim and their imprisonment for a ransom. Search law enforcement databases, and things get jumbled.

By one measure of the crime, however—mentions of the word *kidnap* in newspapers across America—the trajectory stands out in dramatic fashion.

According to a search of the newspapers.com database in October 2020, there were 13,982 uses of the word *kidnap* (including variations such as *kidnapers, kidnaping, kidnapping,* etc.) in American newspapers in 1928, a figure consistent with each of the preceding ten years. The next year saw a slight decrease, to 13,680 appearances of the word. In the first full year of the Great Depression, 1930, there were 16,759 appearances of the word. Another slight uptick occurred in 1931, to 18,367 appearances.

And then the dam burst. In 1932, *kidnap* and its derivations appeared 48,028 times, more than doubling the previous year's count. In 1933, the count increased another 40 percent, and in 1934 and 1935, the number of appearances rose almost 30 percent compared to 1933's tally, to more than 85,000 occurrences in each of those two years.

By the marginally scientific method of counting uses of the word in the nation's newspapers, those years—1934 and 1935—marked the high-water mark of references to that particular crime and, presumably, to instances of the crime itself and its aftermath, such as arrests and trials.

And then, with that 1932 federal law on the books and the subsequent gearing up of Hoover's antikidnapping program, appearances of the word started falling precipitously, to 57,571 in 1936, and continuing a steep decrease until 1941, when the nation's newspapers used the word *kidnap* and its derivatives 9,814 times, an almost 90 percent drop from the peak of six years before.

Over the coming decades, there would be other spikes in the word's usage among the nation's papers. The 1970s saw one jump. *Kidnap* and its derivatives reached just over 56,048 in 1974, before another fall. Appearances of the word peaked again at 47,406 in 2002 before falling steadily to an annual count of below or just above 10,000 between 2013 and 2020.[1]

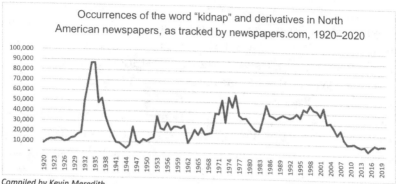

Occurrences of the word "kidnap" and derivatives in North American newspapers, as tracked by newspapers.com, 1920–2020

Compiled by Kevin Meredith

Kidnapping, then, like any crime pattern in the United States, remains cyclical and follows gradual trends—except for the 1930s, when a pronounced spike was followed by a remarkable bottoming out. The Depression was still raging in the mid-1930s, so we can't cite an economic easing for the precipitous drop in that era. No, the credit must go to the federal forces brought to bear against kidnappers, and the Congress that gave them the law to do it, and the high-profile victims—including Howard Woolverton—who forced the passage of that new law in 1932.

Thus restored, America got down to the business of making the modern world. Medicine, television, music, the internet, cell phones, computers, an uncountable array of essential software programs, patents, and remarkable discoveries—these were the creations of a fearless, optimistic people, a people who changed not only their nation but the world, exporting their ideas, their technologies, their example, and growing wealthy in the process—sometimes fabulously so—without ever giving a dime to get free, to escape torture, to get a loved one back.

It was this spirit that won World War II, that won the Cold War, and that continues to inspire the world today.

Thank you, Howard Woolverton.

Should anyone have doubted America's new resolve to crush the kidnapping epidemic, the postconviction lives of the Kellys served as ample notice.

Kathryn Kelly never stopped imagining something better for herself in the days after her sentencing, her stillborn dreams as strange and misbegotten as her deeds had been before incarceration.

The woman who reportedly proposed that Charles Urschel be murdered instead of freed, who probably killed her third husband, and who turned on her fourth husband as soon as she was arrested set about trying to win America's heart as she began her life sentence.

Her charm campaign included posing for a photographer—twice, at least—while still adjusting to prison life.

One such image appeared in the *Medford (Oregon) Mail Tribune* on October 29, 1933. Mrs. Kelly was shown seated in a rocking chair, plainly dressed, holding a needle and working on a garment in her lap. The caption read, "Mrs. Kathryn Kelly, wife of 'Machine Gun' Kelly, is shown as she took up the life of a workhouse inmate in the Cincinnati prison where she began a life sentence for her part in the kidnaping of Charles F. Urschel. Sewing and knitting is the lot of women prisoners there."[2]

In a second image, published widely on the same date, including by the *News and Observer* of Raleigh, North Carolina, Mrs. Kelly was seated behind a basket of flowers, or a cardboard cutout and paper blossoms meant to look like a basket of flowers, it's hard to tell. She is wearing a simple prison smock and beaming broadly.

"Smiling again despite the bleak prospect of a lifetime behind prison bars," the caption read, "Katherine [sic] Kelly, wife of the notorious 'Machine Gun' Kelly and convicted with him for the Urschel kidnapping, is shown in prison garb as she began her term in the penal institution for women at Cincinnati, O. 'I'll try to be a model prisoner,' was Katherine's promise."

Her husband's dreams, such as they were, included escape, something the authorities were determined not to allow.

"I won't be in the spot long," Kelly announced after his sentencing, according to the October 14, 1933, *New York Times*.

The story included a smidgen of pathos in the scene of the couple's final parting after three years of wedded bedlam:

"Be a good boy," Kathryn told her husband and kissed him through the bars of her cell.

"I will," Kelly responded glumly.

Handcuffs and leg irons were kept on him as he took his seat in the railway coach. Justice Department officials said at Washington Kelly would be confined at Leavenworth only temporarily, and that he would be transferred to the government's new prison for dangerous convicts at Alcatraz Island, off San Francisco, as soon as the prison is ready for use.

It's worth noting here that it wasn't until February 1934—four months after the Kellys were shipped off—that Howard Woolverton offered his kidnapping statement to the FBI. Perhaps the peculiar timing of the statement, two years after the crime, was influenced by Woolverton's lingering fears of what happened to snitches that didn't wait until the perps were locked up.

George Kelly never got free, and he followed his wife's instructions, never causing much trouble. So tame became the fearsome Machine Gun Kelly, in fact, that an alternative moniker he'd been given during his trial, "Pop-Gun Kelly," followed him the rest of his life.

That life ended in prison on July 18, 1954.

"A broken and gentle man far different from the swaggering gunman who terrorized the Midwest two decades ago," memorialized the *Daily Oklahoman* on the date of his passing, "he died in the federal penitentiary at Leavenworth, Kan."

He'd been a heart patient in the prison "for some time," the paper said, and it was "coronary thrombosis" that felled him in the end.

How old was he?

Here we have a minor mystery.

Newspaper articles then, and many sources up to the current day, claim Kelly was born on July 18, 1895, meaning he died on his birthday at the age of fifty-nine.

A federal wanted poster issued in August 1933 says Kelly was thirty-five at the time, suggesting a second birthdate, in 1897 or 1898.

However, Kelly's son, Bruce Barnes, gave the date as July 17, 1900, in his book *Machine Gun Kelly: To Right a Wrong*, published in 1991.

A World War I draft registration card filled out in September 1918 for "George Kelley Barnes" and bearing a signature neatly written out as "George Kelly Barnes"[3] also lists July 17, 1900, as Barnes's birthdate, his age as eighteen, and his occupation as "Student."

The card was filled out in Memphis, Tennessee, Kelly's hometown, and names Kelly's father, George Frederick Barnes, as the registrant's nearest relative.

Career criminals lied about things, obviously, and the discrepancies in Kelly's age might be attributed to his own deceptions. But was he already lying about his birthdate when he was twenty-three, trying to pass himself off to the federal draft board as an eighteen-year-old high school student? Probably not.

Mrs. Kelly, who edited a prison newspaper for a time, spent decades incarcerated, but she never stopped pursuing freedom, or stardom, apparently.

It was Hoover's penchant for secrecy (or poor record-keeping, perhaps) when it came to the Kellys that got Kathryn and her mother out of prison after twenty-five years.

Liberation for Kathryn Kelly and Ora Shannon came on June 16, 1958, when new trials were ordered for both women. According to newspaper reports at the time, the pair had claimed that during the Urschel kidnapping trial, their defense attorneys had been investigated by the FBI, and thus were intimidated by the feds while they were trying to keep the women out of prison.

United States District Judge W. R. Wallace ordered the US Department of Justice to turn over their Urschel files, reported the *Daily Oklahoman*, and when the order was ignored, he had the women released on $40,000 bond.

"In the dramatic courtroom scene when the judge's decision was learned," the paper said, "the widow of the late George 'Machinegun' Kelly, kingpin of the $200,000 ransom plot, at first appeared dazed, then burst into tears. U. S. marshals in the courtroom waved down a brief hand-clapping demonstration which followed Judge Wallace's announcement."

Mrs. Kelly, fifty-six, said in her first postprison interview that she learned bookkeeping and other clerical skills while incarcerated and would seek a job to support her seventy-year-old mother.

But one of her employment schemes was quickly shot down.

As reported by the *Daily Oklahoman* on June 19, 1958, "Kathryn Kelly's attorney denied Wednesday that his client will go on the night club circuit to tell of her life since the 1933 kidnaping of Oklahoma City oilman Charles F. Urschel."

Kelly's hint that she might pursue such work had "apparently been misconstrued," said her horrified attorney, James J. Laughlin.

"She has no such thing in mind," Laughlin told the paper. "She is not going to jeopardize her appeal or retrial. She has not thought of any night club circuit."

Mrs. Kelly and her mother never returned to prison, or even to trial. Mrs. Shannon died in 1980, her daughter outliving her by five years. Kathryn Kelly changed her name to Lera Cleo Kelly and lived out her last years in Oklahoma, working quietly as a bookkeeper at a hospital and home for the poor. She died in May 1985, at the age of eighty-one.

The kidnapping of Charles Urschel sent more than a dozen lives spiraling through prison and infamy while it enabled the nascent FBI its first chance to prove the wisdom of a federal kidnapping law—and, by implication, the wisdom of a federal police force.

But why did the Kellys hatch that scheme in the first place?

Because, according to FBI director J. Edgar Hoover, of what happened in South Bend in January 1932.

Hoover gave us part of the story of the Woolverton kidnapping. He couldn't help himself. But he left out one of the most important details, a detail that emerges only now, with the long-buried Woolverton statement.

"That's where they sent my buddy."

—Howard Woolverton, as quoted by his grandson, David Hendry

PART IV

Who Kidnapped Howard Woolverton?

23

The Man with a Cough

IN THE WOOLVERTON KIDNAP story carried by the United Press, the Secret Six agreed to name other victims of the seven "super-criminals," and that's one of the places where the crimefighters' allegations faltered. With the benefits of hindsight, we can conclude that there was no single abduction syndicate, no kidnapping mastermind running everything. The alleged gang of seven was a mirage. The real people-snatchers were, often enough, a single desperate individual or small, independent teams of the antisocial and the opportunistic.

Alex Berg, for example, a wealthy St. Louis furrier who was kidnapped in November 1931, was mentioned by the Secret Six as a victim of the huge kidnapping corporation. By April of 1932, Curtis Medlock, Charles Heuer, Edward Barcune, and George Peak—accused of acting independently of any larger organization—had been convicted of the crime and sentenced to long terms.[1]

Nell Donnelly, a successful fashion designer in Kansas City and one of the few female victims on the United Press list, was threatened with being blinded during her two days of captivity in December 1931. Convicted in 1932 for Donnelly's abduction was another team of go-it-alone entrepreneurs: Martin Depew, Walter Werner, and Charles Mele.[2]

We do find common perpetrators in the kidnappings of two men, identified in the *South Bend News-Times* of January 28, as "James Hackett, Blue Island, Ill., gambler, who paid a reported $200,000" and "James J. (Jack) Lynch, Chicago racing news service owner, (who) paid a reported $30,000."

Both men, authorities were certain at the time, were taken by the gang that came to be known as the College Kidnappers, headed by the infamous "Handsome Jack" Klutas.

So, who kidnapped Howard Arthur Woolverton? The Secret Six said the abduction was ordered by a syndicate, but history demonstrates no such direction was needed in the profession. The FBI said it was Machine Gun Kelly, Eddie Doll, and Kathryn Kelly, and no one else. But was it them? And only them?

Anyone with a bent toward crime, an antipathy toward the well-to-do (a common sentiment in the Depression era), and an eagerness to score cash in well-wrapped bundles, needed to look no further than the nearest newspaper for information about this exciting new business opportunity. Bootlegging had become a crowded and mortally competitive field, and bank robbing wasn't the career it used to be, given all the bank failures around, but kidnapping seemed to be going swimmingly, and helpful advice abounded. In Depression-era America, chapters from the kidnapping for dummies manual were published regularly on the front pages of every daily newspaper, spelling out recommended victim demographics, effective abduction techniques, and, most importantly, the going rate for a job.

What did Howard Woolverton think? While he pleaded ignorance publicly about who'd grabbed him, he seemed to have been more forthcoming in private interviews at the time, and he provided a vital clue toward the end of his federal statement two years later:

> The description of these men: The man who jumped on my running-board and did most of the talking was about 6 feet or possibly a little over, well proportioned, built not stout or thin and well educated. He had a pleasant soft speaking voice using best of English and from the quick glance I had of him on the corner which was not lighted would take him to be from 26 to possibly 32 years of age, fair complexion, neither light or dark. This man I noticed constantly blew through his nose as though he had catarrh, a sort of a hack, in fact, so often that I commented about where he had a cold and he replied, "no, I served the 'god

damned' government in France four months and was gassed and have never recovered." The other man was considerably shorter, about five feet seven or eight in height and much stockier built weighing approximately 150 or 160 pounds. He was darker complexioned and possibly two or three years older, both wore dark rough good looking overcoats with light mufflers, the taller one a black derby hat, the shorter one a gray Fedora, and I believe both wore spats, in fact, they were well dressed. The shorter man did very little talking but spoke good English.

In his statement, then, Woolverton gets us far closer to the identity of one of the kidnappers: he served in the US military, presumably the army, in France during World War I, was close enough to the action to have been subjected to poison gas, and the experience gave him a lasting case of catarrh, or constant buildup of mucus.

This observation narrows the field of suspects down considerably, from any good-looking, well-spoken, midwestern thug to a WWI combat veteran with lingering, obvious health issues. Assuming the kidnapper was being honest about his service, certainly not a given, we can eliminate many suspects. But checking published names against a list of America's World War I soldiers is no easy undertaking. The lists of possible perpetrators published at the time of Woolverton's abduction included aliases, nicknames, misspellings, and errors. John Klutas, for example, was often called Jack Klutas in the press, as well as Jack Klutis and Theodore Klutas. Lining up every published suspect name with World War I service records, which are not necessarily complete or accurate either, quickly becomes an exercise in futility.

It would have been far easier to come up with a short list of viable suspects, of course, had Woolverton shared this recollection publicly as soon as he'd made it home. The police back then, as they do today, kept files on the citizens who made breaking the law a steady habit, and surely military service and continuous hacking would have matched some record somewhere. Had these vital clues been published widely, as they would have if Woolverton had talked immediately and publicly, someone would have come forward, especially if a reward were offered.

But Woolverton, as far as we know, waited two years to say anything to anyone about catarrh and military service, and then did so only in his statement to the feds—a document that was inexplicably buried until now, for reasons we'll get into a little later.

Why didn't he share this most incriminating evidence sooner? For the same reason, we may speculate, that Woolverton scuttled the investigation and did many of the other things he did. Because he knew that if he said anything that got one member of the gang arrested, particularly its leader, those members of the gang still at large could have promptly organized a retribution committee and headed down to South Bend. Woolverton most likely believed the press of the day, certain that his kidnapping had been directed by a large, well-run, multistate syndicate with a brilliant businessman at the helm. Getting revenge on rats, then, would have been an operation as common for such an organization as making a sales call was at any other.

But why did the feds ignore this vital clue? Why did J. Edgar Hoover— as we shall see in just a bit—refuse to divulge any information about the veteran status of this perpetrator? Surely the FBI didn't care that Howard Woolverton was friends with Indiana Secretary of State Frank Mayr, that he was a 32nd degree Mason, that he served on the Indiana Committee of 100, that he was secretary/treasurer of a large manufacturing concern in South Bend.

Most likely, if Judge Farabaugh had called FBI headquarters in Washington, DC, and tried to bluster the bureau into looking the other way, they would have laughed him off the phone.

No, the details that crushed the investigation of the Woolverton kidnapping in Indiana were irrelevant two years later on the federal level.

Other factors were at play, however. Now, almost a century after Woolverton was snatched, not one but two possible new kidnappers emerge, and the FBI's reticence on the subject finally makes sense.

Both were WWI veterans who served in France when the gas was wafting and whose records document injury. Both were on the loose in January 1932.

Both were murderers and robbers, with long, colorful histories of crime. Both were involved in other kidnappings. Both were, in fact, celebrities, remembered today for leading remarkable lives that have yet to be fully explored. This book, in fact, offers new information about both, unearthing the forgotten details of a cold-blooded murder by one, and—with the aid of a World War I historian—casting fresh doubts on the military claims of the other.

And both were close associates of the men Hoover ended up blaming for the Woolverton kidnapping.

No matter who snatched Howard Woolverton and stuck him in a farmhouse basement for one sleepless night, it seems likely the respectable industrialist was in the presence of criminal greatness.

Further, the names of these newly uncovered suspects are linked together in one of the most embarrassing screwups in early FBI history.

And therein, quite possibly, lies the reason the FBI went silent.

24

A Rogue's Gallery of Suspects

WHO KIDNAPPED HOWARD WOOLVERTON?

No one was ever charged with the crime, much less convicted. No one is known to have confessed. So the two new suspects proposed in coming chapters—names concealed for almost a century—must be added to a long list of the bad guys (and a few gals) working the snatch racket in Chicago and the rest of the Kidnapping Crescent around the time Woolverton was grabbed.

John "Handsome Jack" Klutas, king of the band known as the College Kidnappers, comes to mind.

Was John Klutas the "Valentino type" who impressed Mrs. Woolverton, the "tall and clean-cut" man with "a pleasant voice" she spoke of to the papers on the day after the kidnapping?

Klutas was certainly plying his trade in the Chicago area in January 1932. In fact, his gang kidnapped James Hackett twice and defied Al Capone himself when the top gangster ordered Hackett's release during the first kidnapping.[1]

Unfortunately, if Klutas was involved in the kidnapping of Howard Woolverton, he took that secret to his early grave.

Many other names surfaced publicly in the days and weeks after Woolverton was kidnapped.

"The object of the pursuit by police in the Woolverton case is Lee Turner," announced the *South Bend News-Times* on January 28, 1932, "identified by authorities as the leader of a kidnaping gang."

Eight days later, on February 5, the possibilities were expanding—inevitable when there is an utter lack of clues or victim cooperation. As the *News-Times* noted, "Many theories and rumors concerning the kidnaping have been circulated since his return . . . ranging from plausible to absurd and even interweaving the local political difficulties into the affair."

A month after Woolverton's abduction, on February 28, 1932, the *South Bend Tribune* noted in an article datelined in Rochester, Indiana, that two men pleading guilty to charges of forgery the day before had also confessed to involvement in an "extortion plot against Percy Smith, president of the First National bank here."

Smith, the article claimed, "recently had received letters demanding that he place $10,000 and $15,000 in a certain place in a road near Fort Wayne."

"The notes Smith received," the *Tribune* reported, "were said to be almost identical with notes sent the family of Howard Woolverton, South Bend manufacturer, recently, who was held captive by kidnapers."

No further such allegations against these men were published, that lead fading like the rest of them did.

There was also the ad hoc abduction team who grabbed I. C. Kelley, a St. Louis doctor taken in April 1931 and held for a week, in a case with striking similarities to the Woolverton kidnapping nine months later.

Dr. Kelley was at home late in the evening of April 20, 1931, when someone called and asked him to attend to a patient in dire need. When he pulled up to the address he'd been given, a man with a gun got in the car beside him and, as with Woolverton, ordered Dr. Kelley to keep his eyes forward and drive. According to reports of the kidnapping published at the time by the *St. Louis Post-Dispatch* and the *St. Louis Star and Times*, Dr. Kelley was imprisoned in multiple homes, including possibly one in Illinois, and was blinded with goggles that had been taped over (a slight variation of Woolverton's painted or lacquered goggles). The kidnappers added to Dr. Kelley's blindness with a black hood (but they forgot to push him down once, and someone reported spotting a hooded man in the back of a car while Kelley was missing). A machine gun was involved, as with Woolverton, and someone threatened to "smear"

Kelley—or possibly just his front door, the press accounts vary—with it if he talked.

Does being in captivity make one focus on the food one receives? For Woolverton and Dr. Kelley, the answer seemed to be yes. From the police report of Dr. Kelley's kidnapping, published in the *St. Louis Globe-Democrat* on May 2, 1931: "He said they treated him in a friendly way and fed him broiled steaks, very delicious sausage, ham, eggs, etc., and several times offered him liquor, which he refused."

In 1934, a half dozen people were charged with the Kelley kidnapping. Several suspects were already dead, at least one of them believed to have been murdered by others angry about how the Kelley ransom money had been distributed.[2]

Among those charged in Kelley's abduction was a woman, St. Louis socialite Nellie Tipton Muench, who presented another woman's baby as her own during the trial in a bid for lenience. That deception seemed to win enough sympathy from the jury that she dodged the convictions that sent the rest of the suspects to prison, but the baby ruse was found out soon thereafter and eventually earned her and her doctor husband (soon to be ex) ten and eight years, respectively, in the big house.

Did the kidnapping gang that got Dr. Kelley also snatch Woolverton? Their methods were similar to those used against Woolverton nine months later, their number included a woman,[3] and the second ransom note directed them to bring the money to the St. Louis area.

Was it Nellie Muench who called to threaten the Woolvertons? Did Lee Turner grab him? The gang of Jack Klutas? Someone working a political angle?

What did J. Edgar Hoover think?

It turns out the director of the FBI had a lot to say about who kidnapped Howard Woolverton. He named three people: two men and a woman, all of them, conveniently, in prison for life. He wanted credit for locking them up, but he wanted that credit on his own terms, and the peculiar way he shared his allegations about the Woolverton kidnapping raised suspicions at the time and today continues to suggest he was hiding something, orchestrating a coverup that lasted almost a century, because the truth was too embarrassing.

In 1924, J. Edgar Hoover was named director of the Bureau of Investigation, and when that organization became the FBI in 1935, he was still in charge, hanging on to that role until his death in 1972.

It is generally accepted that Hoover pursued his mission zealously, promoting both himself and the Bureau as the best answer to America's criminal scourge.

In the process, he was not above stretching, hiding, or ignoring the truth; taking credit where it was not necessarily due; making unfounded accusations; spying on American citizens who were not suspected of committing a crime; and even storing, for persuasive purposes, the more sordid details from the lives of American politicians and civic leaders from whom he occasionally needed favors.

To the anecdotes illustrating some of these Hoover traits, it seems, we may add the Woolverton kidnapping.

Hoover brought up Woolverton's abduction at least four times in the 1930s, although Woolverton was mentioned only once by name, in October 1935. In that reference, likely the first public accounting by Hoover of the crime, the kidnapping was touched on during a radio program called *G-Men*, a show produced by Phillips H. Lord, with content under Hoover's direct control. On October 12, 1935, in an episode titled "The Case of Eddie Doll," Woolverton was mentioned by name and the kidnappers were publicly identified: Eddie Doll and George "Machine Gun" Kelly.

Two years after that radio show, Hoover put similar allegations in print, in articles published in the *American Magazine* in February and August 1937.

He refrained from naming Woolverton in those articles, oddly, but he added a third kidnapper: Machine Gun Kelly's wife, the infamous Kathryn Kelly.

In his 1938 book *Persons in Hiding*, Hoover repeated allegations from the radio show and borrowed heavily from both magazine stories to present what seemed to be his full and final story of Howard Woolverton's abduction.

According to Hoover, the Kellys got married and traveled the country, mainly the Midwest, running from the law:

> They indulged in new law violations. One of these was the first Kelly kidnapping. It was a bungled job. Kelly and a bank-robbing companion went to South Bend, Ind., from Chicago, where Kathryn and George were staying at one of the big hotels. They looked in the directory and found the name of an influential businessman. Then they shadowed and finally kidnapped him, seeking to obtain fifty thousand dollars.

The ransom notes were hand-printed by Kelly, while Kathryn either directed, edited, or dictated their contents. The victim did not possess the amount of money desired. At last the kidnappers turned the man loose, upon his promise to furnish the money later. Then a conference was called by the kidnappers.

Kathryn Kelly was there as a highly interested principal. The Kelly car had been used to transport the victim. There was the possibility that it might be under surveillance. The Kellys decided to run, and run they did to Kansas City, from which place letter after letter was sent to the kidnap victim, demanding the ransom money. This was before kidnapping had been made a Federal offense.

Recall that Hoover's take lines up with the second ransom note, which instructed Woolverton to drop off $8,000 in well-wrapped cash in Kansas City.

But, Hoover notes, "The efforts failed. The victim did not pay."

In a second passage in the book, Hoover had more to say about Machine Gun Kelly's "bank robbing companion," a man named Eddie Doll, and here he offered up some interesting, possibly dubious, details and got a central fact of the Woolverton kidnapping—how long the man was held—significantly wrong. Hoover said of Doll:

Yet there were many times, when even his wildest efforts at crookedness went for nothing.

There was a kidnapping at South Bend, Indiana for instance, in which he engaged with Machine-gun Kelly, and which was somewhat sketchily described in a previous chapter. They had decided upon an iron manufacturer as their potential victim. While Eddie's wife was left in Chicago, he worked with Kelly in the constant shadowing of their prey until they had catalogued his every action. Then, one night, as the manufacturer and his wife came home, the pair held them up and forced them to drive far into the country, where the wife was released and where the man was bound and his eyes taped. After this, it was necessary to have a hideout. So Eddie Doll, who poses so ably before his wife as an advocate of law enforcement, subjected his own brother to the danger of a penitentiary sentence by using his house to hide the kidnap victim.

Doll, Hoover wrote, had been living under a ruse, telling his wife and family that he was a law enforcement official, and Hoover alleges that Doll explained the kidnapped man's presence as a part of that fable.

"'It's just a fellow who's a witness in a bootleg case,' he told his brother. 'We want to keep him out of the way until the trial's over.'"

Hoover continued erroneously: "The victim was imprisoned in a dark basement for days, while his kidnappers haggled with him over the possibility of ransom and while he insisted that he had no money with which to pay their demands. At last, they released him, threatening death unless he found the money with which to pay them after his return home. Weeks were consumed in waiting, the framing of new demands, long-distance threats by telephone, the naming of meeting spots—all to no purpose. The victim did not pay, and Eddie Doll returned to his wife empty-handed."

Was Woolverton kept in the home of one of Eddie Doll's brothers, or was this another of Hoover's misstatements?

A wanted poster issued by Hoover in January 1934 provided the names and addresses of Eddie Doll's male siblings, both of whom lived in Chicago during the 1930s: Fred Doll at 5816 Navarre Avenue and Harry Doll at 4030 West Lake Street. The Navarre home still stands, a four-bedroom, two-story dwelling built in 1918 that sold for more than half a million dollars in 2020, according to Zillow records published that year. The West Lake Street home has been replaced by a salvage yard. Both homes were city dwellings in the 1930s, neither one the remote farmhouse in Woolverton's federal statement.

Perhaps one of the brothers owned a place in the country, or maybe Hoover was as wrong about where Woolverton was kept as he was about the duration of Woolverton's captivity.

In the next passage of Woolverton's federal statement, he revisits the structure in his memories: "I have never determine[d] where I was held but was told by Mr. Bolte above mentioned that he knew the house at which I was held. If I was ever brought to this place I am positive that I would be able to identify the basement room in which I was held with the four stone walls, dirt floor, and rat holes around the foundation. From the different operators including Mr. Bolte with whom I have talked and described the trip I believe the house was located some where near Kankakee, Illinois, possibly to the South and East."

Mr. Bolte, recall, was mentioned earlier in Woolverton's statement as a former employee of Indiana's Bureau of Criminal Identification, who went on to run a private detective agency.

Almost ninety years after the kidnapping, the record grows thin of homes that Doll's brothers might have owned somewhere west of South Bend. True or false? Who knows?

Was Hoover right about whodunit?

Hoover pointed to George "Machine Gun" Kelly; his wife, Kathryn Kelly; and their bank-robbing buddy Eddie Doll.

These three, according to Hoover, were the final answer to who kidnapped Howard Arthur Woolverton.

Case closed.

No need to file charges, since all three were already safely tucked away in prison on other charges—for life, no less—thanks to the efforts of Hoover and his G-men.

Everyone should have been grateful, but the reporters at the *South Bend Tribune* were not. They were suspicious. They wanted to know more. And they were answered not with, at last, the reassuring evidence that would help the people of South Bend rest at night but instead a continuing wall of silence, represented by a telegram from Hoover himself.

Questions began with the publication of Hoover's February 1937 *American Magazine* article, which received front-page attention from the *South Bend Tribune* on January 16, 1937.[4]

"Woolverton Case Solved?" queried the headline over a story that included this passage: "The Woolverton kidnapping, which threw South Bend into an uproar and attracted the attention of Indiana and Chicago law enforcement authorities, is described without names in Mr. Hoover's magazine article, but the reference to the Woolverton case is regarded as unmistakable. He describes the case as the first kidnaping ever attempted by George (Machine Gun) Kelly and his attractive wife and confederate, Kathryn Kelly."

Doubt seemed to be growing at the *Tribune* the following August, when another *American Magazine* article by Hoover and Courtney Ryley Cooper made a passing reference to the kidnapping.

This article focused on Doll and asserted that he was also there for Woolverton's abduction.

"Hoover Adds New Gangster to Woolverton Kidnaping," announced the headline in the *South Bend Tribune*'s August 17, 1937, edition.

Did the paper believe Hoover? The story beneath the headline fairly dripped with sarcasm: "All the desperate gangsters in the land seem to have been scurrying in and out of South Bend on the night of Jan. 27, 1932," the article began (missing the kidnap date by a day—Woolverton was grabbed late on January 26).

All of them were armed to the teeth and had the same thought in mind—to kidnap Howard A. Woolverton, secretary treasurer of the Malleable Steel Range company. And, strangely enough, most of them succeeded if G-man J. Edgar Hoover has the facts at his fingertips.

In one of his many magazine articles, Mr. Hoover today attributed the kidnaping to Eddie Doll, a mysterious gunman, and George (Machine Gun) Kelly, both of whom are now in prison.

The *Tribune* said it had been alerted to the article by an unnamed subscriber, who attached a note to their copy of the piece, writing: "Mr. Hoover's continued reference to kidnapings of a South Bend manufacturer make it appear everyone here has been kidnaped at least twice. Can you have his ghost writer make it clear only one such case has ever occurred here?"

The newspaper also revealed in the article that, following publication of the January story, it had contacted Hoover directly for more information and had received a prompt, terse reply, from "John Edgar Hoover" himself.

The telegram, dated January 19, 1937, remained in the paper's files until it was passed on to David Hendry. It reads in full: "Reference your telegram of the sixteenth I regret that the confidential nature of the information in our files makes it impossible to disclose further information with respect to the Woolverton kidnapping."

Five years after a man had been very publicly kidnapped and several years after all the alleged perpetrators had been sentenced and confined, what could Hoover have possibly meant by "confidential nature of the information"?

What secrets was he hiding?

And why, we must ask, was Howard Woolverton also ordered to maintain his silence and to tell his extended family the same thing?

As he wrote in the final passage of his federal statement: "Mr. Hartin has advised me that it is absolutely necessary that the investigation of this matter be held in strict confidence and I have advised my relatives to keep this matter quiet and not to divulge any information to anybody concerning this investigation. The above statement is given by me to Special Agent, J. T. Hartin, Division of Investigation United States Department of Justice, and transcribed by Kathryn Allen. The same is true to the best of my knowledge and belief."

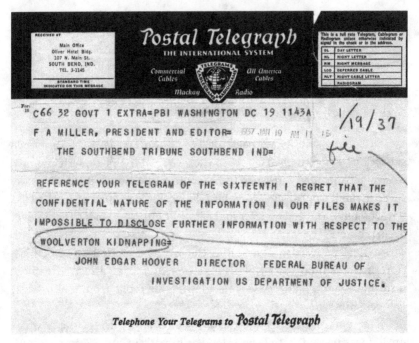

J. Edgar Hoover's mysterious telegram to the *South Bend Tribune*, refusing to divulge any information about the five-year-old kidnapping. *David W. Hendry, Jr.*

Absent charges or any known confession on the part of the Kellys or Eddie Doll, we might, as the *Tribune* had to do, take Hoover's word that the crime couple and their friend kidnapped Howard Woolverton.

We must also take Hoover at his word that Woolverton's abduction inspired a much bigger crime. As Hoover wrote in that February 1937 *American Magazine* article: "Kathryn Kelly did not look upon the flop as a failure. She had seen the real possibilities in kidnapping, their new act, if they played it right."

Thanks at least in part to Howard Woolverton, then, the Kellys' next kidnapping—the final performance of their criminal lives together—would begin on that summer night in 1933, in the Urschel mansion, and prosecution of the crime would provide a critical boost to the perception of the FBI in its first years.

But why would the failed Woolverton kidnapping lead to the Urschel abduction?

Here, we might speculate that the Kellys expected the same behavior from Urschel as they'd enjoyed with Woolverton: the terrified multimillionaire would retreat to his home and deny he'd seen or heard anything.

But Urschel, for some reason unknown to the Kellys, was following a different playbook.

How dare he?

Would the couple have been enraged enough to send their over-the-top missives to Urschel—or written him at all—if they didn't have Woolverton's abject acquiescence as the model of expected behavior? They were likely familiar with the new federal kidnapping law but probably wrote it off as a minor matter. In the lawless land of the Kellys' past experiences, no mere federal statute could protect their wealthy prey from exploitation.

But how sure are we that the Kellys and Eddie Doll were the ones—and the only ones—present for the abduction of Howard Woolverton?

Not even the Kellys' own son, Bruce Barnes, made note of the crime.

Barnes wrote in the preface to *Machine Gun Kelly: To Right a Wrong* that the 1991 book was based on in-person father-and-son meetings at Alcatraz, interviews with family members, and "years of research" through "everything I could find printed about my father." But there is no reference to the Woolverton kidnapping in the work.

Was Hoover being forthright? Did he truly believe Woolverton was kidnapped only by the Kellys and Eddie Doll? Or did he and his FBI have a track record of pretending not to know things once that knowledge became inconvenient?

The odd death of Courtney Ryley Cooper, Hoover's chief collaborationist in the early days of the War on Crime, merits a brief detour.

Cooper, a prolific and successful writer, was Hoover's go-to guy whenever the FBI director needed something in print, a story that needed telling, a tale of Bureau success in the fight against the darkest forces of American crime. His byline appeared on both of those *American Magazine* stories that discussed the Woolverton kidnapping.

Cooper was also a writer of western novels, an essayist, a circus publicist, a moralist, and a Hollywood scriptwriter. He made an estimated $50,000 a year during the Great Depression, an amount equal to almost a million dollars in 2020.

In late September 1940, Cooper and his wife of twenty-four years, the former Genevieve Furey of Los Angeles, checked into the Weylin Hotel in New York City,[5] but on Friday, September 27, he booked a room at the Park Central Hotel,[6] according to the September 29, 1940, *New York*

Times, registering as "C. R. Cooper of the United States Rubber Company, Sebring, Fla."

By Sunday morning, he was dead, his pajama-clad body found hanging from a steam pipe in the closet, his remains identified by his "hysterical" wife. He was fifty-three.

He left a note, which read in its entirety, per the *New York Times* report, "In my clothes is $43 in cash. I think my bill is about $32. Give the hotel $32."

The news stunned his spouse, friends, and colleagues, who hinted at foul play but also tried their hand at guessing why the man would have taken his own life, if indeed he did. The prevailing theory, published in numerous papers after the death, was that he'd uncovered "monkey business" on the part of Nazi Germany in Mexico and had tried to alert Hoover and the FBI, but had been ignored, leading to devastating disappointment.

Mrs. Cooper, according to an Associated Press story, claimed that she'd "told police he had been morose over alleged snubs he had received in Washington when he sought to inform officials of German activities he said he discovered in Mexico."[7]

Her husband, the article said, "had conferred with his close friend and writing collaborator, J. Edgar Hoover. . . . Mrs. Cooper said her husband made an exhaustive investigation in Mexico several months ago and unearthed details of German conditions and propaganda there."

True to form, it might be argued, Hoover and the FBI denied all.

"B. E. Sackett, special agent in charge of the FBI office (in New York), said that neither Hoover nor any other member of the FBI had talked with Cooper about the Mexican matter.

"'We had not seen or heard from him since he returned and we do not know what he did while in Mexico,' Sackett said."

The next sentence of Sackett's statement went further, disavowing Cooper's extensive published work for Hoover and contradicting itself in the process: "Cooper, though a close friend of many of us in the FBI, was in no way connected with the FBI."

Overwork and exhaustion were also blamed by some, as well as the steady psychological toll that might be exacted by researching and writing about crime.

"Cooper always worked too hard when he worked," read one print eulogy, published in the *Los Angeles Times* on October 4, 1940. "He would work all day and then all night and part of the next day without stopping.

He used to write short stories from beginning to end at one sitting. His enthusiasm while the fever was on him carried him irresistibly but was followed by depression. J. Edgar Hoover and the F.B.I. might never have been appreciated as they are if it had not been for Cooper."

Did writing about the kidnapping of that unnamed South Bend manufacturer torment Cooper? Did having to pound out the sordid story of what the Kellys did next trouble the famous author's dreams?

Probably not.

But the kidnapping of wealthy Oklahoma oilman Charles F. Urschel—if not a tale to drive a publicist to suicide—stands out as a gangster-age crime to be remembered, even in an era full of crime, and its successful prosecution remains a bright testament to the clever detective work of Hoover's early FBI.

Hoover could have done worse in naming the Kellys and Eddie Doll as the three, and the only three, abductors of Howard Woolverton.

Each held a special place in American villainy before they were brought down by the feds.

Each represented a laudable success in the early days of Hoover's Bureau, furthermore, so the more crimes Hoover could pin on them, the better. And none of the three were involved in an epic and bloody FBI screwup.

But none of the three were World War I veterans, either, and Hoover accused them in magazine articles and a book, not before a judge and jury in a courtroom. Today, armed with records Hoover possessed but never made public, we may offer our own speculation as to who might have been there on that late January night in 1932.

But what did Howard Woolverton think?

As it turns out, he believed the top G-man.

It was a singular moment in Dave Hendry's life, the only time he can recall his grandfather making any reference to his kidnapping. And the man did so obliquely, offering just a hint before his daughter shushed him.

It was sometime in the mid- to late 1950s, more than two decades after he'd been taken.

Betty Woolverton had grown up. The infant brought into the Woolverton home as part of a hasty and mysterious adoption, the girl who required a police escort to get to school when she was twelve, the subject of such vicious threats from Kathryn Kelly she had to be sent east to school—was now a wife and mother.

Proud father of the bride Howard Woolverton (*far left*) stands beside Betty and her husband, David W. Hendry, Sr., on their wedding day in 1947. On the right is the mother of the groom, Annie McPherson Hendry. *Photographer unknown; David W. Hendry, Jr.*

In 1947, with World War II over, she'd married David Hendry Sr., a navy man she'd met when he came to South Bend to attend 2nd Officers Midshipman's School at Notre Dame.

A decade and a half later, she was living with her family in Piedmont, California, a town across the bay from San Francisco. Her husband, now a navy reservist and naval instructor on Treasure Island in the San Francisco Bay, was also an entrepreneur, running a sprinkler manufacturing company (years later, he would take the reins at the Boye Needle Company as its president and CEO). And the couple had children of their own, including namesake David Hendry Jr.

Woolverton's largesse never waned where his daughter was concerned, the younger Hendry recalled, describing his mother as a "trust fund daughter." Howard Woolverton bought his daughter and her husband their house, with cash. Many years, on his annual visit to the family, he'd buy Betty a new car.

It was during one such visit, sometime between 1956 and 1958—the younger Hendry hadn't quite turned ten—that Woolverton shared a few fateful words with his grandson.

"We were driving across the Bay Bridge, toward San Francisco," Hendry recalled. He and his brother were sitting in the back seat. His father was driving. His grandfather, now a widower, was in the passenger seat, his mother up front as well.

Alcatraz Island, with its infamous prison and its more infamous inhabitants, was clearly visible from the bridge.

"My grandfather leaned over, turned around and was looking at me in the back seat," Hendry recalled, "and he pointed at Alcatraz, and said, 'That's where they sent my buddy.'"

Hendry recalls Woolverton's mood at the moment as jocular, if a little macabre. "He was making conversation, it was light-hearted."

But Betty Woolverton Hendry was not amused.

"My mother scolded him," Hendry recalled. "She said 'Daddy, please, not in front of the children—not a suitable story.'"

When Dave got older, his mother shared her version of the family lore with him, of the kidnapping and its aftermath, but she clearly believed a child younger than ten wasn't ready to hear about gangland skullduggery—even if she already knew what a bootlegger was by the age of three.

But then, she received her introduction to America's underbelly in the early 1920s. By the mid-1950s, the nation was a different place, more genteel, more focused on building, not quite the rough-and-tumble land it had been two decades before.

We may assume that Woolverton knew whereof he spoke that day on the Bay Bridge. He'd seen his kidnappers, despite his initial protestations otherwise. So had Mrs. Woolverton. And when George Kelly became infamous enough in 1933 to get his image published in the newspapers,[8] the Woolvertons must have studied his face.

They must also have paid close attention to the coverage of the Kellys' trial, and several passages in particular must have terrified them. For example, during the Urschel kidnapping trial, George Kelly spotted Urschel, in the courtroom to testify against Kelly and his gang. The *South Bend Tribune* of October 8, 1933, relayed what happened next: "'You'll get yours yet, you—,' the yellow-haired outlaw sneered. Kelly drew his index finger across his own neck in a throat-cutting gesture. Urschel ignored the incident, as an officer quickly hustled the outlaw outside."

Howard Woolverton, during a visit to California in the late 1950s, with daughter Betty and his four grandchildren. Dave Hendry, Jr., is standing on the far right. *Photographer unknown; David W. Hendry, Jr.*

And the *South Bend Tribune* of October 18, 1933, included this promise from Kathryn Kelly as she was taken to prison to begin her life sentence: "George will see me at Christmas. He told me he would break out Christmas and get me out. He always does what he says he will."

The Woolvertons might never have been completely certain about the rest of the kidnappers, however. And it must also be called peculiar that Woolverton did not, in his federal statement, offer a confirmation that it was Machine Gun Kelly who'd abducted him.

But Woolverton did leave us that clue, about a World War I veteran with catarrh, someone who'd served four months in France and been gassed.

Before we consider the two names conjured by that vital clue, we must consider one last name, that of Joseph Barrett. At one time, authorities were certain he was guilty of the Woolverton kidnapping, his story offering another round of twists and turns in a tale full of them.

25

A Ghastly Meeting

A BRIEF, ODD ITEM appeared on page ten of the April 18, 1932, edition of the *Times*, a newspaper in Streator, Illinois.

"Man Is Shot At Lemont Cockfight," announced the headline, referring to a small town on the western edge of Chicago.

"Shot at a cockfight staged in a roadhouse near Lemont," began the story, "Joseph Barrett, 34, of Chicago Heights, was in a hospital here today in critical condition."

The second and final paragraph of the story reads, "While his two women companions were watching the fight Barrett was called outside by a man identified only as 'Roy.' A shot was heard, and the girls ran outside to find 'Roy,' gun in hand, standing over Barrett. The gunman fled in an automobile."

Cockfighting, a battle to the death between roosters now outlawed in all fifty states for cruelty and general bad taste, wasn't the sort of thing respectable men watched or gambled on in the 1930s, but Joseph Barrett was no minor rascal. Five days after news of his shooting was published, and three months after the Woolverton kidnapping, Barrett would be identified, with his brother James, as the leader of a gang of hoodlums. And not just any bad guys.

The gang, authorities were certain, was guilty of twenty-nine bank robberies and at least one abduction: the kidnapping of Howard Woolverton, described in the *Chicago Tribune's* April 23, 1932 report of the arrests as "one of the most daring in Indiana history."

The roundup of the Barrett gang was another project of Patrick Roche, chief investigator for the Illinois state's attorney's office, as well as unnamed Indiana officials who, we might imagine, were still smarting over that scathing *Chicago Tribune* editorial and the kidnapping that provoked it.

"For several months," the *Chicago Tribune* announced in a front-page story on April 23, "Roche and Indiana authorities worked together to seize the gang. Last night was chosen for one grand capture. Half a dozen restaurants, among them the Coney Island, and Columbia, in Chicago Heights, were visited. Homes were entered. In one place one of the men tried to flee, but a bullet from Sergt. Capparelli's revolver pierced his hat and halted him."

"'We suspect this gang of holding up twenty-nine banks,' Roche told the *Tribune*. 'Two of the men, James and Joseph Barrett, we are positive were in on the kidnaping of Howard A. Woolverton of South Bend. Mr. Woolverton will look at them for identification.'"

What made Roche so certain? "Confessions implicating the 13 in the kidnaping of Woolverton were made by . . . other members of the alleged gang," who were arrested on bank robbery charges and identified in the article as "two men and two women . . . already in custody in Racine, Wis., and Hartford City, Ind."

Roche's continuing pursuit of Woolverton's abductors might come as a surprise, given he had said in the first few days after the kidnapping that Woolverton's refusal to cooperate meant he had no choice but to wash his hands of it.

Roche, however, dedicated lawman that he was, couldn't walk away from the crime, it seems, particularly after he learned that Woolverton had been dropped off in Roche's hometown of Chicago by the kidnappers. According to the *South Bend Tribune*, Roche "has personally been directing a systematic investigation into the Woolverton case."

But Roche hit a snag. While their confederates in other cities might have been talking, none of the thirteen Chicago arrestees confessed to kidnapping Woolverton, despite "being grilled for hours by Roche and his assistants."

So Howard Woolverton, one of the kidnapping era's most famously recalcitrant witnesses, was going to have to get involved.

And so was his wife, whether or not her involvement would be publicly acknowledged.

It was a peculiarity of the times that women were treated more or less as second embodiments of their husbands.

Florence Flannery Woolverton was usually referred to publicly by her husband's name, and when something happened to them both, it would often enough be described as something only Howard experienced.

But while some press accounts of the day suggested that only Howard Woolverton had been compelled to go to Chicago to look at a baker's dozen of thugs and ne'er-do-wells, other reports confirmed that Florence went too, and almost a century later, her quiet courage still resonates through a single published anecdote.

The Woolvertons weren't going to Chicago to look at the Secret Six's widely described but most likely imaginary midwestern kidnapping syndicate. The group of arrestees seemed to be entirely self-contained, its headquarters in Chicago only, without additional corporate offices in "Detroit and St. Louis," and without top leadership from a "highly capable business executive."[1]

The Woolvertons weren't going to visit with a gaggle of small-time punks either.

"The operations of the gang spread into all parts of the four states which covered their territory," the *Chicago Tribune* stated, adding that the gang had both the capital and the spunk to operate an "allegedly fake pawnshop."

"According to Roche," the story said, "the gang would return after a robbery and deposit their weapons in the shop. The guns would be tagged with pawn tickets, throwing detectives off the trail."

But now the cops were wise to the group's methods. The article declared: "The gang's arsenal was seized."

In its April 24 story on the arrests, the *Indianapolis Star* (and the *Chicago Tribune*) put the number of those nabbed at fourteen, not thirteen, and attributed "a dozen kidnappings" to the group, not just Woolverton's.

When it came to Woolverton's viewing of the alleged crooks, the *Star's* coverage was typical, ignoring the presence of Florence but noting that Frank Mayr went, perhaps in the hopes of publicly atoning somewhat for his investigation-crushing work of three months before.

"The first witness to view the prisoners was Howard A. Woolverton, wealthy manufacturer of South Bend, Ind., who was kidnaped two [*sic*: three] months ago. Woolverton scrutinized the alleged desperadoes at a 'show up' and said one suspect 'looked a little like' one of his abductors."

Woolverton and Mayr, the article said, "spent considerable time at the Criminal Courts building and at the hospital where Joseph Barrett is confined. Mario Ranieri, 24, was the prisoner who Woolverton said 'looked like' one of his abductors, although he believed the kidnaper in question was a trifle taller than Ranieri. Special attention also was paid by Woolverton to Tony Lungo, 21; John D. Mascio, 29, and James Barrett, on whom authorities said they had evidence of the kidnaping."

It wasn't just Mr. Woolverton and Mayr there, however. The *Chicago Tribune* was one of the few papers reporting that Florence Woolverton also went to Chicago to look at the crooks, and her courage shone through.

The April 24 article stated that the Woolvertons

went from the Criminal court to the Barrett home,[2] where another of the brothers, Joseph Barrett, was under guard, recuperating from a bullet wound suffered a week ago last night in a cock fight near Lemont, Ill.

His face swollen and discolored by infection from his wound, Barrett was difficult to recognize. Woolverton was certain he had never seen him before. Mrs. Woolverton, recalling the cultivated accent of the kidnaper who sent her for the ransom, asked Barrett to speak. The prisoner uttered a few words in broken English. The couple departed, feeling doubtful that Barrett was one of the kidnapers.

Florence Flannery Woolverton, "Illinois Belle" and a "great favorite" wherever she set foot, had been brought to this: going to Chicago to converse with a thug, his face grossly discolored and disfigured by a mysterious shooting at a cockfight.

The fact that she went at all, that she endured the presence of this ghoulishly injured criminal, that she told him to speak, and he did so— these small but courageous strikes against the kidnapping scourge by a refined member of the upper crust should not be forgotten.

Florence Woolverton, like many women appearing in the press at that time and even to this day, was probably not so frail as her portrayals in print.

But in the end, it was all for naught.

"That Howard A. Woolverton will take the stand and testify against any of the gang of alleged kidnapers and bank robbers held in Chicago as his abductors, appeared unlikely Saturday night," reported the *South Bend Tribune* on April 24, 1932, "when it became known that at a 'show-up' in the detective bureau in Chicago during the afternoon, he failed to identify any of the prisoners."

The *Tribune* continued: "In the absence of a positive identification by Mr. Woolverton or Mrs. Woolverton, and in the absence of confessions from the kidnapers themselves, it appeared improbable that any of them will even be placed on trial for the crime."

The fact that Mr. Woolverton took a hard look at some of the suspects, in particular Mario Ranieri, who he said resembled his abductor but was too short, created a discrepancy, and the *South Bend Tribune* hinted as much, stating delicately that it seemed Woolverton had been less than honest about his experiences as a kidnap victim three months before: "This is the first intimation to come from Woolverton that he saw any of his captors. He had let it be known previously that he had been blind-folded during the 24 hours of his captivity and that even if he met them face to face, he would not know them."

So, Patrick Roche couldn't make the kidnapping charges stick, but he had better luck with the bank robbery charges, moving to trial on those counts.

Gang leader James Barrett dodged prosecution there as well, how-ever. On the night before the trial began for bank robbery in June 1932, Barrett used his belt to hang himself in his jail cell.[3]

But what of his brother?

A Joseph Barrett was still alive five years later, according to a short item that appeared in the *Alton (Illinois) Evening Telegraph* on August 30, 1937:

> Assistant U.S. District Attorney Martin Ward said Miss (Betty) Win-ston, Joseph Barrett, and James Mabry Albin were arrested in connec-tion with an investigation by agents of the Federal Bureau of Investiga-tion of an alleged white slave ring.
>
> Barrett and Albin were arrested two weeks ago in Louisville, Ky., on conspiracy charges. They were held under bond for the grand jury. Miss Winston was arrested at the supposed Joliet headquarters of the ring.

The term *white slavery* referred to any transporting of a woman across state lines for immoral purposes, either for prostitution or merely the conducting of an affair.[4]

The feds alleged that Joseph Barrett's white slavery ring "operated in a number of Illinois towns and in Louisville."

Perhaps it was the same man, the bereft brother of James, rededicating himself to vice in remembrance of his sibling. If it was that same Joseph Barrett, he seemed to have dodged those earlier charges and overcome his injury, but not his penchant for breaking the law.

Barrett was never charged with kidnapping Howard Woolverton. No one was ever charged with the crime. We may assume that Machine Gun and Kathryn Kelly and their friend Eddie Doll were in on it, given Hoover's repeated allegations and Woolverton's own veiled corroboration of at least Mr. Kelly's participation.

But almost a century after the crime, Woolverton's mention of a World War I veteran leads to the names of others who may have been involved as well.

26

Frank Nash Gets Revenge

SOMETIME FRIDAY NIGHT OR Saturday morning on March 24 or 25, 1911, four businesses in the tiny town of Gotebo, Oklahoma (population 740), were burglarized.

The burglars focused on the safes at several of the stores, including the Wedel hardware store and the Dixie dry goods store.

"The Dixie store was opened from the rear and some change was taken from the money drawer," reported the *Gotebo Gazette* of March 31, 1911. The safe was also attacked. "The dial knob was pulled out and the handle broken off, but the job was the work of amateurs who had not sufficient knowledge, apparently, to finish the work of getting inside.

"The safe in the Wedel store was similarly treated, and with negative results. Just above the dial on this safe the combination was written in pencil, but if it was noticed the thieves failed to work it properly."

The crime was front-page news, an unusual and major event in little Gotebo, and not something the local police would brush past. Fortunately for the cops, the incompetence of these burglars ran deep.

A search of the area quickly turned up a stash of burgling tools "near the barn back of the Shaw lot on main street."

The equipment included wrenches, a crowbar, and a device for opening safes: "a triangle, a burglar's tool for pulling knobs by means of set screws."

With this last clue, reported the *Gazette*, "Deputy Sheriff W. Z. Smith took the trail. He found a blacksmith at Hobart[1] who claims to have made the triangle for a person called 'Humpy' Wartman, a well-known Hobart character with a police record" who "had no visible means of support and was credited with being a gambler."

Wartman was promptly arrested, as was his close friend, Guy Huber. Both denied any knowledge of the crimes, and Huber was subsequently released. But Wartman—clearly connected to the crime by the triangle—was tried and pled guilty two months later, in May 1911.

Facing a trip to the penitentiary, Nollie "Humpy" Wartman made a fateful decision. According to the May 25, 1911, edition of the *Weekly Democrat Chief* of Hobart, Wartman decided to name his accomplices in the burglaries: "Humpy Wartman was the only one to get convicted and it is said that on last Sunday he concluded to tell on the other boys. It is also stated that he went before the grand jury and told all. He felt that he was getting the worst of it from the other boys, so he 'peached.'"

Based on Wartman's grand jury testimony, Guy Huber was arrested again, as was a second person whose name hadn't come up before: Frank Nash, the twenty-four-year-old son of successful hotelier John "Pappy" Nash.

Frank Nash was a native of Indiana, born in Birdseye in 1887. He was also a veteran, having served in the US Army from 1904 to 1906, according to military records.

And he was a burglar, not just by accident or opportunity but apparently as a deliberate career choice.

Around 1910, at the age of twenty-three, he'd been charged with burglary in Oklahoma's Comanche County and had come to Hobart while on bail, where he'd "made many friends by his jovial way," according to the September 4, 1913, issue of the *Hobart Republican*.

Once in Hobart, he fell in with Guy Huber and Humpy Wartman, already close friends themselves.

But their decision to burgle businesses in nearby Gotebo, Huber's hometown, would prove to be their tragic undoing. Facing a long prison term, Wartman had been promised leniency if he turned on his accomplices, and so he did. Nash and Huber were arrested two months after the Gotebo burglaries, in May 1911, and they responded by lawyering up. The resulting trial two months later was described in the *Hobart Republican* of July 27, 1911, as "one of the most spectacular trials ever held in Hobart."

Under the headline "Huber and Nash Trial Attracting Large Crowd," the paper spoke of the defendants' "large array of counsel," and when Wartman took the stand against his former friends as the trial's star witness, "County Attorney Terral then began to unravel one of the deepest laid plots ever unfolded in any court in this county."

It is difficult, with more than a century having passed since the burglaries, not to find humor in the paper's earnest coverage: They'd broken into the Dixie dry goods store, the paper reported Wartman as testifying, and

> after each had attempted to work the combination and had failed, Frank Nash then put the triangle on the dial. . . . All three worked on the dial before it was finally broken off, and when it broke off instead of pulling out, when it did come out Nash expressed himself as being very much surprised at it having done so.
>
> They then attempted to drive the bolt through the safe. In this attempt to drive the bolt back they failed.
>
> Frank saw a black cat as they went to the lumber yard, and Guy said that it must be an unlucky night for them.

After the burglaries, Wartman testified, Nash went back to his room at Ma's hotel in Hobart, and Wartman and Huber went to stay at Huber's mother's home in Gotebo, where "they were awakened about 9 or 10 o'clock the next morning by Guy's mother who told them that the whole town had been robbed and that they were suspected of having committed the crime."

Wartman testified that dynamite had also been part of the plot, claiming under oath that, at Nash's urging, he went to Gotebo the day before the burglaries and got a friend to buy three sticks of dynamite, along with fuse and caps, for a total of sixty-five cents.

The explosives and accoutrement were turned over to Nash.

"When he returned to Hobart with the dynamite," Wartman testified, "Nash suggested they could dynamite Lyon & Matthews hardware store and make a good haul, but Wartman said he did not care to do this, and Nash said all right, they would go with the other deal."

Without a need for the dynamite, Nash hid it—poorly—at his hotel, according to the testimony of hotel proprietress, Mrs. O'Hara: "With reference to the dynamite she stated that she found the dynamite at her house on Friday before the robbery that night and that she put it out on the back porch (and) at that time she did not know what it was, that on Saturday she found out what it was and that she then called the marshal down there, and he came down and eat supper there and they talked about the dynamite. She did not know who brought it in there or how it got there."

In return for his testimony against Huber and Nash, Wartman went free. Wartman's testimony wasn't particularly compelling, however. The jury acquitted Nash and Huber, setting them free as soon as the trial was over, after a few months' inconvenience in the county jail.

After the trial, Wartman left town for Wichita Falls, Texas, a hundred miles south of Hobart. He should have stayed there, but he got homesick and in early 1913 moved back in with his mother and stepdad, at their farm north of Hobart.

But the farm still wasn't close enough to his old haunts, apparently.

As chronicled in the *Hobart Republican* in stories published on the front page on March 13, 1913, Wartman woke up on March 5 and "felt depressed and was seized with an uncontrollable desire to come to Hobart."

On returning to Hobart proper, Wartman immediately met up with some of his erstwhile buddies, including Frank Nash and Guy Huber.

Despite Wartman's decision to fink a year and a half earlier, there were no hard feelings, it seemed. That evening, a gaggle of young men, including the three burglars, "concluded they would have a little celebration, and to do so procured a quart of whiskey and made a bowl of punch. They drank that, and not being satisfied, got a pint more and drank that, and then another pint."

Satisfactorily pickled at last, the gathering broke up, and Wartman went to a pool hall where Huber later found him and "gave a signal to follow—a signal known only to a certain clan."

Once outside the pool hall, Huber told Wartman he had stolen $1,600 in silks and needed help fencing them. Given that the value of the goods in 2020 dollars was over $40,000, and Wartman stood to gain a decent share of the proceeds for a little work peddling the fabrics back in Wichita Falls, he was in.

As Huber and Wartman walked along a Hobart railway to retrieve the goods from their remote hiding place, Frank Nash happened along.

Now it was just the three of them—Humpy Wartman the snitch, and the two snitchees.

The trio stopped in an out-of-the-way spot not far from the town's sandpit. Nash told Wartman the silks couldn't be retrieved just yet because others were around.

What did they do for light? It was well past dark by this time, the moon the merest sliver, but the weather was clear, affording some starlight. Maybe they lit a fire, a sensible choice with the low for the date in the mid-thirties. The lights of Hobart had been turned off that night due to a dispute between the city and "the electric light people," according to the March 6, 1913, *Hobart Republican*, necessitating lanterns. Maybe the boys had one of those to illumine what happened next.

In trial testimony reported in the *Weekly Democrat Chief* of May 29, 1913, the three decided to discuss the matter of the stolen silks, and they "went over into a field and sat down in a circle, with Huber on (Wartman's) left and Nash on his right side; that while talking, (Wartman) was hit or shot and lapsed into unconsciousness; that when he regained consciousness he found that he was bleeding and cried for help."

The *Hobart Republican*'s March 13, 1913, edition adds more details, stating that it was around midnight that Wartman was "shot at close range with a 32 or 38 caliber pistol, the ball entering the right temple and coming out over the left eye. It is evident that he was shot at short range and by other hands than his own, for the right side of his face is badly powder burned, and there was no pistol upon his person or elsewhere that would tend to prove an attempt at self-destruction."

The bullet just missed Wartman's brain, and he didn't die.

Not then.

Wartman, when he came to, cried out, "Frank, Frank," according to one witness. Two farm boys returning from a show heard him and brought him to the Paul Hotel in Hobart, where he had a room. Someone thought to call a doctor, and the police got involved.

But Humpy Wartman, who snitched on his friends in 1911, refused to talk this time. As reported by the *Hobart Republican*: "His statements as to how he came by the wound are not at all clear. In fact he insists that he was not shot. He says he left town and walked down the railroad, and after leaving it near the place where the shooting occurred he met two men, one of whom asked for a match, and while he was accommodating him the other one struck him on the head."

The sheriff's office searched the scene of the crime and found Wartman's hat, "a bloody cloth," and two pairs of footprints that faded out. Bloodhounds were summoned but couldn't follow the trail.

"The officers are making a heroic effort to run the matter to earth, but there is so little to work from that it is doubtful if they will succeed, unless Wartman should divulge the secret which he is guarding so carefully."

He was no more forthcoming with the surgeons than the police. Just before he was put under for surgery on his wounds, he was warned that he "might not survive the ordeal" and should consider spilling the beans on his assailants.

Wartman replied that he "guessed he'd come through all right."

The *Hobart Republican* noted that "even his mother could not induce him to make a confession."

But Sheriff Lewis Terry had an idea. They'd gone through Wartman's clothes and found the name of his sweetheart, a girl named Viola Carson, whom he'd met while in Wichita Falls, Texas.

If we brought your honey to town, the sheriff asked the injured young man, would you tell your story to her?

Wartman agreed, the girl was brought, and on March 8, three days after he'd been shot, Wartman told her who'd done it, how, and when.

Frank Nash and Guy Huber were promptly arrested.

Still blind but recovering, it seemed, Wartman returned to Wichita Falls with Carson over his mother's objections. He died there a few weeks later, on March 28, of an infection and a blood clot on the brain, his Viola still by his side.

Charges against Guy Huber and Frank Nash were immediately upgraded to murder. This time, although it was presented posthumously in court, Wartman's testimony stuck.

Less than three months after the shooting, the twenty-year-old Huber dodged the death penalty but was sentenced to life.

"Huber's face, blanched from several months confinement in the county jail, was even whiter," reported the *Gotebo Gazette* on May 29, 1913. "He paled as the clerk read the verdict."

Nash had to be tried twice because the jury couldn't reach agreement the first time, but in August, at the age of twenty-six, a second jury reached its decision.

At 8:30 Saturday morning, August 30, Nash was brought from the jail to learn if his peers would find him guilty, and, if so, if they would sentence him to death or life in prison.

Facing the prospects of exoneration, execution, or permanent incarceration, "Nash was brought in, bright and cheerful as on every day of this trial and the preceding one," reported the *Hobart Republican* on September 4, 1913.

In fact, a sunny disposition seemed to follow Nash no matter his circumstances, the paper asserted.

"During Nash's confinement in the county jail he has been a model prisoner, always cheerful, and especially to the other unfortunates with whom he is surrounded."

After Huber had been sentenced to life two months earlier and brought back to the jail, the paper noted, "Nash was the only one to offer him words of cheer, and told him not to mind such a little thing as a life sentence."

Now Nash had come to hear his own fate, recounted the *Hobart Republican*. The jury of twelve men found him guilty of murder and sentenced him to "imprisonment in the state penitentiary for life."

Nash's response? In a word, aplomb.

"During the reading of the verdict, occupying but a few seconds time, Nash steadily gazed at the jurymen, and without a change of countenance or waver of eyelid, took the verdict as an every day occurrence."

One important question remained, however, that had not been settled by the jury.

While Frank Nash and Guy Huber were both convicted of the murder of Humpy Wartman and received the same sentence, only one of them could have pulled the trigger.

Which one did it?

Frank Nash, most likely. Recall that the bullet entered Wortman's right temple, and Nash was seated at Wartman's right when the three sat down to discuss retrieval and resale of the stolen silks.

Nash, further, as a soldier in the army for two years during the preceding decade, had presumably more experience with firearms than Huber.

Nash's assignment as the gunman also makes sense from the perspective of division of labor.

We might imagine Nash and Huber marveling over the reappearance of Wartman in Hobart that day in March, and the opportunity it presented to serve a little cold vengeance on the turncoat. After some discussion, the two presumably agreed that Huber, who had been the better friend of Wortman, would summon him from the pool hall and get him to a remote area, where Nash would serve as the triggerman.

The fact that the bullet missed Wartman's brain entirely and came out over his left eye is telling. While bullets can do odd things on encountering bone and passing through tissue, ricocheting this way and that, we might guess that the pistol was not placed perpendicular to Wartman's temple, where he might have noticed it out of the corner of his eye. Instead, it was fired slightly from behind, at an angle, Nash's trembling hand probably inches in front of Wartman's right ear.

That was that, then: one young life cut short, a mother and a lover bereft, two other young men sent up the proverbial river.

But if you assumed Guy Huber and Frank Nash lingered in prison for decades and perhaps died there, you would be underestimating Frank Nash.

Frank Nash and Guy Huber, sentenced to life in prison in 1913 for the cold-blooded revenge killing of Humpy Wartman, were freed by the governor of Oklahoma five years later, an act of commutation reported in papers around the state in April 1918.

While America has never made it a practice to release murderers wholesale to serve in the military, it appears that was the condition of Nash's release, as he promptly signed up and was shipped off to France.

The reason for Huber's release is more difficult to ferret out. Perhaps Nash's preternatural good cheer and persuasive abilities got both the men free, although only Nash went on to fight.

From that day forward, Huber went straight, reverting to his full given name, William Guy Huber, and going to work for the Oklahoma Publishing Company, a newspaper firm.

William G. Huber lived to sixty-one, dying of a heart attack at the dining table in Edmond, Oklahoma, July 1954.

According to his obituary, published in the *Daily Oklahoman* of Oklahoma City on July 5, 1954, he'd been a member of the Methodist Church and the Elks club, and left behind a wife, a daughter, and two grandchildren.

Frank Nash went straight as well, but only briefly. There would be crime galore and quite possibly one or two kidnappings, including one in South Bend, Indiana, in January 1932. But first, he had to serve his country.

By the time Nash got out of prison, World War I had been going for four years, since 1914. America joined the conflict in 1917, and able-bodied soldiers were at a premium for the rest of the war.

Frank Nash, with previous military experience, would have been an especially desirable enlistee, and a murder conviction might not have given the recruiters much pause, given the nature of war.

Now, recall Woolverton's description of the kidnapper who jumped on his running board: "This man I noticed constantly blew through his nose as though he had catarrh, a sort of a hack, in fact, so often that I commented about where he had a cold and he replied, 'no, I served the 'god damned' government in France four months and was gassed and have never recovered.'"

Does this part of Woolverton's narrative line up with Frank F. Nash's history?

Yes.

On March 16, 1919, the USS *George Washington* sailed out of Brest, France, carrying members of the Le Mans Casual Company Number 1230. Casual companies were formed from soldiers injured or incapacitated in the war.

Among those on the ship: Frank F. Nash, a private in the infantry, with an address listed as "Nash Hotel, Hobart Oklahoma." The hotel was most likely owned by Nash's father.

Nash's second draft registration was filled out in June 1918, five months before the end of the war, and he left France in March 1919, four months after Armistice. Was gas used in France in the waning months of WWI? Yes. The Hundred Days Offensive comes to mind, a series of allied victories in France that overcame gas attacks launched from weakening German lines.

Now, was Nash in the Chicago area in early 1932? And did he consort with the Kellys?

Yes, on both counts.

But how Frank Nash ended up in Chicago, how we know he was there, and the reasons the FBI never mentioned him as a possible kidnapper, are questions that add new twists to the already very twisted tale of the kidnapping of Howard Arthur Woolverton.

Trouble is also a recurring theme of the story.

Within months of his return to America, Frank Nash was again earning police attention.

Early on Saturday, October 18, 1919, three men held up the Korn State Bank in Corn, Oklahoma, blasting open the safe with dynamite and leaving with $1,262.75 worth of bonds and savings stamps.[2]

Later that day, the three were arrested as they waited for a ferry to bring them and their car across a river near the crime scene.

The stolen securities were found sewn into the upholstery of the car's rear seat.

Charged in the crime were three ex-convicts: George Myers, Edward Wade, and Frank F. Nash, and all were quickly sentenced to twenty-five years in the state penitentiary.

Nash's appeal of the sentence was rejected in August 1921, but good behavior got him another sentence reduction, and he was out in time to help notorious Oklahoma gangster Al Spencer steal $20,000[3] in Liberty bonds and other loot from a train near Okesa, Oklahoma, on August 20, 1923.

Nash was one of fifteen people arrested for the crime, and in March 1924, he was sentenced to twenty-five years at Leavenworth, Kansas, according to the March 6, 1924, edition of the *Hobart Democrat-Chief.*

"Judge, I am not guilty," the paper reported Nash declared before his official sentencing. "This is the second time I will have been sentenced to 25 years imprisonment for a crime of which I was innocent. I know of only one other case of persecution which parallels mine and that is the crucifixion of Christ."

Nash was just being dramatic. He wasn't executed. Nor did he serve his entire sentence.

Less than six years into his term at the federal penitentiary in Leavenworth, Kansas, Frank Nash—convicted murderer, bank robber, train robber—had somehow earned the status of trusty there, a role that got him outside the prison walls.

On October 19, 1930, he simply walked away.

"No trace had been found today of Frank Nash, 43-year-old trusty, who escaped last night from the federal penitentiary here," reported the Associated Press in a story published in papers around the region the next day. "Nash had been detailed to duty at the home of F. L. Morrison, deputy warden."

Like many hardened criminals who had just escaped from prison, Nash didn't lay low and didn't go straight. In fact, he stayed remarkably busy with criminal enterprises, if even half the allegations are true.

According to United Press stories published in several papers on June 17, 1933, including the *Columbus Telegram* of Columbus, Nebraska, Nash's name came up "in connection with a number of bank robberies in Nebraska" while he was on the lam from Leavenworth.

He was also, the United Press reported, suspected in not one but two prison breaks, "implicated . . . in the outbreak of seven convicts from the Leavenworth prison Dec. 11, 1931," and suspected as "one of the plotters in the outbreak of 11 convicts from Kansas state prison at Lansing" on May 30, 1933.

In the Leavenworth break, Nash and an accomplice, Harold Fontaine, "were responsible for shipping arms and nitroglycerine into the prison in a barrel of shoe paste."

Things didn't go particularly well for the escapees, however. "Three of the escaped convicts were trapped and killed near Leavenworth and the other four were captured."

The Lansing prison break was more successful.

And here the underworld network of those who may have been involved in the Woolverton kidnapping, or were closely connected to the abductors, grows a little more complex.

There are not one but two World War I veterans—Frank Nash and a former South Dakota sheriff who went very bad. There's another notorious bank robber. There were other people and other crimes and kidnappings, along with that moment when some of these lives came together with disastrous consequences. And there were the cover-ups generated by the FBI itself.

Along with other career moves while Nash was free between 1930 and 1933, he may have dabbled in two kidnappings, one involving Howard Woolverton, and one in Minnesota, where he was, according to the July 8, 1933, *Belvidere (Illinois) Daily Republican*, "linked by local police with the kidnaping of William Hamm, Jr., millionaire brewer."

Hamm had been grabbed off a St. Paul, Minnesota, street in June 1933 while walking to lunch. Like Howard Woolverton seventeen months before, Hamm was blinded by goggles and held briefly in Illinois. He was released unharmed after a few days' captivity when a ransom of $100,000 was paid.

Authorities who investigated the crime, the *Columbus Telegram* reported, "accepted it as fact that Nash was associated with the Hamm kidnapers when fingerprints taken in a house in St. Paul, which the abductors are believed to have used as their base of operations, tallied with Nash."

Although Nash seemed to be popping up all over the Midwest, he spent most of his time in Chicago, where he joined up with other hoods, including Machine Gun Kelly. How did they know each other? They'd done time together at Leavenworth, and Nash had reportedly taken the younger man under his wing, advising him on the best ways to knock off banks.

While in Chicago, Nash also got married.

A July 12, 1933, article in the *Kansas City Times* identified Nash's wife as Frances Miller (Frank Nash's aliases included the last name Miller). She told federal authorities she was thirty-one, that she thought her husband's name was Frank Harrison (another alias), and that they made their home in Chicago after they got married eighteen months before— which would suggest a ceremony that took place in January 1932—the month of Woolverton's kidnapping.

Other reports date the wedding more than a year later, in May 1933. Perhaps Frank and Frances started cohabitating on that earlier date— living in sin for sixteen months—a moral quandary Frances resolved by backdating the nuptials.

The couple lived with Frances's seven-year-old daughter, Darnell, a child from an earlier marriage. Nash came into the union with an unlikely cover story, the paper reported, telling his new bride "he owned a chain of roadhouses in Chicago."

Whether the couple got married in early 1932 or mid-1933, their happy union didn't last long.

But before we get into that, it should be acknowledged that the Woolvertons' descriptions don't entirely line up with Frank Nash. Although their observations may be questioned as having been made under duress, in the dark, while being threatened with unpleasantries, they're worth noting again here.

Recall that Howard Woolverton described the man on his running board, the veteran with catarrh, as twenty-six to thirty-two, while Nash, born in February 1887, was almost forty-five on the day Woolverton was kidnapped.

And Florence Woolverton's description of the lead kidnapper—again, the man on the running board—as a "Valentino type" doesn't quite hold up. In a side-by-side comparison of movie star Rudolph Valentino and

Frank Nash, one must notice that Nash's nose was considerably larger and not as straight as Valentino's.

George Kelly and Eddie Doll had perhaps more of the leading man looks than Nash, so possibly the Woolvertons were confused about who was in charge. Nothing in the records indicates the hoodlums began the abduction by outlining their hierarchy.

Maybe the feds could ask him after his inevitable return to prison?

No, probably not. Frank Nash wouldn't live that long.

27

The Kansas City Massacre

ON THE AFTERNOON OF June 16, 1933, a quiet man who called himself Doc Williams and was known as a good tipper was minding his own business at the White Front cigar store in Hot Springs, Arkansas, when three men walked in and bought cigars.

They didn't just walk out with the smokes, however.

Instead, according to an Associated Press story picked up widely, including by the *Iola (Kansas) Register* of June 17, 1933, the men "drew revolvers and surrounded 'Williams' as he was drinking a bottle of beer."

The story continued:

Two of them shoved their guns into his stomach while the third stood watch outside the store beside an automobile.

"Put that beer down and get into that automobile," commanded one.

"Williams" complied reluctantly and was pushed into the car.

As the automobile sped away toward Little Rock, police received reports that some one had been kidnapped or "taken for a ride" and immediately sent out requests to officers in neighboring cities to watch all highways and stop the sedan.

But this was no kidnapping, and the man who'd been grabbed was no doctor. "Doc Williams" was the escaped convict Frank Nash, and his captors were three government men, including federal agent Frank Smith.

In a long interview with the *Kansas City Star*, published June 17, 1933, Smith offered a slightly differing, firsthand version of the arrest of Nash after almost three years on the run.

Smith said he had traveled to Hot Springs with federal special agent F. J. Lackey and Otto Reed, chief of police in McAlester, Oklahoma.

"We pegged Nash right in front of the White Front pool hall and race booking joint," Smith said. "He was standing out in front drinking a bottle of beer. . . . I knew that he was very bald, with only a fringe of hair. There was a full head of brownish hair on his head when we arrested him in Hot Springs. He wore a black mustache, too, and had on nose glasses."

Smith recalled that when confronted by the officers, "Nash didn't resist. . . . He saw our revolvers and knew we meant what we said. He entered our car and we tore out on the highway, taking the road to Joplin, so that we could throw anyone off who tried to follow."

Smith handcuffed Nash and tugged on the man's hair. Off came the wig.

"'That's a good toupee,' Nash said. 'I paid $100 for that in Chicago.'"

Smith recalled that Nash, true to form, "never caused us a bit of trouble. He was polite. He was saying 'thank you' to us and 'please' and asking our permission to smoke. I was impressed with his good manners."

Smith believed the kidnapping reports were called in by Nash's friends in a bid to disrupt his return to prison, and in fact the car was stopped once, twenty miles outside Hot Springs, but waved on after things were explained to the officer.

On the drive, Smith told the paper, Nash revealed that he'd been in Chicago since he escaped from Leavenworth. "He told me on the way up from Arkansas that he had a good set-up in Chicago. He had a joint up there, beer and other stuff like that. He told me that he had some slot machines working there too, and was making money on them."

The officers and their prisoner had dinner in Russellville, Arkansas, then headed to Fort Smith, where they caught the overnight train to Kansas City, Missouri.

In the meantime, the phone lines hummed, the underworld buzzing with news that one of their own, a leading light in the criminal universe, had been clawed back to custody by the feds. One or more of those calls might have been made by Nash's wife.

And thus was history made.

About 7:00 a.m. the next morning, according to the Associated Press, Smith, Lackey, and Reed were met at the Union Station in Kansas City by four more officers: R. E. Vetterli, chief of the US Bureau of Investigation for Kansas and Western Missouri; Raymond J. Caffery, a Bureau investigator; and two Kansas City detectives, W. J. "Red" Grooms and Frank Hermanson.

According to the version of the AP story published on the front page of the *Iola Register* on June 17, 1933, "The seven escorted Nash, handcuffed, through the station to Caffery's car, waiting outside and across the street near the parking lot. . . . The officers had planned to drive to Leavenworth with the prisoner rather than wait for a train."

They never even got the car started, but reports of what happened next have never been entirely ironed out.

"I was putting an invalid in a taxicab," a station employee named W. H. Pemberton said, "when I noticed a group of men walk across the platform into the street toward some parked automobiles."

Someone near him speculated that the men were taking Pretty Boy Floyd to prison, Pemberton recalled.

"Some of the officers got in the right hand side of their car and at least one walked around the car to get in the left side," Pemberton said. "I looked away at that moment and then heard a shot. . . . One of the men was firing at another one with a submachine gun. He was standing within a foot of the man he was shooting."

According to Lackey, who survived the shooting, "Two men stepped out from between cars" parked near the police vehicle, "either with shotguns or rifles. I do not believe they had machine guns."

Lackey said the shooting started when one of the gunmen said, "Let's let them have it."

The surprise attack left the officers helpless, according to Lackey.

"There were shotguns and other weapons in the car, but we could not get at them."

Even on the day of the attack, and even among surviving members of the team escorting Nash, details were fuzzy.

Blame the fog of war.

"Accounts differed as to the number of men in the killers' party," the newspaper reported:

One eye witness said he saw only two men. Another reported the firing came from two automobiles and some officers expressed belief four men were involved.

The killers fled in one or more automobiles after pouring a murderous fire into a parked car which the officers and their prisoner were boarding just south of the east door of the station.

Veterli, the paper reported, "received a slight wound as the bullets tore through his clothing." He described the attack this way:

> Just as we started to get in Caffery's car in front of the station, they opened on us with sub-machine guns. . . . I don't know how many machine guns were opened up on us, but there was more than one. It sounded like four to me but I didn't know positively.
>
> All I know is that they were hidden behind cars and opened up on us.

Not in doubt: the names of the dead.

"They killed Nash first," Vetterli said. "The bullets were flying so thick about us by then that I don't know who went next."

"Then I saw the officers falling and some of them firing from machine guns as they fell," reported Moore, the cab driver, who said he thought at first he was hearing firecrackers. "I also saw the car at the curb with its windows shattered by gunfire and the figure of Nash, his head lolled back over the back of the front seat of the car and very bloody."

Also dead: Caffrey, Grooms, Hermanson, and Reed. McAlister, Oklahoma, had lost its police chief, Kansas City was down two detectives, and the killers had taken the life of a federal agent.

"All the dead were shot in the head," the Associated Press reported.

Vetterli received a minor injury to his arm, but Lackey was more seriously wounded, with three bullets in the back.

Lottie West, a Travelers' Aid worker at Union Station, told the *Fort Worth Star-Telegram* she was curious and followed the lawmen and their prisoner out of the station, where she

> saw them direct Nash to get in the front seat of the motor car. Some of the officers went on each side of the car. The two carrying sawed-off shotguns leaned these against the left-hand fender of the car. Just at that time a large man, who weighed about 200 pounds, stepped out from behind the lamp post. . . . He was carrying one of those guns with a cylinder on top of it. He started shooting right into the backs of the two officers. At about the same time two men stepped out from behind my automobile, which was parked a little west of the officers' car and facing north. Both were small men. One had what appeared to be

a shotgun and the other a machine gun. They started shooting at the other officers. The officers fell to the ground.

West offered some interesting speculation about who actually killed Frank Nash.

One of the agents in the car was able to return fire, she said. "He started shooting at the two men back of my car. He was shooting right by Nash and I believe he shot Nash."

Unlike other witnesses who said Nash went first, West said Nash was the last to die.

The attack took less than a minute and sent commuters and station employees scurrying for their lives. Not a single bystander was hurt, but the building itself bore signs of the rampage: "Windows in the station were broken and marks were left on the front of the big stone structure."

The Associated Press also reported, unsurprisingly, that "there was consternation among the large crowd of travelers."

A more colorful description of crowd reactions was provided by the *Columbus (Nebraska) Telegram* on June 17, 1933: "The rattle of machine gun fire and groans of the dying men brought a crowd rushing from the station. Women screamed and men cried in awe of the spectacle."

Agent Smith, the only one of Nash's escorts left unscathed in the attack, told the *Kansas City Star* he played dead as soon as the bullets started flying, after he realized his "six shooter" was no match for "a man aiming a machine gun at the car. It was shooting a red flame in our direction."

After dropping, Smith said, "I felt my friend Reed sag down upon me . . . Agent Lackey began to groan . . . I put my arm under Ott Reed's head. I tried to comfort Lackey. I noticed that Lackey's revolver handle had been splintered by a bullet. Maybe that was why he wasn't killed outright, like the others."

Mike Fanning, a motorcycle cop parked at the station, was the first police officer to respond to the shooting, telling the press he "fired three times with his pistol at the slayers' car as it was pulling away. He said some of the men were still shooting from the running board. He said he was certain there were four men in the automobile."

The return of Frank Nash to Leavenworth to complete his sentence had been a complete and bloody failure. Not only were the prisoner and four officers dead; the car (or cars) of the villains made a clean getaway.

"The assailants fled west," the Associated Press said, "but eluded police cars which rushed to the scene."

Ultimately, the feds were to blame. This was a federal prisoner, being brought back to a US prison. The government agents knew Frank Nash had many friends in low places but—other than keeping a stash of weapons they couldn't get to in time—they took little in the way of precaution, parading their prisoner through a crowded public area to a lot filled with cars—perfect for hiding behind and shooting from. Three local cops had paid for the screwup with their lives, along with the federal officer. Considering the number of bullets flying around crowded Union Station, it's a wonder more people didn't die.

Almost a century after the attack, important details of the massacre remain murky. Some reports had the gunmen shouting, "Up! up!" as they approached, suggesting they had hoped the officers would submit without a fight. The weapons used were reported variously as machine guns, shotguns, and rifles. Some saw one car, some two.

Compounding the contradictions and mysteries of the massacre, J. Edgar Hoover and his young FBI muddied the waters with what has been described by multiple researchers and authors as a cover-up.

In the wake of the Kansas City Massacre, Hoover and the Bureau had their work cut out for them, and Hoover wasted no time. The bodies were still warm when the Bureau brought up the name of the notorious hoodlum, Charles "Pretty Boy" Floyd.

"Floyd and his companion, Adam Richetti," reported the Associated Press in stories that appeared the day after the massacre, on June 17, 1933, "were considered a factor because the two had released their hostages at Lee's Summit, southeast of Kansas City, only a few hours before."

One of those hostages was no less than William "Jack" Killingsworth, sheriff of Polk County, Missouri. He'd made the mistake of walking into a Bolivar, Missouri, garage where the two desperadoes were getting their car patched up. Richetti, fearing he and Floyd were about to be identified, pulled a gun on the sheriff (as well as several other hapless shop visitors), and the two criminals then borrowed someone else's car, ordered Killingsworth into it, and drove off. Killingsworth was released unharmed that evening, declaring Floyd to have been "as clean a fellow as I ever run into" who "treated me nicer than I ever expected."

According to an Associated Press story about the kidnapping carried in the June 18, 1933, *Fort Worth Star-Telegram*, Killingsworth said of the two, "I don't believe they had anything to do with those Kansas City killings this morning."

Indeed, it is unlikely that Floyd and Richetti decided, amid a desperate run from justice, to pause their journey long enough for a little freelance prisoner rescue work, heading into a crowded city where many knew their names and had seen their wanted posters.

More likely, according to those who have studied the massacre's many eyewitness and official accounts, and the trail of underworld connections and loyalties that ran to and from Frank Nash, Hoover threw Floyd's name into the ring to boost pursuit of the criminal, a notorious bank robber and murderer whose successful life on the lam served as an ongoing affront to the young FBI and its director.

In the months following the slayings, other names were floated. In a story distributed by the Newspaper Enterprise Association in October of that year, reporter Robert Talley placed suspicion on Verne Miller, Harvey Bailey, Wilbur Underhill, and Robert C. Brady, the latter two "desperadoes who escaped from the Kansas penitentiary in the daring break led by Bailey last Memorial Day."

That Lansing prison break, recall, received assistance from Frank Nash. Maybe they thought they owed him one?

Over the decades since the Kansas City Massacre (also known as the Union Station Massacre), many have reviewed the incident, accessing records and testimony not available to the press of the day.

In *The Kidnap Years*, published in early 2020, David Stout summarized his own research, along with other writers' theories about who was involved in the massacre and why it was undertaken. Citing work by Jay Robert Nash (no relation to Frank Nash) and Robert Unger's 2005 book, *The Union Station Massacre: The Original Sin of J. Edgar Hoover's FBI*, Stout surmised that the massacre was orchestrated by Kansas City crime boss John Lazia, who enlisted Verne Miller and two gunmen, brothers Homer and Maurice Denning.[1] And the objective was not to free Nash but to kill him, to make sure he never spoke of the criminal gangs he'd run with in his nearly three years of freedom.

But Nash, according to this narrative, was not killed by the three hoodlums, an assertion that matched some witness accounts. Instead, Lackey, who was sitting behind Nash and wielding a shotgun he wasn't familiar with, fired in panic when the shooting began.

"The back of Nash's head was blown away," Stout wrote, "a massive wound characteristic of a shotgun blast from *behind* [emphasis Stout's] at point-blank range."

And yet, to this day, the FBI claims that Miller was joined by Floyd and Richetti to do the killing, and their goal was to get Nash free.[2]

No one disputes that Nash died at Union Station and that Miller was there with a gun, and that is why the story is important here. One or both men may have been involved in the kidnapping of Howard Woolverton.

The massacre and the dubious FBI claims that followed it suggest a reason for the federal cover-up of Woolverton's kidnapping.

The Woolverton abduction was important to Hoover. It was mentioned twice in those *American Magazine* articles, in Hoover's book, and in radio programs he helped create. Strangely, however, Hoover didn't name Woolverton in either article or in the book that borrowed heavily from them. And it was Hoover who sent that 1937 telegram to the *South Bend Tribune* citing "the confidential nature of the information" and refusing "to disclose further information with respect to the Woolverton case." And Woolverton himself was sworn to secrecy over the kidnapping. Recall that in the last passage of his federal statement, he'd said he'd been advised by federal special agent J. T. Hartin "that it is absolutely necessary that the investigation of this matter be held in strict confidence and I have advised my relatives to keep this matter quiet and not to divulge any information to anybody concerning this investigation."

Why the secrecy? Why was Woolverton ordered not to talk?

Was Charles Urschel, kidnapped a year and a half later, subjected to such restrictions? Of course not. Even though a federal man was there to greet Urschel late the night he returned home from his kidnapping, no one prevented him from meeting with a bevy of newspaper reporters the next morning to share the tales of his exploits. In kidnapping after kidnapping in the era when that crime raged, both before and after the Woolverton abduction, victims talked to the press, posed for the press, wrote books, blabbed without any interference from Uncle Sam.

What was so sensitive about the Woolverton case, a case not even under the purview of the federal government when it occurred?

In 1937, five years after the crime, with everyone involved either dead or cooling off in prison, we can guess at "the confidential nature of the information."

In a word, PR.

Hoover wanted it both ways—he wanted credit for apprehending the masterminds of one of the biggest abductions of the era, a crime that spawned a military-level, three-state mobilization of police, led to a new way of covering kidnappings by the press of the day, and played an important role in the new federal kidnapping law. But Hoover didn't want anyone taking too close a look at that feather in his cap.

And for almost a century, the plan worked.

There was that very awkward matter, however, toward the end of Woolverton's federal statement of the gassed World War I veteran.

Frank Nash was a veteran, wounded in the war, living in Chicago at the time of the kidnapping, and running in the same circles as Machine Gun Kelly and his wife, Kathryn.

And then there's Verne Miller, who allegedly led the Kansas City Massacre. He was also a World War I veteran who had made claims of being gassed in the war and was also connected to Chicago and Machine Gun Kelly.

In fact, Kelly, Nash, and Miller were all part of the same gang of crooks active in Chicago between 1930 and 1933, a fact brought up during Kelly's trial in the Urschel kidnapping: "The government rested its case that Kelly himself admitted connections with a gigantic kidnaping and robbery ring centered in Chicago," the United Press noted during the trial, adding that after the Urschel kidnapping, Kelly sought some kind of help from Miller.

Sometimes called the Holden-Keating gang after its two founding fathers, members included Harvey Bailey.[3] In an interview Kathryn Kelly gave just before she was sentenced to life for the Urschel kidnapping, she offered a rundown of crooks she knew in the gang, including Bailey, Albert Bates, and Verne Miller. Of Miller, she said, he "doesn't look like his picture. He's older."[4]

When Hoover talked about the Woolverton kidnapping, bringing up other names or details of the perpetrators wouldn't help, so Hoover left all that out, including any reference to the World War I veteran in Woolverton's statement or who he might be. Given that one of them led that Kansas City fiasco, and the other had died in it, why give them any more publicity?

And what became of Verne Miller, the former lawman who went bad? The feds couldn't bring him to justice either.

Like Nash and the Kellys, Miller had lived boldly and recklessly, but he could also fit in with polite society when circumstances called for it.

He even joined a country club.

28

Vernon Miller:
Veteran, Lawman, Criminal, Killer

AS SOON AS FRANK Nash was picked up in Hot Springs, Arkansas, phones were picked up and orders were given, either to free Nash or to rub him out.

One of those calls (presumably with the former objective in mind) was allegedly placed by Frances, the soon-to-be-bereft bride, who called for help from her husband's associates in Chicago, who in turn called someone in Kansas City.

A story written by Robert Talley and distributed by the Newspaper Enterprise Association says a shoot-out postmortem by the authorities included a look through the phone records.

"Tracing telephone calls," Talley wrote, "they located the Kansas City bootlegger to whom the message from Chicago had come," finding "a home in the residential section of Kansas City where Verne Miller, posing as 'Mr. V. C. Moore,' had lived in quiet respectability."[1]

Maybe Verne Miller, who shared the home with his wife and her daughter by a previous marriage, was trying to go straight after a decade of crime. He even joined the Milburn Country Club, still a going concern in 2020.[2]

Those other members of the Milburn club might have been surprised to learn that "V. C. Moore" was probably born in North Dakota in 1896

310

(the date is in some dispute, as is often the case with people who lie for a living), served in France during World War I, and returned from there with claims of having been injured and gassed—claims that now appear to be dubious but that elevated him to the status of war hero and propelled him by the early 1920s to the rank of sheriff of Beadle County, South Dakota.

One must wonder how "V. C. Moore" paid his Milburn membership dues. Did he peel off a few twenties from a wad tucked into his jacket? Did he retrieve it from a bag of cash under his bed, in the back of his closet, in the icebox? Might a little of that dues money have come from a ransom payment wrapped tightly by one Howard A. Woolverton before it was dropped on the side of the road on Highway 40 between Columbia, Missouri, and Kansas City?

Verne Miller's life of crime began while he was still supposed to be enforcing the law. According to the *Black Hills Weekly* (Deadwood, South Dakota) of August 11, 1922, Miller had last been seen the previous month, on July 16, his disappearance corresponding with a total shortage in sheriff's accounts of $4,771, the equivalent of almost $65,000 in 2020 currency. In a subsequent investigation, authorities determined that Miller "withdrew from the City National bank $600 in two checks and from the James Valley bank $2,025, this leaving a balance of about $46.70 in two banks."

According to the rumors that attended his abscondment, Miller was headed to Minneapolis to receive medical treatment, allegedly for lingering war infirmities.

That's where he was caught. The following spring, he pleaded guilty, was ordered to pay back $5,200, and was "given an indeterminate sentence of from two to 10 years in the state penitentiary."[3]

Miller did his time, got out, and got down to the business of doing very bad things.

Along with bootlegging and the occasional gangland killing, he is credited, in partnership with Machine Gun Kelly and others, with the July 15, 1930, robbery of the Bank of Willmar, Minnesota.

In a summary of the crime the next day, the *Star Tribune* of Minneapolis reported on the front page that "in less than 10 minutes the Bank of Willmar was robbed of $67,000 in cash and negotiable bonds."

The paper reported that "five men roared into Willmar at 10:15 a.m.," where they "subdued 25 employees, officials and customers of the bank."

As they left the establishment and fled from town, the paper noted, "they caused citizens of Willmar to retreat, terrified, under the wilting, raking fire of a machine gun."

The bandits, the story said, "left behind them a city literally 'shot up,' with windows shattered and buildings spattered with bullet marks."

Despite all the flying lead, only two injuries were reported, and no deaths at press time. Bystander Mrs. Emil Johnson took a bullet to the chest. Her daughter, Mrs. Donald Gildia, was hit in the leg.

One of the presumed robbers was injured as well, dropped off eight hours after the crime in Sioux Falls, South Dakota. He'd been shot in the head, and because his description matched that of the driver of the getaway car, authorities quickly concluded he was one of the hoods, although his cohorts had done their best to deflect suspicion.

"When brought into the hospital," the paper reported, "the man was without trousers, hat or shoes, apparently having been divested of part of his clothing to avoid identification. The men who carried him into the hospital disappeared immediately."

The man was "semi-conscious" but kept repeating, "Give me a highball and let's go."

In subsequent stories, the Sioux Falls patient was identified as a local man who'd attempted suicide and had nothing to do with the robbery, and the amount of the haul was adjusted upward, to $142,000, or the equivalent of more than $1.8 million in 2020 dollars.

Surely Miller's share of the loot was enough to retire on, and perhaps he moved to Kansas City to do just that.

But he couldn't leave well enough alone. Frank Nash got captured, someone made a phone call, and Miller headed to the train station.

After the Kansas City Massacre, Verne Miller fled the city. Officials thought they'd cornered him in a forest preserve west of Chicago on August 15, 1933.

"More than 200 city police, county, and federal operatives began a frantic search" for Miller, read that day's *Belvidere Daily Republican*. "A federal government airplane cruised over the western city limits" looking for Miller, and federal officers were on hand "to stop every car approaching the city over two main highways and scrutinize the occupants."

Despite a manhunt of historic proportions, Miller not only was not caught; he remained in Chicago and reportedly perpetrated at least one more outrage on the city.

The crime was detailed in a United Press story carried nationwide, including on the front page of the September 22, 1933, *El Paso (Texas) Herald Post*.

"Six machine gun bandits held up a federal reserve bank automobile in the loop today," the article began, referencing, incidentally, the Chicago Loop where Howard Woolverton caught that train home after his kidnapping. The gunmen, the article continued, "seized four money bags and fled under cover of a dense smoke screen, killing a policeman in the escape."

Authorities immediately believed they knew who did it, according to that *Herald Post* wire story: "Two nationally notorious gangsters George (Machine Gun) Kelly and Verne Miller, are suspected, police disclosed today."

Evidence of Miller's involvement was indicated by machine gun clips that "fit only a special, small type of weapon constructed by Miller."

The robbery, "in the heart of the financial district," happened before the doors of the federal reserve building at Jackson and LaSalle Streets, beginning when the robbers pulled up and "huge clouds of black smoke poured from their machines and blinded their victims."

The five machine gunners met no resistance from the guards, but as they sped away from the scene of the crime, the *Herald Post* related, "they collided with an automobile in which three girls and three boys were riding. Both cars overturned."

When Chicago patrolman Miles Cunningham, thirty-five, stepped over to investigate the wreck, "three machine gunners opened fire. He fell with a dozen slugs in his body."

The criminals commandeered another car and made a clean getaway, leaving behind an impressive array of bank-robbing equipment.

"In the wrecked bandit car, police found two sets of Minnesota license plates, one set each for Illinois, Georgia and Florida, five automatic pistol clips, one machine gun drum and three automatic rifle clips. The car was equipped with red and green lights, similar to those used by ambulances, a short wave radio, a police siren, (and) a complete set of first aid equipment, including a tourniquet."

The car, it should be noted, was later traced back to Kelly.[4]

Verne Miller and his fellow gang members knew how to pull off a crime. But the man was not well. He also, quite possibly, was lying about his military achievements.

Despite the intelligence and forethought indicated by his gang's preparations when it came to robbing banks, something was bugging Verne Miller. We might blame childhood anguish brought on by the divorce of his parents or unhappy times on his uncle's farm, where he was sent to live after the split. Maybe it was the stress of life as a lawman in the hard-bitten Dakotas. Some have blamed syphilis.

Or was it the war, which left him with injuries both visible and invisible, the aftereffects of a poison gas attack plus the ravages of what we now call post-traumatic stress disorder?

But did Verne Miller really suffer in the war?

World War I historian Robert Laplander has his doubts.

Laplander, author of 2006's *Finding the Lost Battalion: Beyond the Rumors, Myths and Legends of America's Famous WW1 Epic*, summarized his reservations in June 2020, under an online biography about Miller published by *South Dakota Magazine*.[5]

Laplander wrote that he had "so far found no evidence that Miller was in combat."

In his comment (which I confirmed was authentic in a July 2020 phone conversation with Mr. Laplander), the author noted that Miller's service records indicate he "went to France as a stable sergeant with the 163rd Infantry of the 41st Division" and remained "among this permanent support staff" throughout the war. The job of the 41st Division, later redesignated as the 1st Depot Division, was not combat, Laplander noted. Instead, they "served as a funnel for replacements to combat units that had suffered casualties," and Verne Miller was one of those who stayed with the unit: "They ran the division, trained the replacements, and then shuffled them to where they were needed."

Added Laplander, all-capping his comment for emphasis at times: "He stayed with the horses . . . I have seen conflicting reports that he was wounded twice, gassed severely, promoted on the field, decorated with the Croix de Guerre, trained as an expert machine gunner, trained as a sniper, and came home a decorated hero, however I have found NOTHING that supports ANY of that. Miller did not suffer from PTSD from his time in France, though he MAY have been gassed SLIGHTLY at some point, but nothing more."

Thirteen years after Verne Miller and Frank Nash left France and sailed back to the United States on troop ships, Howard Woolverton was kidnapped by a man who claimed to have been gassed in the war.

Was it Verne Miller? Was it Frank Nash? Was it some other veteran? Or was it merely a liar, someone claiming to have served in WWI in the hopes Woolverton would share that detail with the police, thereby throwing suspicion onto Miller, Nash, or some other denizen of local crime who'd seen action in Europe?

Most, but not all, of the evidence points to Nash. His documented time in France of about four months and his documented injury there match what the kidnapper said to Howard Woolverton. Miller, on the other hand, was in France well over four months, and his claims to have been gassed or injured in any other way are suspect.

But it must be noted that Miller, unlike Nash, bore a striking resemblance to movie star Rudolph Valentino, as did one of the kidnappers, according to Florence Woolverton.

Whether it was Nash, Miller, both, or neither, one would have expected Hoover's FBI to follow up on that detail from Woolverton's 1934 statement or at least toss that fact to the local cops, but there's no evidence they did either. In the first years after the abduction, Hoover refused to discuss the crime other than in magazine allegations, and he ordered secrecy from everyone else involved.

Why? Here we must speculate: If word got out that a WWI veteran was a perpetrator, people might quite logically have pointed to Nash, Miller, and their stories—neither bringing any credit to the FBI—the former dying at the latter's hands, the latter escaping justice time and again, even slipping through a two-hundred-man dragnet that included a federal plane and federal agents.

Nor was Verne Miller's death anything to brag about: the feds looked for him for months, but they never got him; the crooks did, in Detroit. And it wasn't pretty.

"The nude body of the outlaw," reported the *Chicago Tribune* on November 30, 1933, "was found yesterday in a ditch by a roadside just outside the city limits. It was identified today. Miller had been beaten to death. His skull was crushed in. The slayers had wrapped the body in blankets and tied the covering with a clothesline."

Police speculated Miller had been killed somewhere else, "probably in some haunt of the Detroit underworld, and the body conveyed to the lonely roadside for disposal."

The speculation published in that day's edition of the *Chicago Tribune* remains today the favored explanation for his murder. Miller "was

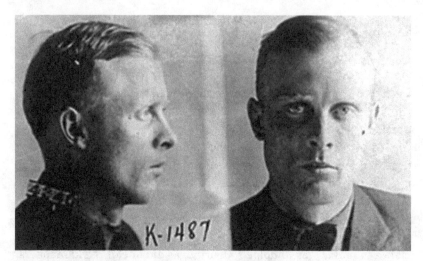

Vernon "Verne" Miller, shown here in a prison mugshot from the 1920s. While not named as a suspect in the Woolverton kidnapping, he could pass for Rudolph Valentino, and his war service and criminal history are a general match. *Photographer unknown; public domain image.*

1920s movie star Rudolph Valentino. Florence Woolverton said one of the kidnappers looked a lot like him. *Photographer unknown; public domain image.*

Frank "Jelly" Nash wasn't going to be confused with Rudolph Valentino under any but the most extreme environmental conditions, and he was never named as a suspect in the Woolverton kidnapping, but his World War I service lines up precisely with what one of the kidnappers told Howard Woolverton. *Photographer unknown; from the US Federal Archives.*

George "Machine Gun" Kelly in a federal prison mugshot from 1933. Might pass for Rudolph Valentino in a dark alley. *Photographer unknown; from the US Federal Archives.*

Taken February 23, 1930.

Eddie Doll, from a 1930 federal wanted poster. Another passable Valentino lookalike. *Photographer unknown; from the US Federal Archives.*

believed to have gone to Newark, N.J., a few weeks ago to hire himself out to the Longie gang as a killer" and "became quite friendly with a gangster named Al Silvers and cooperated with the latter in several killings."

Miller and Silverman (his actual name) had killed the wrong person or people, it seems, and both had been marked for death. Two weeks before the discovery of Miller's body, they found Silverman's in Connecticut, murdered in a "strikingly similar" way, noted the December 1, 1933 *Hartford (Connecticut) Courant*: Silverman's "nude and mutilated body, wrapped in a blanket, was found, with one foot resting on a fence off a side road in Somers on the morning of November 20."

Ultimate justice had come to Verne Miller, but it wasn't meted out by the federal government. And not for want of trying.

"So important did the government regard Miller," the *Chicago Tribune* reported, "that it had published 40,000 circulars in the last few months, giving his description and urging his capture. He was wanted for kidnaping and robbery, as well as for murder."

The outlaw's death was an embarrassment to the FBI, as was his life. When J. Edgar Hoover set about chronicling the early victories of his G-men, people like Frank Nash and Verne Miller needed to be left out, not only because both pointed up government failure but also because talking too much about them might inspire another look at the Kansas City Massacre. There were skeletons there, and Hoover wanted them kept in the closet.

And yet, the temptation to claim victory for solving one of the era's biggest kidnappings proved too great for the lawman. So Hoover played both sides, making obvious references to Woolverton but withholding his name and asserting that all the people who'd grabbed him were safely tucked away in prison, thanks to the feds.

Hoover didn't need to drop Woolverton's name to take credit for solving the crime, of course. The right people knew who he was talking about. And if he gave the name, that might get people wondering again. In the days of published phone books and operator assistance, Woolverton would have been simple to track down, and some enterprising reporter unfamiliar with the case might get curious, call, catch the man in a talkative mood, and dig up that little detail of the World War I veteran with a cough, which might lead down other trails to a not-as-tidy-as-advertised kidnapping denouement, not to mention a bloody shoot-'em-up in Kansas City that the FBI would just as soon forget.

History, it has been said, is written by the victors, and the FBI scored enough victories in its early days to write a lot of history.

In the end, we can probably forgive Hoover for his transgressions against the truth. The 1930s were a desperate time in America, where a brutal new economics might lead the suffering common people to favor the outlaws over the banks they blamed for the crisis, or the cops trying to protect said banks.

America needed a national police, and the national police needed America to believe in it, so perhaps a lie here or there, a cover-up, a little selective editing of a massacre or a kidnapping served a higher truth.

And why drag the name of Howard Arthur Woolverton through the mud again? He didn't want to be kidnapped, didn't want to be talked about, never asked for fame. He, at least, must have been grateful that Hoover granted him anonymity.

Howard Woolverton, like most of America, just wanted to be left alone, to resume his life, to go about his business unbothered by the Depression-era scourge of robbers, kidnappers, and machine gun–wielding murderers.

There was a little more reckoning to be done, but in the end, Woolverton, like the nation, got his wish.

29

The Woolvertons Move On

THE 1930S PROVED A pivotal decade in American history, a painful transition from the wealth and frivolity of the 1920s to the cataclysmic 1940s, when the nation rose to its feet, rolled up its sleeves, helped destroy tyrants around the globe, and set about making the modern world.

The 1930s might also, with a century's hindsight, seem almost funny today, full of bad guys wielding tommy guns they pulled out of violin cases, knocking over banks, hauling liquor, fleeing in clunky sedans pursued by cops driving clunky roadsters, talking tough even on their way to prisons, which, often enough, proved unable to hold them.

We can be confident, however, that the fear was very real for those living through it, especially for the wealthy and successful, who had far more to lose.

Kidnapping, in particular, ensured that surviving those difficult years—the Public Enemies Era, it is sometimes called—was not a spectator sport. For the Woolvertons and the many others who'd had a brush with abductors and extortionists, it was their own names in the daily headlines or the names of people they knew.

The Woolvertons, who subscribed to at least two papers—the *South Bend Tribune* and the *Chicago Tribune*—and surely more, received a near-daily barrage of personally germane coverage for years after their encounter with kidnappers. Not only was Machine Gun Kelly a regular player in the annals of the day, but so, too, were his friends and people like him—Frank Nash, Verne Miller, Pretty Boy Floyd, Jack Klutas, Creepy Alvin Karpis, John Dillinger, Bonnie and Clyde, Ma Barker and her sons. They robbed, murdered, kidnapped, went to jail, and broke out of jail.

But the Woolvertons, like the nation, never gave up hope, and by the mid-1930s, the cops were winning, and the bad guys were dying in the streets or going to island prisons they couldn't leave, tracked down by federal officers with new federal powers.

Indeed, even when things must have seemed most hopeless for the Woolvertons, with those who'd grabbed Howard still at large and threatening the life of their daughter whom they'd had to send east, the couple kept on, and the same hometown newspaper that recorded the crimes against them (infuriating them in the process, at times) chronicled their refusal to give in, to give up, to withdraw.

Half a year after he was kidnapped, Howard Woolverton was partying with the same people that had played vital roles in the case that preceding January. It was the Fourth of July, America was 156 years old, and the people of South Bend wanted to celebrate. As the *South Bend Tribune* reported: "One hundred and fifty guests attended the dinner last evening at the South Bend Country club, many more going out later for the dance and to see the display of fireworks. Bob Helmcamp's orchestra played for dancing. Woodson Carlisle was host to twelve guests and Miss Eleanor Carlisle entertained a smaller group. Another party included Secretary of State Frank Mayr and Mrs. Mayr, Mr. and Mrs. J. M. Studebaker, Mr. and Mrs. G. A. Farabaugh and Mr. and Mrs. Howard A. Woolverton."

A few months later, Florence Woolverton was in the paper, and, once again, we see not a shrinking violet, not a woman given to hysteria and fainting spells in the face of unpleasantness but an outspoken and confident member of the South Bend community.

"Poor Relief Abuses Charged," announced the headline across the top of the front page of the *South Bend Tribune* on September 23, 1932.

At issue were the allegedly high costs of medical care in St. Joseph County, which had prompted a blowup at a meeting of the county's Central Service Appeals Board the day before.

"$34 Expense for Setting Broken Arm of Dole Youth Starts Fireworks," a subheadline noted. Adjusting for inflation, the cost of that treatment in 2020 dollars would be around $700, still arguably a bargain in America's current medical regime, but too high for those responsible for the budget in that age, including Florence Woolverton:

> Mrs. Howard A. Woolverton, who had voiced her approval of more stringent economies in poor relief administration, declared that the medicine and drug costs in the township are becoming excessive.
>
> During the months of April, May and June, she said, the township paid out $1,573.75 on the drug prescriptions of physicians for indigents. At this rate, she said, the cost of this item alone would be more than $6,000 a year.

Despite Howard Woolverton's protestations of poverty when his life was on the line, it seems unlikely the family ever wanted for money. Whatever the man's fortunes while the Great Depression ravaged the 1930s, he was neatly on his feet in 1940. According to census records of that year, the Woolverton household consisted of Howard, Florence, and Betty Woolverton, and three live-in employees: cook Hannah Scheibel, maid Karin Pedersen, and laundress Sylvia Powell.

Among the business dealings of Mrs. Woolverton (who, recall, brought her own wealth to the marriage, thanks to her inheritance of half of the Boye Needle Company) was a favor for two dear friends of hers, George and Bess Studebaker. The Studebakers owed more than $20,000 on that storied property at 110 N. Esther Street, where the Woolvertons had visited just before they were kidnapped. At some point in the 1930s, as the Studebaker family fortunes dwindled, Florence Woolverton had guaranteed half the loan to help keep her friends in their home. However, the Studebakers were forced to move to an apartment in 1936 and rent the grand home to Harold S. Vance and his wife.[1] The rent being paid by the Vances didn't cover the mortgage and expenses, unfortunately, and by 1939, according to documents maintained by Dave Hendry, the Studebakers had moved to California and Mrs. Woolverton was on the hook for $18,000—or about $330,000 in 2020 dollars.

She appears to have eventually extricated herself from the obligation with the sale of the home to the Vances.

In a sad footnote to the story, an auction was advertised in the *South Bend Tribune* on November 14, 1939, offering "all personal effects of Mrs. George M. Studebaker," including twenty rugs, original paintings, china, cut glass from around the world, a "scarcely used" sterling silver set, fine furniture, a refrigerator, and a Cadillac.

Mrs. Woolverton lived another twelve years after the kidnapping, until a heart attack took her at the age of sixty on August 12, 1944.

"Although she had not been feeling well for the past few days," the *South Bend Tribune* reported, "her ailment had not been considered serious. However, she complained of shortness of breath this morning and Mr. Woolverton decided to summon a physician for her. She died in the living room of her home about 15 minutes after the doctor arrived."

In the end, the newspaper gave the woman her due, dismissing once and for all the caricature of a frail, hysterical woman conjured by the press during that kidnapping.

"Mrs. Woolverton underwent terrific strain when she and her husband were kidnaped the night of Jan. 27, 1932," the *Tribune* recalled, getting the date wrong by a day. "However, her bravery under the terrifying circumstances stood her in good stead and after being released, although her husband was held, she had the courage to drive her car from where she was released to South Bend and police were notified [clarification: she stalled her car at the light and a patrolman noticed her]. Throughout the awful affair she bore up bravely."

The article noted Mrs. Woolverton's service of nearly thirty years to the American Red Cross in South Bend and identified her as a founder of the Visiting Nurses' Association.

Mrs. Woolverton's obituary also offered up perhaps one small clue as to how she ended up adopting Betty.

"In connection with the nurses' association," the obituary continued, "Mrs. Woolverton devoted much of her time to the establishment's free baby clinic. Although her work was not widely known, she was intensely interested in private philanthropies and gave much of her time and finances to individual cases which she considered worthy of aid."

Howard Woolverton, widower, served in his later years as chairman of the board of St. Joseph's Bank & Trust Company, which he helped to found in 1939 as the merger of two of the businesses his father had founded decades before: the St. Joseph Loan and Trust Company and the St. Joseph County Savings Bank. And the bank seems to have been where Woolverton's true passions lay. According to Dave Hendry, his mother told him more than once that her father would be due to work at Malleable Steel Range on occasion but chose to "play hooky," going to the bank he founded to stand in the lobby and greet customers.

Florence Flannery Woolverton (*standing at the first table*) in her role as a Red Cross volunteer. The grateful organization named a wing of the local Red Cross building after her. *Photographer unknown; David W. Hendry, Jr.*

Woolverton's bank existed under its original name until the 1980s, undergoing multiple mergers and name changes until its soul—if banks had souls—had become an unrecognizable amalgam.

Howard Woolverton never remarried after the death of his wife, but he continued doting on his daughter. The girl who needed a police escort when she was twelve had her father's arm to hold when she walked down the aisle on her wedding day in 1947. The ceremony was held at the storied Woolverton estate, but she and her husband, David Hendry Sr., soon moved to California, where she bore a daughter and three sons. Howard Woolverton would visit annually, buying her a home there and a car now and then as well.

After six months of declining health, he died of pneumonia at 11:45 p.m. on January 27, 1960. He was seventy-nine.

To his final chagrin, we might imagine, his obituary in the *South Bend Tribune* made extensive reference to the kidnapping. Not helping things was the time and date of his death, a detail the *Tribune* did not fail to notice.

"His death, coincidentally," the paper noted, "occurred on the 28th anniversary of the night and almost the hour that he returned home,

Florence Woolverton left behind an eclectic collection of bracelets, pins, and other jewelry—Victorian, art deco, art nouveau, retro. Some of these items were worn by Betty Woolverton as well. *Photo by Greg Stanfield.*

unharmed, after a 24-hour kidnaping ordeal that began the night of Jan. 26, 1932, when a car in which Woolverton and his wife were riding was stopped a few blocks from their home."

The "bizarre kidnaping case," the obituary said, "threw South Bend into a turmoil and attracted the attention of law enforcement authorities both in Indiana and Illinois, as well as the Federal Bureau of Investigation."

The newspaper chose to go with its own disputed version of how Woolverton was freed, making no mention of the counterclaims published ten days after the kidnapping in the *South Bend News-Times*, which had long since gone out of business.

According to the *Tribune*, "it subsequently was disclosed that his release had been arranged by a go-between acting for the Secret Six, a Chicago crime-fighting organization. It was reported that an $8,000 ransom was paid."

In the *News-Times*'s version of things, recall, published on February 5, 1932, Woolverton had negotiated his release with a promise to pay $8,000, and the Secret Six was not involved in either the arrangements or the payment itself. This narrative (which matched Woolverton's subsequent federal statement, of course) was based on information provided exclusively to the *News-Times* by (presumably) Woolverton family attorney G. A. Farabaugh. But all of that had been conveniently forgotten by the *Tribune* in the intervening decades.

By the time Mary Elizabeth Woolverton Hendry died at age seventy-eight of congestive heart failure, on June 11, 1998, the kidnapping was all but forgotten. She was, for one day, the most famous girl in Indiana and one of the very few twelve-year-old girls in American history publicly threatened with death, but her brief obituary in the *South Bend Tribune*'s June 21 edition made no mention of the crime.

And, although almost half of Howard Woolverton's *Tribune* obituary recounted the kidnapping and its aftermath, the story made no mention of the broader significance of the crime, its impact on kidnapping coverage in the newspapers, or the part it played in the federal kidnapping law.

The snatching of Howard Woolverton was certainly not called America's most important kidnapping in the piece.

But can the case truly be made that it was?

30

The Closing Argument

CALL IT THE GANGSTER era or the Public Enemies Era; the age of Prohibition, of organized crime, or of the G-men, the years from the early 1920s to the mid-1930s represented a singularity in American history, a time when a multitude of forces aligned to produce a variant on human nature not seen before or since.

Outlawing alcohol in 1919 brought every drinking American into the arms of the nation's criminals, and those outlaws became rich.

The competition for commercial turf among the bootleggers led to other crimes, including murder. The automobile, introduced a few decades before, meant a new approach to killing: lure the target into the car or toss him in, drive him a little beyond city limits, and end his life there.

From that practice sprang the idea of kidnapping for ransom—grab your fellow crooks, but let them live if they paid up.

From there, the commercial harvesting of the innocents was just one more point on the continuum, a franchise of crime webbing out from midwestern gangster strongholds to the rest of the nation, sucking the lifeblood from the wealthy, the successful, the innovative, destroying the American Dream one abduction at a time.

With kidnapping, the gangsters had come into their own, following a business plan that took them out of the crosshairs of their liquor-toting

329

competitors. Now they had only terrified captives to deal with and dis-traught family members who couldn't pay the ransoms quickly enough.

Cars and a growing network of good roads made all the difference here, enabling the bad guys to drag their victims to remote places, far from their homes and well outside city or state jurisdictions.

All the while, with the nation under attack from within, the federal government watched from the sidelines, the forces of darkness winning.

Without any laws to back him up, Uncle Sam could do nothing.

America, it might be said, was out of balance, advancing in certain ways, being held back in others, becoming in the process the ideal petri dish for the culturing of malevolent gangsterism. Cars, roads, and new firearms coupled with a hamstrung national police and a rudimentary information system meant criminals could become famous as they wan-dered at will from bank to bank and victim to victim, no one recognizing them until after the deed was done and the survivors had a chance to leaf through the mug shots.

There was long-distance travel for the first time, but still no televi-sion, no internet. In the 1930s, the best way to disseminate the images of those at-large was the newspapers, which provided the pictures to paying subscribers only, as space allowed. The FBI's famous Ten Most Wanted campaign, its pictures hung in post offices across the nation, didn't launch until 1950.

Gangsters, prowling the nation in search of lucrative opportunities, would happen on kidnapping inevitably. A single abduction could raise as much money as a month of bootlegging or several armed heists, with-out the risks of liquor-fueled turf battles or the bullets that often con-cluded a bank job.

And no crime—not bank robbery, arson, burglary, not even mur-der—had the power to sap American creativity like kidnapping. Extor-tion might run a distant second, in which money is demanded of the well-to-do and successful based on threat alone. But kidnapping is the consummated violation, a profane intrusion into the sanctity of the personhood, the family—the home, often enough.

Awful as other crimes might have been, they were for the most part equal-opportunity violations, inflicted on all classes, not a torment re-served for the well-to-do. And as costly as financial and property crimes are, they do not invade the psyche like being made a prisoner.

By the early 1930s, America was finished wringing its hands. The first step: get a picture of the scourge.

Beginning in mid-1931, the Secret Six gathered anecdotes and assembled speculation about kidnapping, and the St. Louis Police Department collected hard (and probably much more accurate) data, mailing surveys to police departments around the nation. Between them, they had a powerful story to tell, of both raw figures and the flesh-and-blood terror behind the numbers: the innocent, respectable victims; the tortures; the cold, businesslike, and growing nature of the enterprise.

It was a story that needed telling, and on January 24, 1932, the Secret Six had some success, getting their version of things put out on the wire and published in papers here and there around the nation.

But to really capture the nation's attention, they needed a fresh victim.

And not just any victim.

Ideally, the abductee would be a wealthy, successful man, but not a tycoon, not a celebrity. Someone who went to work every day. Someone people could relate to, realistically aspire to become. He should be a family man, with a wife and children, or at least one child, preferably a girl, preferably at a maximally sympathetic age. Twelve would be perfect—old enough to understand the danger her family was in but too young to protect herself.

He should be gone for at least a day, so the daily newspapers could spend a full news cycle screaming about the man who'd been taken. And it would be best if he were snatched in front of witnesses—ideally his wife—who could offer a terrifying, believable, first-person account of exactly how her husband had been grabbed. There needed to be a ransom note, of course, preferably containing dramatic prose and a few thuggish threats against life and limb.

And timing was important too. Not the weekend. Tuesday night would be best, so the story would run on a Wednesday, the middle of the workweek, when the whole nation was up and about. And if it could happen within a few days of that Secret Six report, that would be ideal.

Enter one Howard Arthur Woolverton, secretary-treasurer of the Malleable Steel Range Manufacturing Company, wealthy but not ridiculously so, well known in South Bend but no celebrity. A family man, he went to work every day, just like anyone else who had a job back then, and he came home every day to his wife and twelve-year-old daughter.

In some respects, Woolverton's kidnapping was most noteworthy for how insignificant it was. He was gone for twenty-four hours before he returned home unharmed. He was out $8,000, a solid chunk but not a devastating loss to someone like him. The kidnappers apparently never got the money, which meant that was $8,000 they couldn't invest in the next snatch.

But Woolverton's station in life, the details of his capture, and the perfect timing gave his abduction a power that arguably no other kidnapping in American history possessed.

Just before Woolverton was grabbed, both St. Louis Police Chief Joseph Gerk and the Secret Six announced their kidnapping findings, and that might have been it, another crime trend for Americans to worry about when they weren't fretting over bank robberies and murders, saber-rattling by Japan and Germany, and the economic despair that attended the Great Depression.

But Woolverton's kidnapping served as the lit match, dropped onto the tinder of dry facts and distant anecdotes, and his became the face of a new kind of kidnapping coverage in the newspapers, beginning literally hours after he was taken, and continuing for six critical weeks in early 1932, culminating in the preparation of multiple comprehensive reports about this horrifying new trend, which by supreme happenstance were ready to roll within a day or two of the abduction of Charles Lindbergh Jr.

Was it the Woolverton case that inspired Bruce Catton to start work on his series for the Newspaper Enterprise Association? Did Fred Pasley of New York's *Daily News* begin researching his sixteen-chapter kidnapping compendium because of what he read about our man in South Bend? We know both writers were well aware of Woolverton because they featured his case prominently. And the timing fits.

Their stories, riding on the coattails of the sensational Lindbergh case, played well, getting picked up by papers around the nation and emulated by other publications. The *New York Times*, for example, ran its take on abduction a few days after Pasley's series began.

And surely, the nation's sentiments, provoked both by the taking of baby Lindbergh and the press's characterization of the crime as part of a terrifying new American epidemic, weighed heavily on Congress. A federal kidnapping law had been proposed in late 1931 and then set aside. The Woolverton case in January 1932 single-handedly revived deliberations.

That august body must have been influenced as well by the letter from Woolverton and support from Indiana's police chiefs, who mentioned

Woolverton explicitly in their February 1932 plea from the middle of the Kidnapping Crescent.

Further, Woolverton's silence, coupled with connections that gave him a unique ability to quash the investigation at its outset, lent the crime an additional dimension of terror. Kidnapping occupied a special class of offense, his fellow citizens must have concluded, something the victim would not talk about and the authorities wouldn't pursue. Get snatched, and you're on your own. Just hope they don't come for you twice or abduct every member of your family, one by one.

So Congress dismissed budgetary and state's rights concerns to pass in summer 1932 the federal law that brought the nation's full resources to bear against kidnapping. The Lindbergh case still gets virtually all the credit for passage. The Woolverton case, which arguably served as the law's primary catalyst, gets none.

Did the law work?

Yes.

The measure of press uses of the word *kidnap* and its derivatives dropped precipitously soon thereafter, falling by almost 90 percent from 1935 to 1941. By that yardstick, the new law was a dramatic success, the incidence of the crime dwindling significantly in half a decade.

The American Dream was saved, and America's citizens went on to lead the world—for almost a century and counting—with ideas both good and profitable.

Other results of the Woolverton kidnapping, while not as significant as the new federal law, added to its importance.

The crime prompted renewed vigor among authorities, particularly in Chicago, in prosecuting a form of lawlessness that had been too often ignored in the past. And it has been argued by J. Edgar Hoover himself that Woolverton's kidnapping served as a dry run for the abduction of Charles Urschel, a crime whose effective prosecution not only burnished the image of the FBI as a national police force but also led to the arrest and imprisonment of a cadre of crooks, including Machine Gun and Kathryn Kelly and two other notorious criminals, Albert Bates and Harvey Bailey. All of them might have remained at large for years, committing more crimes if the Kellys hadn't made the mistake of grabbing Urschel, a man who was determined to work with the G-men to bring them to justice. And they might not have grabbed Urschel if they hadn't tried their hand at taking Woolverton first. Much about the Woolverton abduction, it should be noted, went swimmingly for the kidnappers. Woolverton went home, lied to protect the thugs, and did all he could to cover up the crime. The only thing he didn't do, apparently, was get that money into the kidnappers' hands. Thus the band of people-snatchers decided to keep Urschel locked in that shed until they had the lucre— giving Urschel enough time to plant fingerprints and make the mental notes essential to the federal investigation.

Finally, might we credit Woolverton with not just that new federal kidnapping law but also, to some smaller degree, with the federal laws against other crimes Congress passed in subsequent years? Bank robbery was declared a federal crime in 1934, for example. Was Congress inspired by the successful federal prosecution it had enabled of the Urschel case the year before?

Today, Americans take for granted that the feds will show up to address a wide array of serious offenses beyond kidnapping. Indeed, it is an idea embedded in American myth: the arrival of the G-men ensures that truth, justice, and the American way shall, often enough, prevail.

It was not always so, and most observers would agree that the changes wrought in one of our nation's darkest eras made for a more perfect union.

Thank you, Howard Arthur Woolverton.

Getting himself kidnapped was, historically, the most important thing Woolverton did, but it was not the only thing. In the same way that each kidnapping should be understood in its historical and cultural context, each victim must be viewed as a whole person. In Woolverton's case in particular, examining his life before and after the crime sheds essential illumination on the story. It also adds a human element to the tale, valuable on its own merits.

Howard Woolverton lived a long, comfortable life, but it was not without its pain.

He lost at least one child. He lost his wife, spending the last fifteen years of his life a widower. And for just under twenty-four hours in the winter of 1932, he lost his freedom to a band of thugs, at least one perhaps a World War I veteran, and some surely cold-blooded murderers.

It was, we might argue, a small price to pay for the good his kidnapping did. But would Woolverton agree? If he were alive today, would he portray himself as a pivotal figure, the man of the hour, the person whose small sacrifice was worth the greater good?

Probably not.

In Woolverton's first moments of freedom after he stood on that Chicago curb, he approached two women. Where am I? he asked them. What city am I in?

The women looked at him like he was drunk, Woolverton recalled the next day, and he was content to let them believe so.

He didn't share his name or his terrifying story with them, nor did he go to the police or call his family in South Bend. Instead, it seems, he called his lawyer. Then he came to South Bend on the South Shore Interurban and rode a taxi home from the station with a state cop working for his good friend and neighbor, Indiana Secretary of State Frank Mayr Jr. The taxi pulled up to his house, Woolverton dashed through his front door and, for the most part, clammed up.

And that's the way he played the incident the rest of his life, not spinning tales of his brush with the underworld, not seeking credit for what followed, perhaps not even remembering certain details.

Traumatic experiences have a way of vanishing from the mind.

"He never talked about it in front of us kids, other than that one slip going over the San Francisco Bay Bridge," Dave Hendry said in a 2019 interview. "I'm guessing that he never talked about it to friends or anyone else but his closest family. There's enough misinformation out there, that it tells me he rarely talked about it and had no interest in talking about it and correcting the story."

If we could sit down with Howard Woolverton today, to ask him for his recollections, to propose he had helped to change history, how would he respond?

"He'd probably underplay it," Hendry said. "That was the way he dealt with it his whole life."

ACKNOWLEDGMENTS

LIKE THE KIDNAPPING OF Howard Arthur Woolverton and its aftermath, the story of how this book came to be features a few twists and turns, a lucky break or two.

David "Dave" Hendry, Jr. encountered the kidnapping of his grandfather as family lore, a story told incompletely through the generations, whispered about at times but something he knew needed research and a professional telling to a wider audience.

A graduate of Weber State University, Hendry went back to his alma mater for help, and the state institution in Ogden, Utah, rose to the challenge of turning an alumnus's unique family history into a book.

The school helped with agreements, provided fiscal oversight, and—most importantly, from my perspective—signed on to help Hendry find an author to research and write the story. Enter Sarah Langsdon, head of special collections at Weber State, who had worked with my mother-in-law, Dr. Jean Andra Miller (an early proofreader of this book as well), to maintain and build the Carl Andra Collection (a remarkable memorial to her late husband). Sarah, whom I'd met as a donor to the collection, remembered that I had a history as a writer, reached out to Jean to get in touch with me, and provided the initial introduction between Hendry and me.

Subsequently, no less than Brad Mortenson, president of Weber State University, got involved in executing the agreements that established the framework for the book's creation.

And, almost two years later, with the book in its first rough-draft form, Weber State stepped up again with the services of Gene Sessions, Weber State's Brady Presidential Distinguished Professor of History. Dr. Sessions, a gifted and oft-recognized teacher, and the author of historical books of his own (including *Mormon Thunder: A Documentary History of Jedediah Morgan Grant* and *Prophesying upon the Bones: J. Reuben Clark and the Foreign Debt Crisis, 1933–39*), proved an ideal editor as well, making his way bravely through a (very) rough draft and gently pointing out a great many areas for improvement, from typos to the book's overall composition.

The Weber State University Ski Team and its coach, Coach J. Earl Miller, also helped indirectly. "If you fall, get up and finish the race" was the steady refrain of Coach Miller, a philosophy that guided the tenacious Dave Hendry through the years and kept him working on the research that eventually led to this book.

Many thanks to Barbara Mackowiak, an associate in Dave's jewelry insurance business who also just happens to have an exceptionally good eye for typos, logical errors, and poor turns of phrase. As this book's first editor, she had to cut a new course through the dense vegetation of the initial draft, making the way easier for all who followed, editor and reader alike. The last to make that literary journey before publication, editor Dan Crissman of Indiana University Press, was also the most comprehensive, slashing thousands of words, reorganizing important passages, and, it must be admitted, greatly improving the work. Greg Stanfield, also affiliated with Dave's business, lent vital effort with Photoshop, turning several pictures of a Pierce-Arrow Five-Passenger Car into works of art. Others who made the car image possible: James Sandoro, founder and executive director of the Pierce-Arrow Museum in Buffalo, New York, and Robert Waver, owner of that beautiful car.

Special research acknowledgment goes to Michael Moriconi, branch manager of the St. Joseph County Public Library, who went above and beyond in poring through ancient microfiche of the long-defunct *South Bend News-Times*, some of it misdated. Without his work, we would never have known some fascinating details of the crime and its aftermath, including that journalistic battle royale between the Woolvertons and the *South Bend Tribune* waged on the pages of the *News-Times*.

Many others offered historical knowledge, encouragement, insight, or a kind word along the way, thus making the book better and/or the lonely work of writing a little more bearable: Elana Rosario, Martin Grame, Michael Newton, and Jack Major all deserve credit and thanks.

More personally, Dave thanks his wife, Sandra Beck-Hendry, for her continued support and encouragement.

I also thank my wife, Dr. Michelle Andra, who allowed me to read some of the earliest sections of the book to her, who listened patiently as I pontificated endlessly for three years on all things Woolverton, and who offered endless support. Birthing a book does not hurt like childbirth, but the pain lasts longer, and she held my hand and kept me breathing through it all.

And then, finally, my mother and father, Patricia (another of the book's sharp-eyed proofreaders) and the late Michael Meredith, who answered every single question I ever asked to the best of their abilities, creating a child who believed—for better or for worse—that nothing could not be known.

NOTES

1. "THIS IS A STICKUP"

1. The Granada was opened in 1927 and razed in the 1970s. The movie they saw that night? *The Guardsman*, starring Alfred Lunt and Lynn Fontanne, whose Oscar-worthy performances earned them Best Actor and Best Actress nominations in the Fifth Academy Awards.

2. WAR, FLAPPERS, BOOZE, AND THE KIDNAPPING CRESCENT

1. Dominic Sandbrook, "How Prohibition Backfired and Gave America an Era of Gangsters and Speakeasies," *Guardian*, August 24, 2012.

2. Emphasis on *allegedly* here. Ma Barker was built up as a criminal mastermind by J. Edgar Hoover's FBI, but those who have explored the records found her to be a simple woman who was fond of jigsaw puzzles.

3. One of the papers that used Gerk's findings was the January 27, 1932, edition of the *Daily Independent* of Murphysboro, Illinois.

4. "Let Murderers Hang," *Los Angeles Times*, December 21, 1927.

3. "OTHERWISE, I WOULD BE KILLED"

1. Minor corrections and clarifications to Woolverton's statement will be noted in brackets, as here.

2. That home is gone, replaced by fashionable apartments.

4. THE MYSTERY DAUGHTER

1. We will be learning more about Ulga Fraid shortly.

2. Most of the word "SAWDUST" is still visible on the other side of the page.

5. UNSATISFACTORY LODGING

1. Elmo Roper, "The Fortune Survey," *Fortune*, August 1930 (as reported by the *Visalia Times-Delta* [Visalia, CA], August 29, 1939).

6. MANUFACTURING THE TRUTH

1. *South Bend Tribune*, October 20, 1930, p. 11.

2. At the time of Woolverton's kidnapping, a single *p* was the convention in the words *kidnaping* and *kidnapers*. Two *p*'s is now the convention, and that is what's used in this book for all but direct quotations from newspapers. Some other peculiarities of 1930s spelling, punctuation, and capitalization will also be preserved without correction in direct newspaper citations. For example, "clew" instead of *clue*, "indorse" in place of the modern *endorse*, "to-day" instead of *today*, "Jefferson boulevard," not *Jefferson Boulevard*, and "Frank Mayr, jr.," not *Frank Mayr, Jr.*, etc.

3. Almost $20 million and $10 million, respectively, in 2020 dollars.

7. A MESSAGE FOR THE KIDNAPPERS

1. The number 20 is a peculiar one for a license plate, of course, even in the days when cars were not as plentiful. In that era, Indiana's plate sequencing system ran to six numbers, in two groups of three, e.g., 341 880. The kidnappers might have been referring to the last two digits on the plate. Or maybe it really just said 20; in some states, low license plate numbers have been passed down through families, where they still adorn cars and serve as status symbols.

2. *Hysterical*, from the Greek for *uterus* and the origins of *hysterectomy*, is considered a sexist term today, but in Mrs. Woolverton's day, it was thrown around all the time, typically to describe a woman experiencing normal emotions.

8. THE SECRET SIX

1. Kathleen McLaughlin, "Kuhn Wins over Secret Six. Youth Is Given $30,000 by Jury in Arrest Suit," *Chicago Tribune*, December 3, 1932, p. 1.

2. "Crime Board Scorns Secret 6 Plea for Merger. Extra Legal Groups Hard Pressed for Funds," *Chicago Tribune*, January 10, 1933, p. 3.

9. PANDEMONIUM IN SOUTH BEND

1. G. A. Farabaugh, the Woolvertons' attorney and friend. His central role in the kidnapping cover-up will be explored in the coming chapters.

2. Namesake of its builder, James Oliver.

12. THE MYSTERY OF THE PHONE CALL

1. The terms *newspapermen* and *newspaper men* were used regularly to refer to the throng of reporters working the Woolverton case. Perhaps only men were covering that particular crime, but the term was already an anachronism in 1932, women being an important force in American journalism, including crime reporting, since the previous century.

13. THE MAN WHO CAME HOME

1. "Judge Farabaugh Dies at Age of 77," *South Bend Tribune*, January 7, 1961, p. 1.

2. At the time of the kidnapping, Dr. Martin Luther King Jr. Boulevard was known as Michigan Street.

14. KIDNAPPING? WHAT KIDNAPPING?

1. Kuespert, a native of Bavaria, Germany, was replaced as chief of police at the end of 1934. He died at the age of eighty-four on March 14, 1967, in Fort Lauderdale, Florida, where he'd retired eight years before. He left behind his wife, a son, two daughters and two stepdaughters.

2. The same thing that killed Patrick Roche in 1955, oddly enough.

16. THE WOOLVERTONS GET EVEN

1. Now a parking lot.

2. Recall that Risher was named by multiple newspapers as the man who picked up Woolverton in a taxicab at the train station.

17. TALES OF TERROR AND TORTURE

1. Col. Robert Randolph, one of the less secret members of the Secret Six, was frequently mentioned in the press as speaking for the group, and he appeared in Howard Woolverton's statement as someone who interviewed him the night he returned home from his abduction.

2. Sadly, Stout died two months before its publication, in February 2020.

18. FEAR AND LOATHING IN SOUTH BEND

1. The letter was sent in response to a request for information from the Webber College of Business and Financial Management for Women, which has no relation to Weber State University in Ogden, Utah, which played an important role in the genesis of this book.

19. LAW ENFORCEMENT TAKES A STAND

1. The amount demanded varied in media reports.

2. Boehne was probably referring to that nationwide survey conducted by St. Louis Police Chief Joseph Gerk, which reported 279 kidnappings in 28 states in 1931.

3. No arrests would be made in the case for another two and half years. Bruno Hauptmann was charged with the kidnapping and murder in September 1934, found guilty, and hanged in April 1936.

4. The kidnapper did use the US mail to send ransom demands, also made illegal under the new laws.

20. THE RULES HAVE CHANGED

1. According to the company's website, consulted in 2020.

2. For corroboration of Hoover's story, see, for example: Bill McDougall, "S. L. Pair Admit Kidnaping; Hideout in Spokane Found," *Salt Lake Telegram*, June 10, 1935, p. 1; "Guilty," *Chicago Tribune*, July 28, 1935, p. 95; and "Mrs. Waley Starts to Prison Gladly," *Kane County Standard* (Kanub, UT), July 25, 1935, p. 1.

3. Frequently referred to by the alias "William Mahan" by the press at the time.

4. Throughout her life, Mrs. Urschel's first name appeared in newspaper articles and official documents as either "Berenice" or "Bernice." The first spelling seems slightly more common and is used here.

5. In other accounts, neither he nor Jarrett identified themselves.

6. The equivalent of about $4 million in 2020 dollars.

7. The Kansas City Massacre, a tragedy with important links to the Woolverton kidnapping, will be discussed in coming chapters.

8. As is the case with most War on Crime killings and arrests, who did what and said what remains in dispute with the Bailey apprehension. According to some press reports, Bailey's first words on waking up to guns pointed at him were "It looks bad for me now."

9. "Texas Family Balks at Fort Worth Hearing," *Oklahoma News*, August 24, 1933, p. 2.

21. THE LOVE STORY OF KATHRYN AND GEORGE "MACHINE GUN" KELLY

1. John Toland, "Kellys Tried Two Kidnappings Before Getting Any Ransom," *Dayton (Ohio) Daily News*, May 9, 1963.

22. THE END OF AN ERA

1. More recent statistics may have been skewed by other factors, such as the trend of newspapers to go online beginning in the 1990s and choosing at that point to keep their pages out of other organizations' databases.

2. Was Mrs. Kelly using needles manufactured by the Boye Needle Company, half owned by Mrs. Woolverton? Quite possibly.

3. While his name was misspelled "Kelley" on occasion, the correct spelling was "Kelly," with no second "e."

23. THE MAN WITH A COUGH

1. "Berg Kidnaper's Plea for Parole Up Thursday," *St. Louis (Missouri) Star and Times*, November 1, 1937, p. 1.

2. "Louisville Case Recalls Kansas City Kidnapings," *Pittsburgh Press*, October 11, 1934, p. 6.

24. A ROGUE'S GALLERY OF SUSPECTS

1. "Kidnap Leader Shot to Death in Police Trap," *Baltimore Sun*, January 7, 1934, p. 1.

2. The payment of a ransom was never confirmed, nor was the amount demanded, although $100,000 was referenced in some press reports.

3. Recall that a woman called the Woolverton home regularly to threaten the family over the lost ransom money.

4. Although dated February 1937, the copies went out the previous month, apparently, one reaching the sharp-eyed reporters of the *South Bend Tribune* in January 1937.

5. The Weylin Hotel, built in 1921, was converted to an office building in the 1950s.

6. The Park Central Hotel, built in 1927, still stands on 7th Avenue.

7. "Hanging Death Puzzling End to Ryley Cooper Career," *Fort Worth Star-Telegram*, September 30, 1940, p. 1.

8. George Kelly's picture appeared in the *South Bend Tribune* several times in 1933, including on September 28 and October 8.

25. A GHASTLY MEETING

1. As asserted by the Secret Six in that kidnapping package written by Bruce Catton for the Newspaper Enterprise Association and distributed nationally in March 1932.

2. Other articles placed the injured Barrett in the hospital, not his home. Given he was under arrest and being guarded by police, Barrett was most likely not in his own bed.

3. "Bank Bandit Cheats Law by Hanging; James Barrett Hanged Self with Belt in Hartford City Jail," *Tipton (Indiana) Tribune*, June 10, 1932, p. 1. (Many other papers carried this item, distributed by the United Press.)

4. In the mid-twentieth century, federal laws against "white slavery" were sometimes enforced against Black celebrities who took their white girlfriends across state lines, regardless of the women's willingness to be taken.

26. FRANK NASH GETS REVENGE

1. A bigger town about 13 miles from Gotebo.

2. Value in 2020 dollars: about $19,000.

3. About $265,000 in 2020 dollars.

27. THE KANSAS CITY MASSACRE

1. Jay Robert Nash, Annals of Crime, http://www.annalsofcrime.com /indes.htm#03-05, accessed April 2021.

2. "Famous Cases and Criminals," FBI, https://www.fbi.gov/history /famous-cases/kansas-city-massacre-pretty-boy-floyd, accessed April 2021.

3. See various articles, for example, in the *Kansas City (Missouri) Star*, August 14, 1933, pp. 1, 2.

4. Lee Hills, "Fear-Ridden Life Spent with Desperate Gang and Gunmen Revealed by Kidnaper's Wife," *Rock Island (Illinois) Argus*, October 11, 1933, pp. 1, 5.

28. VERNON MILLER: VETERAN, LAWMAN, CRIMINAL, KILLER

1. Robert Talley, "Crime on the Run," *Pantagraph*, October 10, 1933, p. 5.

2. Based in Overland Park, Kansas, the club billed itself on its 2020 website as "the ideal community-gathering place" with a "warm and welcoming environment" and offering "a one-of-a-kind recreational and social experience for the whole family."

3. "Record Reached in Penitentiary," *Argus-Leader* (Sioux Falls, SD), April 4, 1923, p. 5.

4. Robert Talley, "Winkler Dodged Cops; His Own Pals 'Got Him,'" *Los Angeles Evening Post-Record*, October 11, 1933, p. 9.

5. Brad Smith, "The Verne Miller Story: From Lawman to Outlaw," *South Dakota*, https://www.southdakotamagazine.com/the-verne-miller-story (consulted in April 2021).

29. THE WOOLVERTONS MOVE ON

1. Bess Staples, "Society," *South Bend Tribune*, November 5, 1936, p. 14.

BIBLIOGRAPHY

Barnes, Bruce. *Machine Gun Kelly: To Right a Wrong*. Perris, CA: Tipper, 1991.

Blackford, Mansel G., and Kathel Austin Kerr. *Business Enterprise in American History*. Boston: Houghton Mifflin, 1994.

Burrough, Bryan. *Public Enemies: America's Greatest Crime Wave and the Birth of the FBI, 1933–34*. New York: Penguin, 2004.

Hoover, J. Edgar. *Persons in Hiding*. Boston: Little, Brown, 1938.

Newton, Michael. *The Encyclopedia of Kidnappings*. New York: Checkmark, 2002.

Stout, David. *The Kidnap Years: The Astonishing True History of the Forgotten Kidnapping Epidemic That Shook Depression-Era America*. Naperville, IL: Sourcebooks, 2020.

Warburton, Clark. *The Economic Results of Prohibition*. New York: Columbia University Press, 1932.

INDEX

Kevin Meredith worked as a reporter, editor, photographer, and columnist at newspapers in Hillsborough, North Carolina, and Savannah, Georgia, where he covered local politics, education, business, crime, and, when necessary, the weather. After seven years in journalism, he received a business degree and has since earned his keep in marketing, public relations, and technology sales. He is married and the father of three adult sons.